PORSCHE

ANDERS DITLEV CLAUSAGER

GALLERY BOOKS
An Imprint of W. H. Smith Publishers Inc.
112 Madison Avenue
New York City 10016

Published in the United States of Amercia
in 1988 by Gallery Books,
an imprint of W.H. Smith Publishers Inc.,
112 Madison Avenue, New York, NY 10016

Printed and bound in Spain by
Gráficas Estella, S. A. Navarra.

ISBN 0 8317 7090 2

CONTENTS

INTRODUCTION

Porsches are without doubt the most charismatic cars in current production. In the market place as well as on the race track, Porsche is the leading sports car make in the world. We may have become accustomed to the successes achieved by the sleek cars from Zuffenhausen, and it is only too easy now to take Porsche for granted and become blasé about the 928 and the Turbo. Yet the fact is that Porsche has reached its position today from very modest beginnings and in a very short timespan; the history of Porsche as a car maker spans only 35 years, and during this time the growth and achievement of the company has not been matched by any potential competitor.

But if Porsche the car is a comparatively recent phenomenon, let us not forget that the engineering heritage which is the real foundation for the company goes back a further half-century, to the very dawn of motoring in the distant 1890s when a young Austrian engineer, Ferdinand Porsche, first started work on a horseless carriage. This background provides a great deal of the fascination of Porsche, and the story of Professor Porsche's achievements is worth recounting in its own right. The Professor has rightly been acclaimed as one of the greatest geniuses among automotive engineers, and it is a credit to the house of Porsche today that the spirit and the heritage which he founded are still so jealously guarded.

Few car makers can lay claim to the triple distinction of commercial success in the market place, a distinguished record in motor sport and outstanding achievements in the field of engineering — but to Porsche all these have come naturally, almost casually. This is how it might seem to the outside observer who only perceives the surface of things, and fails to see and analyze what goes on beneath the surface. Porsche's watchwords might be commitment and dedication; these have helped the company to achieve perfection in its undertakings, the kind of perfection which is so difficult to reach yet looks so disarmingly simple once it has been achieved.

Although the Porsche family comes from Austria, there is undoubtedly something very German in the Porsche story. Single-mindedness, commitment to perfection, dogged persistence and dedication to hard work are all very Germanic virtues. However compared to other German car makers Porsche has a more international outlook, and perhaps a rather more sophisticated way of doing things. This approach is necessary when making sports cars for the world; the customers are international, sophisticated, probably wealthy and certainly self-indulgent. It is no bad thing to be on the same wavelength. If Porsche is then at times considered rather frivolous by other German car makers – well, the men at Zuffenhausen can probably live with that.

I am near enough the same age as the Porsche car although I rather doubt whether that entitles me to any special distinction — and I can certainly not claim to have grown up with Porsches. But I remember in the 1950s I was as keen as most small boys to talk cars, and we rather looked down on those funny-looking Porsches, while the most knowledgeable would point out that they were only souped-up Volkswagens anyway . . . we knew all about Beetles and held them in mild contempt. When it came to sports cars we were nurtured on a diet of Austin-Healey, Jaguar, MG, and Triumph; besides, real sports cars were open so Porsches were obviously for amateurs. Looking back now, I rather doubt that many of us in school had ever even seen a Porsche but no one is more unshakeable in his conviction than a small boy who is mad on cars and has read all the right magazines . . . suffice it to say that I have had occasion to change my mind since. Obviously Porsche knew a thing or two that I did not know; this may be why Porsches are still made but very few of those that were the "real" sports cars to me and my school friends 25 years ago.

Porsche is a name that today as much as ever inspires respect and admiration among the cognoscenti of fine machinery, and the enthusiasm for the marque is legend. I hope that in the pages which follow, I have been able to put across some of the fascination which I have found in the Porsche story.

ACKNOWLEDGMENTS

I would above all like to record my sincere thanks to all members of staff in the Porsche companies who gave so much invaluable help during the writing of this book. Mr Snook and Ms Day of the Press Office of Porsche Cars Great Britain were instrumental in giving me an introduction and arranging my visit to Porsche at Zuffenhausen. I was most kindly received there by Herr Klaus Reichert of the PR department, and a very special thanks must go to Herr Klaus Parr, Porsche's archivist who patiently let me rifle his photographic files and produced numerous prints (many of which appear in this book), and also showed me the fascinating archives established by his predecessor Ghislaine Kaes, nephew of and secretary to Professor Porsche. I must also mention Chris Martin and Ing. Austen who showed me around the sales and service department at Ludwigsburg, and my old friend Robert Powell who offered me generous hospitality in his home during my visit to Porsche.

In Britain, Peter Brockes and Philip Scott of the library of the National Motor Museum were as helpful and competent as ever. I am delighted that so many of Neill Bruce's excellent color photographs appear in this book. Thanks also to my colleagues at the British Motor Industry Heritage Trust who still have to put up with my writer's moods.

No writer is an island and although the following is by no means a complete bibliography of works which I have consulted these books may also be of interest to the reader who wishes to learn more about Porsche. The most important are: Karl Ludvigsen's *Porsche—Excellence was Expected*, which is the Porsche enthusiast's bible, Boschen and Barth's *The Porsche Book* which is a typically thorough German *Typengeschichte*, and Paul Frère's books on the Porsche 911 and the Porsche racing cars which provide an exceptional degree of technical insight. Michael Cotton, formerly the PR Officer of Porsche Cars Great Britain, has written concise and informative books on the 911 and the Turbo, while for a unique blend of light-hearted entertainment and plenty of information Denis Jenkinson's books on *Porsche—Past and Present* and the Porsche 356 are unbeatable. Richard von Frankenberg's *Porsche—The Man and His Cars* in Charles Meisl's elegant translation is the classic biography of Professor Porsche while Ferry Porsche's reminiscences written with John Bentley, *We at Porsche* is equally interesting. Jerry Sloniger's book on the 924, 928 and 944 models is an unfailing guide to the more recent history of the company and its products.

In addition, reference works such as Georgano's *Complete Encyclopedia of Motorcars* and *Encyclopedia of Motorsport* were invaluable, as were Oswald's *Deutsche Autos 1920–1945* and *Deutsche Autos 1945–1975*; Graf von Seherr-Thoss' *Die Deutsche Automobil Industrie*; Merritt and Millar's scholarly source book of Porsche sales literature 1948–1965; together with magazines and periodicals such as *Autocar*, *Automobil Revue* (catalog issues), *Auto Motor und Sport*, *Autosport*, *Car magazine*, *Classic and Sportscar*, *Motor*, *Motor Sport* and *Thoroughbred and Classic Cars*. It is only appropriate to thank the authors and editors of all these publications.

Anders Ditlev Clausager

2
13

1: INGENUITY FOR SALE

The Porsche family came from the area around Reichenberg on the river Neisse in Northern Bohemia, close to the German border. Until 1918 this was part of Austria-Hungary, and the German-speaking Porsches always considered themselves Austrian. When the break-up of the Austrian empire occurred after the First World War, Bohemia became part of the new Czechoslovak state, but Reichenberg was in the Sudetenland—the disputed Czech border area which was annexed by Hitler in 1938, so the Porsches could be described as Sudeten Germans. Czechoslovakia was re-established after the Second World War and Reichenberg is today called Liberec. Porsche's father Anton was a tin-smith in the village of Maffersdorf east of Reichenberg, and Ferdinand, born on 3 September 1875, was the third of five children.

Ferdinand was at first apprenticed to his father but as a youth showed both interest and aptitude for the new-fangled discovery of electricity. A local factory owner became his patron, and secured a job for him at the Bela Egger company in Vienna, manufacturers of electrical equipment; the young Porsche moved to Vienna at the age of 18. Here he attended the Technical University as a part-time student—the only formal technical education the future honorary Doctor and Professor was to have.

After four years at Bela Egger, he was offered a position by Jacob Lohner, a coachbuilder who held the Imperial and Royal Warrant. Lohner intended to make motor cars but not nasty, smelly and dirty gasoline-engined ones—he saw a greater future for electric cars and wanted to employ a young designer who was familiar with electrical equipment. Within three years the Lohner-Porsche electric car had been developed to a stage where it could be shown at the Paris exhibition in 1900. It attracted great attention in the contemporary press because of its novel design—Porsche had hit upon the idea of installing the electric motors in the hubs of the front wheels, thereby eliminating the shaft, chain or belt which would otherwise have been necessary to transmit the drive. That the Lohner-Porsche was also one of the first practical front-wheel drive designs was to some extent incidental. In some later designs, Porsche installed electric motors in all wheels and thus gained the advantage of four-wheel drive.

Porsche stayed with Lohner until 1905, and during these early years also developed the "mixed" drive—instead of storage batteries, electric current was generated by a dynamo driven by a gasoline engine. The idea was taken up by Austro-Daimler as well as Mercedes, but found little use on private cars in later years, although the American Crown Magnetic used a similar system well into the 1920s. The principle of an internal combustion engine coupled to a generator which in turn drives electric motors is however accepted practice in the railway world, and is also used on some very heavy road vehicles—Porsche himself would later employ such drive systems on his large military road trains, tractors and tanks.

In 1905 Porsche was appointed technical director of Austro-Daimler, Austria's most important car manufacturer which was originally an offshoot of the German Daimler company. Porsche was only 30, and it speaks volumes for the respect he already commanded in his native Austria that he was given such an important position. Initially he continued work on the mixed drive system but in 1909 designed his first conventional gasoline-engined car, a 32hp model, which was developed into the sports model and won the 1910 Prince Henry Trial. He also initiated the development of aero engines even before there were any aircraft in Austria; a 1912 aero-engine design was an air-cooled four cylinder engine with the cylinders positioned in a flattened almost horizontal X—not quite a flat-four but in spirit perhaps a Volkswagen ancestor.

Previous page: The Porsche-designed Auto-Union was the most extraordinary racing car of the 1930s. This is the original P-Wagen driven by Ernst Delius at the Nürburgring in 1934.

Right: Porsche at the steering wheel of a mixed-drive Lohner, outside the family home at Maffersdorf in 1902.

Below right: Among Porsche's designs for Austro-Daimler during the First World War was the petrol-electric "C-Zug" which was capable of pulling some of the heaviest artillery pieces.

Below: The young Ferdinand Porsche showing the electrical installation he devised for his parents' house in 1893.

Above: The first small car designed by Porsche was the 1921 Sascha for Austro-Daimler. The racing model was successful in the Targa Florio. This car is now in the Porsche Museum.

Porsche rose to become managing director of the Austro-Daimler company and during the First World War he developed gun tractors—some with four-wheel drive—motorized artillery pieces and other forms of military transport, such as the remarkable petrol-electric "C-Zug", a road train with powered trailers. After the war, Porsche for the first time turned his mind to small car design—on the suggestion of a Count Kolowrat whose first name Sascha was adopted for the car. This had an 1100cc (67.1cu in) four-cylinder engine with a single overhead camshaft, developing over 40bhp. The car was timed at 89mph (143km/h) and won its class in the Targa Florio, driven by a certain Alfred Neubauer who later became famous as the Mercedes-Benz racing team manager. Porsche was keen on motor racing—he had driven a Lohner-Porsche in a hill climb as early as 1900—but his views were not shared by his fellow directors at Austro-Daimler, especially not after a works driver had a fatal accident in one of Porsche's cars at Monza in 1922. Further differences of opinion resulted, and Porsche eventually accepted an offer from Daimler in Stuttgart to become their technical director, with a seat on the board.

He stayed at Daimler for almost six years. His family settled down in Stuttgart and commissioned the building of a large villa in the Feuerbacherweg. Porsche adapted readily enough to Germany, but to the end of his life he retained the typical Austrian lilt to his voice, and he was also rather more temperamental than the local German people, the *Schwaben*. Porsche's most famous design for Daimler was the large seven-liter, six-cylinder supercharged Mercedes, which began life as the K and S series but was gradually developed in SS, SSK and SSKL forms. He was also working on Diesel engines for trucks, aero engines and had a very advanced racing car with swing-axle suspension on the drawing board. After the merger with Benz in 1926, the combined Daimler-Benz board decided to stay with somewhat conservative and stolid side-valve designs in the middle and upper price brackets, and rejected Porsche's ideas for ohv engines, and for a small one-liter (61cu in) car. So at the end of 1928 Porsche left Daimler-Benz; his successor was the erstwhile Benz

Right: This Saoutchik-bodied tourer from 1924 is an example of Porsche's Mercedes K-type, the 24/100/140 model with a supercharged engine.

chief engineer Hans Nibel.

Nibel rented the villa in Feuerbacherweg, and Porsche returned to Austria—not to Austro-Daimler but to Steyr. As if wanting to compete with his former employers in Vienna and Stuttgart, he began the design of a large luxury car with a straight-eight 5.3-liter (323.4cu in) engine, the almost mythical "Austria" which was a sensation at the 1929 Paris Motor Show. But this had hardly gone into production when Steyr's backers, a Viennese bank, collapsed and was taken over by another bank which was allied to Austro-Daimler. As a result the Austrian motor industry was reorganized, the "Austria" was dropped and Porsche's contract canceled. His only other design for Steyr was the type 30 (or XXX), based on Steyr's existing chassis with rear swing axles but with Porsche's 2-liter (122cu in) ohv six-cylinder engine. In April 1930 at barely 55 years of age, Porsche was without a job—or, in modern parlance, redundant.

Far from despairing, Porsche wasted no time in carrying out a plan which he had considered for some time. He returned to Stuttgart and set up an independent design bureau for automotive engineering. In a small office at Kronenstrasse 24 he gathered round him a select staff of engineers, all Austrians, many of whom he had worked with for years and who were all to play their part in the development of the Volkswagen and Porsche cars. The chief engineer was Karl Rabe who had joined Porsche at Austro-Daimler in 1913; the others were Mickl, aerodynamicist and brilliant calculator, Komenda the body designer, Reimspiess who designed the Volkswagen engine, also Fröhlich, Kales, Zahradnik and Porsche's 21-year-old son Ferry. Porsche's son-in-law Dr Piëch, a lawyer in Vienna, was a partner in the company, as was Adolf Rosenberger, the first commercial manager. Rosenberger later became Porsche's representative abroad—he was Jewish and wisely chose not to stay on in Germany after 1933. Porsche's new company was officially registered in April 1931, and originally carried the rather grandiose title of *Dr. Ing. h.c. Ferdinand Porsche GmbH, Konstruktionsbüro für Motoren-Fahrzeug, Luftfahrzeug und Wasserfahrzeugbau*—Porsche thereby declaring his readiness to tackle any form of transportation, on land, sea or in the air.

Their first design which was given project number 7 was however a fairly staid car for Wanderer, at that time an independent company with a factory at Siegmar near Chemnitz (now the Karl Marx Stadt in East Germany). This had a six-cylinder engine of 1.7 or 2 liters (103.7 or 122cu in) capacity and came on the market in 1932 as the Wanderer W.17 or W.20, but was replaced in the following year by the W.21/22 series for which Porsche had designed a swing-axle rear suspension similar to that used by Steyr. Wanderer had also commissioned Porsche to develop an eight-cylinder car but only one prototype was built before Wanderer merged with Audi, DKW and Horch to form the Auto-Union group. The eight-cylinder car had streamlined bodywork designed by Komenda and the prototype was used by Dr Porsche personally for a number of years.

Other customers soon came along to the Porsche bureau. Historically important was the contract given by Fritz Neumeyer of the Zündapp motorcycle factory to Porsche for the development of a small car, christened by Neumeyer the *Volksauto*—the people's car—but referred to by Porsche more prosaically as the type 12. Three prototypes were built in 1931–32, before an upturn in the motorcycle market decided Neumeyer to abandon the project. The type 12 had a rear engine, with five cylinders arranged radially and a capacity of 1192cc (72.7cu in). The suspension was independent all round, the wheelbase was 2500mm (97.5in) and two of the prototypes carried streamlined saloon bodies (built by Reutter) which were scaled down from Komenda's earlier design for the large Wanderer and already pointed toward the eventual Volkswagen design.

In 1932 Porsche took out the first patents for the torsion bar independent front suspension with trailing arms and transverse torsion bars enclosed in a tube; a number of variations on this theme were designed in later years for companies as diverse as Citroën and Morris, and this suspension was used on the Auto-Union racing car as well as on the Volkswagen and Porsche 356. However, the early years in Stuttgart were still a difficult period and the bureau was in almost constant financial difficulties. Then in 1932, Porsche was approached by a Russian delegation which invited him to visit Soviet Russia as a guest of the state, to inspect all the engineering and manufacturing facilities. Porsche's trip to Russia lasted several weeks, and he was taken all over the country; finally in Moscow, he was offered the position of State Designer, with a free hand to oversee all vehicle production and at whatever salary he would care to name. But he would have been obliged to stay in Russia for the rest of his life, and it was doubtful whether under the Soviet political system he would have been able to fulfill his ambition of designing a small peoples' car and a world-beating racing car. So Porsche turned down the Russian offer and returned to Stuttgart.

An opportunity to further Porsche's ideas on small car design soon came along. Fritz von Falkenhayn, chairman of the NSU motorcycle company at Neckarsulm, which had once made cars of its own and subsequently assembled Fiats for the German market, came to Porsche with a request for another small car. Type 32 was designed in 1933, and took the basic ideas from the Zündapp a stage nearer the Volkswagen concept as the NSU featured an air-cooled flat-four engine in the rear together with Porsche's torsion bar suspension, in combination with swing axles at the rear. The engine capacity was 1470cc (89.7cu in) and the wheelbase was 2600mm (101.4in). Three prototypes were built again—of which one miraculously survives to this day as part of the Volkswagen Museum at Wolfsburg—before NSU decided to cancel the project. Apparently the company's contract with Fiat prevented them from making their own cars again.

Meanwhile, the bureau had started the design of a racing car on its own initiative. In the autumn of 1932 a new Grand Prix racing formula had been decided; this limited maximum weight to 750kg (1650lb) but did not stipulate a maximum engine size and did not prohibit the use of superchargers. Porsche drew up a specification for a car with a 4.4-liter (268.5cu in) supercharged V-16

Right: Members of the Porsche family, including Ferdinand and Ferry, found time to line up for this group photograph with a Steyr type XXX in front of the family villa at Feuerbacherweg in 1930.

Right: Ferry is at the wheel of the first design from the Porsche bureau, the 1.7-liter Wanderer number 7, here undergoing prototype trials in 1931.

engine behind the driver's seat, with a tubular chassis frame and torsion bar suspension. With some 295bhp, the expected top speed was 180mph (290km/h). Design work started, and a separate company—*Hochleistungsfahrzeug GmbH*—was set up, the intention was that this company should build and race the car. There was even a project for a three-seater road-going sports version of the same basic design but this never got off the drawing board.

As we shall see in the next chapter, the change of government in Germany in January 1933 had far-reaching effects on the motor industry, and one of the first acts of the Nazi government was to make a large sum of money available to a German company willing to enter Grand Prix racing under the new formula. The obvious candidate was Mercedes-Benz but the Auto-Union group also showed a desire to go in for state-supported racing. The Auto-Union directors went to Porsche and asked him to design a racing car; they must have been pleasantly surprised when Porsche declared he already had the design in his pocket. Auto-Union took over the type 22 project, which became known as the P-Wagen, and Porsche together with representatives for Auto-Union went to make a presentation of the project to Hitler who agreed to split the state funding between Mercedes-Benz and Auto-Union.

The Auto-Union was ready to race for the 1934 season, and from then on until 1939 the big silver cars from Germany won almost every important

Left: Berndt Rosemeyer was the most famous of the Auto-Union drivers but he was tragically killed in 1938.

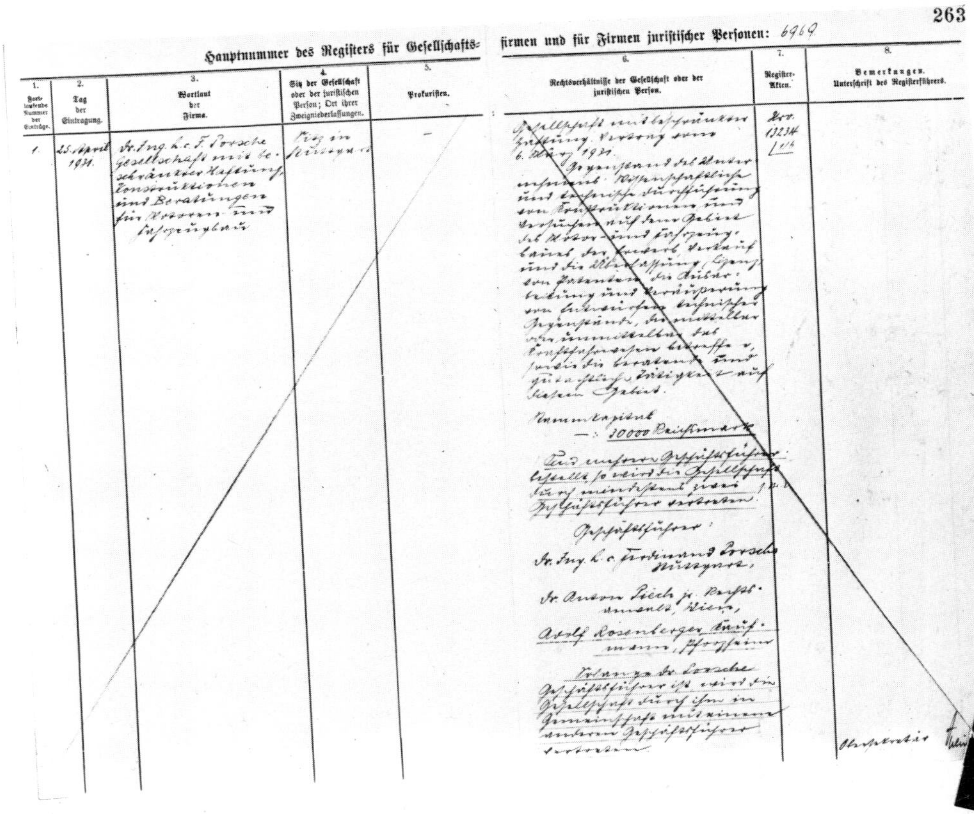

Grand Prix race in the world, the honors being divided between those wearing the four-ring symbol of Auto-Union and those wearing the three-pointed star of Mercedes-Benz. With their rearward weight bias, the enormous amount of power transmitted through what today look like incredibly narrow tires and their swing-axle rear suspension, the Auto-Union were difficult to drive and acquired a rather unsavory reputation. Not many drivers were able to get the best from these cars, which were capable of frightening oversteer and it has been said that Auto-Union's best drivers—like Berndt Rosemeyer—were those who had come straight from motorcycle-racing without ever having raced conventional cars. However, the success of experienced racing drivers such as Hans Stuck (senior), Tazio Nuvolari and Achille Varzi seems to disprove this argument.

Apart from racing, there was constant rivalry between Mercedes-Benz and Auto-Union in the field of record-breaking. These record-breaking attempts took place over closed sections of the newly-built Autobahns—the German expressways—usually either at Dessau or on the Frankfurt-Darmstadt Autobahn. The Grand Prix racing cars were used but normally fitted with all-enclosing highly streamlined bodywork, and the speeds achieved were and still are remarkable, in view of the fact that they were recorded on public highways. In a Mercedes, Caracciola had set a Class B record over the flying kilometer of 430km/h (over 268mph) and on 28 January 1938, Rosemeyer set out in his Auto-Union on the Frankfurt Autobahn to beat this. He was killed in the attempt—it was a windy day and the science of streamlining was as yet not perfectly understood, so it seems that the highly sidewind-sensitive car was literally blown off the road. A dignified memorial next to the expressway marks the spot of Rosemeyer's death to this day.

This unhappy event caused Dr Porsche much anguish as he had personally advised that the attempt should not take place under the prevailing weather conditions, but he was now rather less directly involved with the Auto-Union design and the running of the racing team. In the early years, one was sure to see Dr Porsche in the Auto-Union pits during a Grand Prix race, fiddling perhaps with carburetor adjustments or pulling the stopwatch out of his waistcoat pocket; but by 1938 he was preoccupied with other matters and the design work for the last generation of Auto-Union racers (a much improved 3 liter (183cu in) V-12) was in the hands of Eberan von Eberhorst who had joined the Porsche bureau in the previous year.

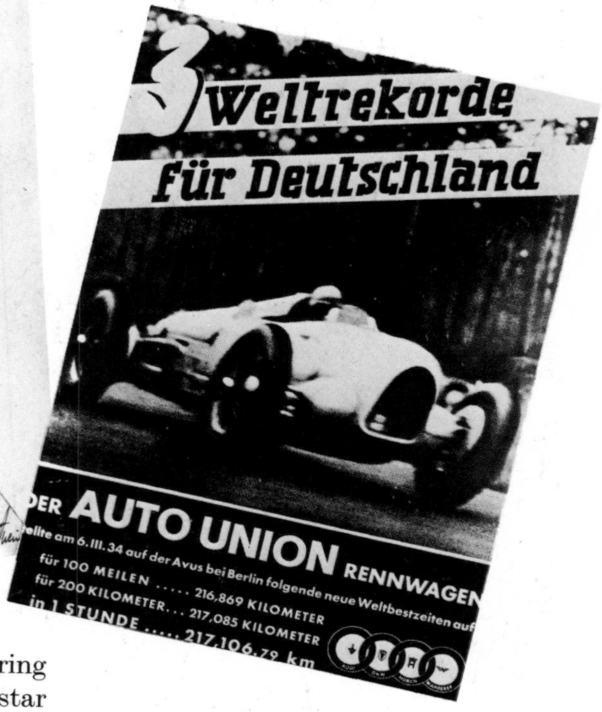

Above left: This was how the Porsche bureau was entered in the Stuttgart commercial register for 25 April 1931.

Above: The Auto-Union began its record-breaking career in 1934 when Hans Stuck set three new world records at the Avus track in Berlin.

Far left, center: The NSU prototype of 1933 was an important step on the way to the VW design. This car stands in front of the Porsche office in Kronenstrasse.

Far left: The 1931 Zündapp photographed at Feuerbacherweg was Porsche's first rear-engined small car and was clearly a Volkswagen ancestor.

2: ON THE FUHRER'S ORDERS

Previous page: During 1937 the VW 30 prototype series was undergoing extensive tests at the hands of picked drivers of the SS.

The German President Hindenburg—a veteran field marshal and general from the First World War—accepted the resignation of the government and called on the leader of the largest party in the German parliament, the Reichstag, to form a new government on 30 January 1933. This was not a particularly unusual event, especially not in the German Weimar Republic which was not noted for the longevity or stability of its governments. But the party leader who was called upon to become Chancellor was Adolf Hitler, of the National Socialist or Nazi Party. Thus began the period in German history known as the Third Reich—12 years that many Germans still find difficult to come to terms with. From 1933 to 1939, the Nazis sought to transform German society completely; from 1939 to 1945, their ambition spread worldwide with the horrifying results, with which we still live.

Within a few weeks of that fateful date, the Reichstag had voted to give Hitler what amounted to dictatorial powers, and when Hindenburg died in 1934, Hitler took the dual office of prime minister and president, appointing himself Führer of Germany. Hitler, and Nazi Germany, have come under close scrutiny in any number of learned works but few have considered the aspect of the Führer's character that concerns us here—his interest in motoring. Hitler was, if not precisely a car enthusiast, well aware of the advantages of motorization, and of the prestige attached to success in motor sport. It is perhaps significant that already in 1923, the Nazi Party spent a large proportion of its meager funds on the purchase of a Mercedes car for Hitler's use, although he rarely drove himself—entrusting this task to his chauffeurs, one of whom was Erich Kemptka who helped to burn Hitler's body in Berlin in 1945 and who after the war became an employee of the Porsche company.

One of Hitler's first official speeches after he came to power was when he opened the Berlin Motor Show on 11 February 1933. In this speech he outlined the points which became the cornerstones of his program for popular motorization: car taxes and licenses were to be abolished, there would be a large-scale program of road building, motor sport would be encouraged—and there was a hint that the state would take a much more direct interest in motoring as distinct from other forms of transport. Apart from encouraging Germany's youth to become familiar with cars and motorcycles and organizing driving tuition in the *Hitler Jugend*, the Nazi instrument for controlling motoring in general and motor sport in particular was the NSKK—the National-Sozialistische Kraftfahrer-Korps—under the leadership of Korpsführer Hühnlein. As might be expected this was no ordinary motoring club but a uniformed corps organized on semi-militaristic lines.

Hitler's mentor in matters relating to motoring was Jakob Werlin, whom he had met in the early 1920s when Werlin was in charge of the Mercedes branch in Munich, and it was from Werlin that Hitler bought his first car. After 1933 Werlin became a director of Daimler-Benz, aided undoubtedly by the fact that he was the Führer's confidant. Perhaps it was Werlin who first suggested the idea of a *Volkswagen*—a people's car—to Hitler, and it was certainly Werlin who arranged the meeting between Hitler and Porsche in Berlin toward the end of 1933 when the idea of the Volkswagen project was first put to Porsche. Strangely enough, Porsche and Hitler had first met eight years earlier when both were present at a race-meeting at the Solitude circuit on the outskirts of Stuttgart. Porsche was then the technical director of Daimler-Benz and Hitler an aspiring politician and the guest of another Daimler-Benz director who performed the introduction. They had also met when Porsche was a member of the Auto-Union delegation securing state funds for the GP car.

Hitler and Porsche soon agreed on the basic specification of the Volkswagen —not a small car but large enough to be really practical for a wide variety of uses, it should accommodate four to five people with luggage, be capable of a top speed of 100km/h (62mph) with a fuel consumption of 8 liters (1.76gall) per 100km (62 miles), it should be air cooled for simplicity and be very cheap to service and repair. But Porsche was taken aback by the Führer's demand that such a car should sell for RM1000 or less (then the equivalent of approximately £90 or $360). Nevertheless, Porsche agreed to prepare a memorandum containing preliminary details of the Volkswagen design, and this was submitted in due course, bearing the date of 17 January 1934.

This *Exposé relating to the construction of a German Volkswagen* is one of the most fascinating and important documents in motoring history. In broad outline and in drawings, it contains the basic specification and design of the Volkswagen, with the air-cooled rear engine and the all-independent torsion bar suspension. There were however some differences; the chassis consisted of two parallel tubes, with three cross tubes—at the front and rear containing the torsion bars, with a central cross tube supporting the bodywork. The drawings show the flat-four engine but Porsche made the suggestion of an alternative engine: a three-cylinder two-stroke radial engine, while at a later date a double-piston two/four cylinder two-stroke engine was also considered. The outline of the body as shown was clearly derived from the Zündapp and NSU projects, and was almost like the final design for the Beetle as we know

Below: Professor Porsche continued to use a VW 38 model after the war. His nephew and secretary Ghislaine Kaes took this photograph during a holiday in the Austrian Alps in 1950.

Left: The VW-based Kübelwagen *became the standard German jeep vehicle in the Second World War and proved the capabilities of the design in the African desert as well as the Russian winter.*

Left: With Albert Speer at the controls and an apprehensive-looking Professor Porsche perched beside him, the Ferdinand tank goes on trial.

it. An appendix to the memorandum gave specifications of comparable German small cars costing from RM1700 to RM3500—Porsche costed the Volkswagen at RM1550, but pointed out that with a reduction of the cost of raw materials in Germany the price could well be reduced further and added that the state already controlled the German light alloy industry. . . .

By the standards of the mid-1930s the Volkswagen specification was very much in tune with the most recent developments in car design. Not only Porsche but many other designers in Central Europe were convinced that the future belonged to rear-engined streamlined cars. Ledwinka of Tatra, Nibel of Daimler-Benz, the editor of *Motor-Kritik* Josef Ganz and the Hungarian Barenyi were all thinking along the same lines. High gearing and streamlining would give adequate top speed with low fuel consumption on the new expressways. Rear engines would make it possible to build cars lower, and permitted effective streamlining of the front end; and independent swing axle suspension would cope equally well with the poured concrete of the Autobahn, and rutted mountain tracks in remote areas. Of the numerous designs of this kind developed in the 1930s, only the Volkswagen, its Porsche derivative and on a

Above: The final design for the VW was displayed at the Berlin Motor Show in 1938. In this photograph Porsche demonstrates the features of the chassis to Hitler and his entourage.

Below: Almost a Porsche: the VW Streamliner built for the projected Berlin-Rome race in 1939.

very small scale the Tatra had any lasting success, and neither of these cars can be said to owe their continued success exclusively to the original design parameters.

The Volkswagen was of course unique as it had to be built down to a price. In the 1930s, some British manufacturers (Morris, Ford and Austin) had managed to squeeze the price of their most spartan small cars down to £100 (or $400); in America, Ford had brought the price of the cheapest Model T down to $260 (around £65) in 1926 but by the early 1930s, the cheapest car on the US market was the Continental Beacon at $335 (£85). Despite much increased production after 1933, the German motor industry could not hope to match such figures—in 1937 the cheapest German cars were the Opel P.4 at RM1450 and the DKW Reichsklasse at RM1650 ($528 or £132 and $600 or £150 respectively). The Opel was shown to Hitler at the Berlin Motor Show by an Opel executive who proudly proclaimed, "This is *our* Volkswagen, Mein Führer!"—but history records that the Führer was not amused.

Nevertheless, the Volkswagen was not as unrealistically priced as one might think, when it is remembered that the car would be bought direct from the factory without any intermediate distributors or dealers, and that the purchasers would have to pay for their cars in full, through the famous Kraft durch Freude (KdF) savings system, before accepting delivery. There was also a mandatory insurance premium of RM200 to be added to the basic cost of RM990. Furthermore production was planned to start at 500,000 cars per year—not such a large figure by modern standards but it must be compared to the total German production of private cars of 277,000 in 1938. This goes some way toward explaining the hostility shown to the Volkswagen project by the established German motor industry, and it has been argued that the weakness of the project was that the German market was simply not capable of absorbing the planned number of cars.

Porsche's memorandum in 1934 convinced Hitler that the project should go ahead. Porsche suggested that his bureau should undertake the design and build of prototype cars—which he, rashly, promised to have ready within a year—and that the government should discharge all the costs involved. Should it be decided to produce the car in series, he reserved the right to a royalty paid on each car made. In June 1934 the German Society of Motor Manufacturers (RDA) gave Porsche the contract to develop the type 60—as the Volkswagen was known internally in Porsche's bureau—and the first prototype was ready before the end of the year. Further prototypes followed in 1935, and in 1936 some 30 pre-production cars were made by Daimler-Benz. These were subjected to rigorous endurance testing in the hands of picked drivers from the SS, who conveniently enough were already sworn to secrecy and loyalty to the Führer.

The decision was taken to go ahead with production of the car, and the design of the production version—the VW 38—was readied in 1937–38. The DAF or Deutsche Arbeits-Front—in effect, the state-organized trade union—undertook to produce the car, through its Kraft durch Freude (Strength through Joy) organization which looked after the recreational needs of the German worker. From these initials the Volkswagen derived its first official name—the KdF-Wagen—and in 1938 Adolf Hitler laid the foundation stone of the Volkswagenwerke near the village of Fallersleben in Lower Saxony. The site chosen was on the Mittelland Kanal, not far from the Hannover–Berlin Autobahn in the heart of prewar Germany; but it was well away from the established motor industry and the components manufacturers, and also far removed from the sources of raw material in the Ruhr district. Plans were already in existence for a whole township, Stadt des KdF-Wagens, which was subsequently renamed Wolfsburg after an ancient castle nearby. At the foundation ceremony, the perfected Volkswagen design was shown to the public—in all details similar to the 20 million Beetles that have left Volkswagen factories worldwide since.

While Dr Porsche was a director of the Volkswagenwerke GmbH, and one of two managers (the other was Dr Bodo Lafferentz of the DAF) appointed to oversee day-to-day affairs of the new factory, he and his staff were also involved with many other projects. The most remarkable of these was perhaps the world land speed record contender developed in great secrecy for Daimler-Benz—the aero-engined T.80 which due to the outbreak of war never ran but is still preserved in the Daimler-Benz museum. The Porsche bureau began design work on light tractors, with the intention of using the Volkswagen engine, and Porsche also turned his mind to sports cars based on the VW. At first he was discouraged from doing so, as the Nazis did not see any point in popular sports cars, but when Hühnlein of the NSKK had the idea of arranging a road race from Berlin to Rome to celebrate the Axis partnership between Hitler's Germany and Mussolini's Italy, the authorities relented and Porsche was allowed to develop a team of three sports coupés based on the Volkswagen chassis. Komenda designed a lower, lighter and more aerodynamic body which still retained a clear resemblance to the standard Volkswagen. This Berlin–Rome model proved capable of 145km/h (90mph). However, the Berlin–Rome race which was scheduled for September 1939 never took place as more pressing matters then faced the German nation. Luckily, one of these cars still exists in Innsbruck in Austria, owned for many years by the remarkable one-armed racing driver Otto Mathé.

The Berlin–Rome car was a true predecessor of the Porsche car to be, in spirit as well as in style. There were other projects on the Porsche drawing board which pointed toward the future. The most remarkable was the type 114, which was a kind of missing link between the Auto-Union racers and the future Porsche. The type 114 shared Auto-Union characteristics in its V-engine mounted between the driver's seat and the rear wheels, although this engine was an unsupercharged 1.5 liter (91.5cu in) V10 with two overhead camshafts per bank—surely one of the most extraordinary engine designs ever conceived. There was also the Volkswagen type 64 which was to have the VW engine enlarged to 1.5 liters (91.5cu in) and an aluminum body, with a top speed around 150km/h (93mph). Both these projects resembled the Berlin-Rome car and did in fact predate it; neither of them reached very far beyond the drawing board stage, as after the outbreak of war Dr Porsche became involved in the design of military vehicles instead.

First of these, and again as a result of a direct order from Hitler, was the military version of the Volkswagen—the type 82 Kübelwagen which was largely developed by Ferry Porsche and despite initial resistance from the army's Military Supply Office was adopted as the standard "jeep" for the German armed forces in the Second World War. Then there was the amphibious version of the Volkswagen, the Schwimmwagen developed to a brief from the SS. Porsche also received orders for tank designs, and the Professor (he was appointed honorary professor by the Stuttgart Technische Hochschule in 1940) became chairman of the Armor Commission under Reichs Armament Minister Albert Speer although after differences with Speer, he was kicked upstairs with the title of Reichs Armaments Councillor. Tank designs included the Tiger, the Ferdinand and the colossal 180-ton Maus—all of which featured the mixed drive with an internal combustion engine driving hub-mounted electric motors, a straightforward throwback to Porsche's early days at Lohner. Finally in 1944 at the end of the war, he designed a one-ton tracked

Above: At least the former sawmill at Gmünd enjoyed a spectacular setting. Note the Porsche sign at the gate. The VW in the drive is a one-off prewar cabriolet used by Ferry just after the war.

personnel carrier which never really got off the ground. Toward the end of the war, with foreign armies already on German soil, Porsche was ordered to evacuate his staff and works from Stuttgart to Gmünd, a tiny remote village in the Austrian province of Kärnten. Their accommodation here was a former saw-mill soon nick-named the *Vereinigte Hüttenwerke*—which may mean the United Smelting Works, but in German *Hüttenwerke* can also mean a factory consisting of huts.

It is difficult now to evaluate the position of Professor Porsche, his family and associates in the context of Hitler's Third Reich. Porsche probably considered himself to be if not German, at least Austrian, although he held Czech citizenship until Hitler bestowed honorary German citizenship upon him. While he was not a member of the Nazi party, it cannot be denied that the Nazi government was the best customer for the services of the Porsche design bureau (which extended its staff from 19 in 1931 to 291 in 1940). The Nazis also conferred a number of honors on Dr Porsche who was quite happy to work for Hitler and his cronies. Porsche considered himself above politics and by all accounts never treated Hitler with the customary obsequiousness; he normally addressed the Führer as plain "Herr Hitler" much to the horror of party officials present. The Porsche family found the Nazi rituals and pre-occupation with uniforms more than a little ridiculous; Ferry was given an unwanted and completely unwarranted colonelship in the SS on Himmler's personal instructions which was to cause him brief embarrassment in postwar years, but he refused to wear even the NSKK uniform.

The Porsches certainly enjoyed the trust and respect of Hitler and in consequence had rather greater freedom than most—not many Germans could have traveled abroad as much as Porsche, who for instance paid two visits to the USA in 1937 to study the American motor industry. Not all of Hitler's minions shared the Führer's good opinion of Professor Porsche—Göring thought the Volkswagen project was a waste of time when the Luftwaffe needed more aircraft, and an exasperated Speer who had had enough of Porsche tank designs once suggested to the Professor that even he might end up in a concentration camp. But Speer also stated after the war that it was stupid to arrest Dr Porsche who had never had anything to do with politics.

The fact is that the Porsches, if not politically naive, were as unaware as the vast majority of the German population and saw Hitler and the National Socialists as leaders out of the morass left behind by the depression, inflation, unemployment and ineffective policies of previous governments.

3: A FAMILY AFFAIR

The choice of Gmünd as a temporary home for the Porsche bureau proved very fortunate. In the spring of 1945 Allied forces were advancing rapidly across Germany from both east and west, but the push from the south following the invasion of Sicily in July 1943 had ground to a temporary halt when the British and American forces came up against the dual obstacles of Field Marshal Kesselring and the Apennine Mountains. By April 1945 Germany itself had been split in two, but the Allied armies had yet to reach the Po valley, and the Alps and Austria beyond. In the last stages of war in Europe, "Germany" had effectively become an area shaped like a squeezed figure 8, stretching from Northern Italy through Austria and Czechoslovakia into Southern Germany. Gmünd was almost at the center of this area and was not reached by Allied forces before the hostilities had almost ceased. It was also fortunate that American troops reached the Western part of Austria before the Russians; otherwise Professor Porsche might have had to accept the 13-year-old offer of becoming state designer in Russia on an involuntary basis!

While American troops reached Gmünd, it was the British who first reached the Professor, who had been staying at the family estate at Zell am See. It seems that the occupying forces were rather surprised at finding Porsche and his bureau, but the Porsches' activities were obviously well known to the Allied powers and the family was subjected to thorough investigation. The

Previous page: The 1951 Porsche 356 coupë. This car, owned by Betty Haig, is one of the oldest Zuffenhausen-built cars in existence, possibly the only one with the 1100cc (67cu in) engine still fitted.

Below: A rather unusual Porsche: the diesel-engined tractor built by the Allgaier Company.

Professor was interned for some months in the late summer of 1945 in a castle near Frankfurt from where he emerged cleared of any charges, and was allowed to return to Austria. Things were rather complicated here as Gmünd was in the British zone, and the Porsche estate at Zell was in the American zone which made communications difficult. The Porsche factory in Spitalwaldstrasse in Stuttgart-Zuffenhausen (inaugurated in 1938 to accommodate the design bureau which had outgrown the combined premises at Kronenstrasse and the garage of the Porsche villa in Feuerbacherweg, where the first Volkswagen prototypes were built) had been commandeered by the American army for use as a motor pool and a return was, and for many years would be, out of the question.

At Gmünd, the Porsche engineers occupied themselves mainly with tractor designs but were also assisting with the repair and maintenance of the ex-army VW Kübelwagens which were just about the only cars available. Their

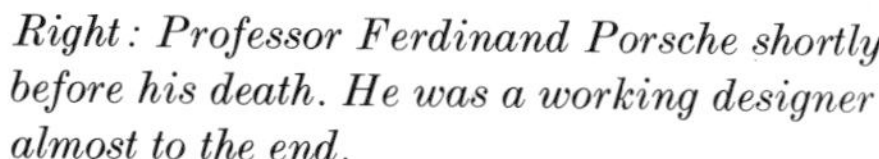

Right: Professor Ferdinand Porsche shortly before his death. He was a working designer almost to the end.

The Cisitalia racing car, which is now kept at the Porsche Museum. It was built in the Auto-Union tradition but featured four-wheel drive.

workload steadily increased even if new car designs were as yet only dreams for the future. Toward the end of 1945, Professor Porsche was approached by the French occupation authorities who were considering the possibility of taking over the Volkswagenwerke as war reparation, and wanted to enlist Porsche's help in moving the factory to France. At a meeting in December 1945 at Baden-Baden in the French zone of Germany, the Professor was arrested on the authority of the French Minister of Justice, as were his son Ferry and his son-in-law Anton Piëch. No explanation was given but it eventually transpired that the arrest was due to rivalry between political factions in France, and opposition on behalf of the established French motor industry to the idea of a French Volkswagen factory.

Ferry was freed after a few months in custody, but the Professor and Piëch were transferred to France and were kept in custody first in Paris, later at Dijon in gradually worsening conditions. For a long time the French were trying to gather evidence to put the Porsches on trial as war criminals because of their dealings with the Peugeot company during the war. Peugeot had supplied parts to the Volkswagenwerke, and the Gestapo had imprisoned Peugeot executives after alleged sabotage in the factory. It was eventually established beyond doubt that Porsche had nothing to do with this, and had even attempted to intervene with the Gestapo on behalf of the imprisoned Frenchmen. But Porsche's imprisonment in France nevertheless lasted until August 1947, and even then the French demanded the considerable sum of one million Francs to release him. While in custody in Paris, the Professor had at one time been given quarters at the Renault factory and had been consulted about the development of the Renault 4 CV, another small rear-engined car which had been designed in secret during the war and would go into production in 1947; this has sometimes been taken to mean that Porsche designed the 4 CV which was not the case, although it has been stated that the Renault engineers did heed the advice he gave them.

Already during the winter of 1944–45 Porsche's health had given cause for concern and he had been ill for some time; he was taken ill again while in prison in France, and he never regained his former vigor after his return to Austria. In his absence, the bureau had taken on a new customer, the Italian industrialist Piero Dusio who had begun to make the Cisitalia 1100cc (67cu in) sports cars based on the Fiat 1100. This contact had been brought about by Carlo Abarth and Rudolf Hruschka, both Austrian engineers living in the Italian Tirol who had been appointed the Porsche bureau's representatives in Italy. (Both were later to achieve fame in the Italian motor industry; Abarth under his own name, Hruschka as the designer of the Alfa-Sud.) Prompted by no less than Tazio Nuvolari, Dusio now decided to have a new Italian Grand Prix car designed, and through Abarth and Hruschka placed a design contract with the Porsche bureau, not only for the Grand Prix car but for a sports car, a tractor and other projects as well. The fees paid by Dusio incidentally helped to raise the bail to free Professor Porsche from the French prison.

In Porsche's absence Karl Rabe, Ferry Porsche and the other members of the design team went ahead with the design of the Grand Prix car in the early months of 1947. None of the other Cisitalia projects ever came to anything but let us consider the Grand Prix car which became Porsche type 360. This had a supercharged flat-twelve engine of 1498cc (91.4cu in) supposed to develop an estimated 450bhp although this was never achieved in practice. The engine was installed behind the driving seat in a tubular chassis frame and there was provision for four-wheel drive. Another feature was the typical Porsche torsion bar suspension, and for the first time Porsche's synchromesh was used in the gearbox. By 1949 one complete car and parts for a second car

existed but by then Dusio's company was in financial difficulties. Dusio accepted an invitation from the Argentine President Peron to transfer his organization and build up an Argentine motor industry, and the Cisitalia Grand Prix car moved to Argentina with Dusio. Here it was eventually track tested in 1953 (with rather disappointing results) and was then forgotten about for six years before being brought back to Europe and exhibited in Porsche's first factory museum which opened in 1959. The second Cisitalia was also rescued and was finished with a British-made replica body before going on display in the Donington Park racing car museum.

When the Professor came home in the summer of 1947, he found not only the Cisitalia design in progress, but also another design, type 356, for a small sports car built from Volkswagen parts. In effect this was a return to the prewar VW sports car plans described in the previous chapter, and it is possible that renewed impetus for this kind of car had come from contact with Dusio's Cisitalia company which was building their small sports cars using commonly available parts from the Fiat 1100. But the important difference between the type 356 and all previous Porsche designs was that this was going

to be a Porsche car. The first prototype, an open two-seater roadster with the VW engine mounted in front of the rear wheels, Auto-Union fashion, was completed in the middle of 1948, and thanks to orders received from export markets, enough capital was gathered to build a series of 50 cars at Gmünd. These had the engine behind the rear wheels similar to the Volkswagen and most had coupé bodywork. But the story of the birth of type 356 belongs properly in the next chapter.

While still at Gmünd, Ferry Porsche had got in touch with the Volkswagenwerke at Wolfsburg, well on their way to the miraculous recovery led by ex-Opel man Heinz Nordhoff. Ferry's main concern was to safeguard a supply of Volkswagen parts with which to build the Porsche cars, but as it turned out Nordhoff was also interested in employing the Porsche bureau as consultant engineers to the Volkswagen company. The agreement which came out of their negotiations in 1949 gave Porsche a royalty on every VW built to their design, said to be DM5 per car; but Porsche was not to design a possible Volkswagen competitor, either for their own manufacture or for any other company. The parts supply was agreed, and it was agreed that Porsche cars could be sold and serviced through the growing VW dealer network in Germany and abroad. Through a subsidiary company in Austria, eventually established at Salzburg under the direction of Ferry's sister Louise Piëch, after the early death of her husband, Porsche was also given the VW importation for Austria. In return, Porsche patents could be used by Volkswagen free of charge, and Porsche engineers would act as consultants and advisors to Volkswagen.

With this important agreement as a safeguard for the future, and with growing difficulties in continuing the small-scale car production at Gmünd, it became obvious that the Porsche firm had to return to Germany. The American army motorpool showed no sign of vacating the premises in the Spitalwaldstrasse, so the Porsche garage at Feuerbacherweg was once again pressed into service, this time as a design office. Later the design and sales offices moved to a prefabricated building adjoining the Reutter coachworks, also in Zuffenhausen and just across the road from the Spitalwaldstrasse. At the same time Reutter was given the contract for the bodywork for the first 500 Porsche cars, and some 500 square meters of space was rented from Reutter

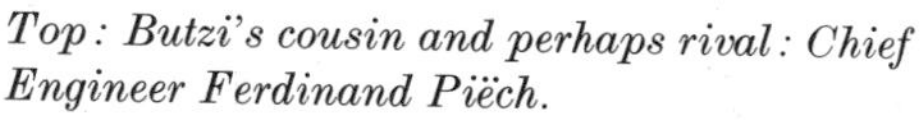

Top: Butzi's cousin and perhaps rival: Chief Engineer Ferdinand Piëch.

Above: Ferry's sister, Louise Piëch, is a shareholder in the Porsche company and was in charge of Austrian operations.

Left, top: On his 75th birthday, the Professor attended a gathering of Porsche owners at the Solitude and was presented with a new 356 Coupé.

Left, center: Ferry Porsche in a relaxed mood.

Left: The third generation: "Butzi" Porsche, the Chief Stylist, and his work, a 911 Targa.

Top right: At the Pebble Beach Concours in 1982 spectators were treated to the appearance of the Porsche number one with bumpers.

Top, center: At the same concours there was also a Gmünd-built aluminum coupé.

to accommodate final assembly of Porsches. The first cars left this improvised factory in the spring of 1950.

On 3 September that year, Professor Porsche celebrated his 75th birthday. At Schloss Solitude near Stuttgart there was a gathering of Porsche owners paying their respects to the founder of the marque, and the Professor was ceremoniously presented with a new 356 Coupé. This car, nicknamed "Ferdinand", later covered 200,000 miles as a development car, and may be seen today in the Porsche museum. In October 1950 Porsche attended the Paris Motor Show where Porsches were exhibited for the first time, but a month later he suffered a stroke from which he did not recover; he was partially paralyzed and was bedridden for the last months of his life. Professor Ferdinand Porsche died on 30 January 1951, and was buried in a chapel on the family estate at Zell am See.

After his death, ownership of the Porsche company—which by now had become *Dr. Ing. h.c. F. Porsche K.G.*—passed jointly to Ferry and Louise Piëch. In later years they divided their holdings with their children; each had four so eight Porsche and Piëch children each took one tenth of the stock of the Porsche company, the remaining two portions were kept by Ferry and Louise. In 1972 the company became an *Aktiengesellschaft* or AG, which is a joint stock company. Also in 1972, Ferry Porsche retired from the post as chairman of the executive board (the *Vorstand*—a position which is equivalent to managing director) and became chairman of the board of directors (the *Aufsichtsrat*).

Old Porsches never die and many of them continue to race. Note that the Speedster (No 11) and the Cabriolet (No 268) have been fitted with wheelspats for the 1982 Laguna Seca Races. The appearance of the 1939 VW Berlin-Rome car (top left) in this event was very unusual.

Following page: Further studies of Betty Haig's delightful all-original 1951 car. The early 356 shape was much cleaner and more attractive than later models, which had more prominent bumpers.

11

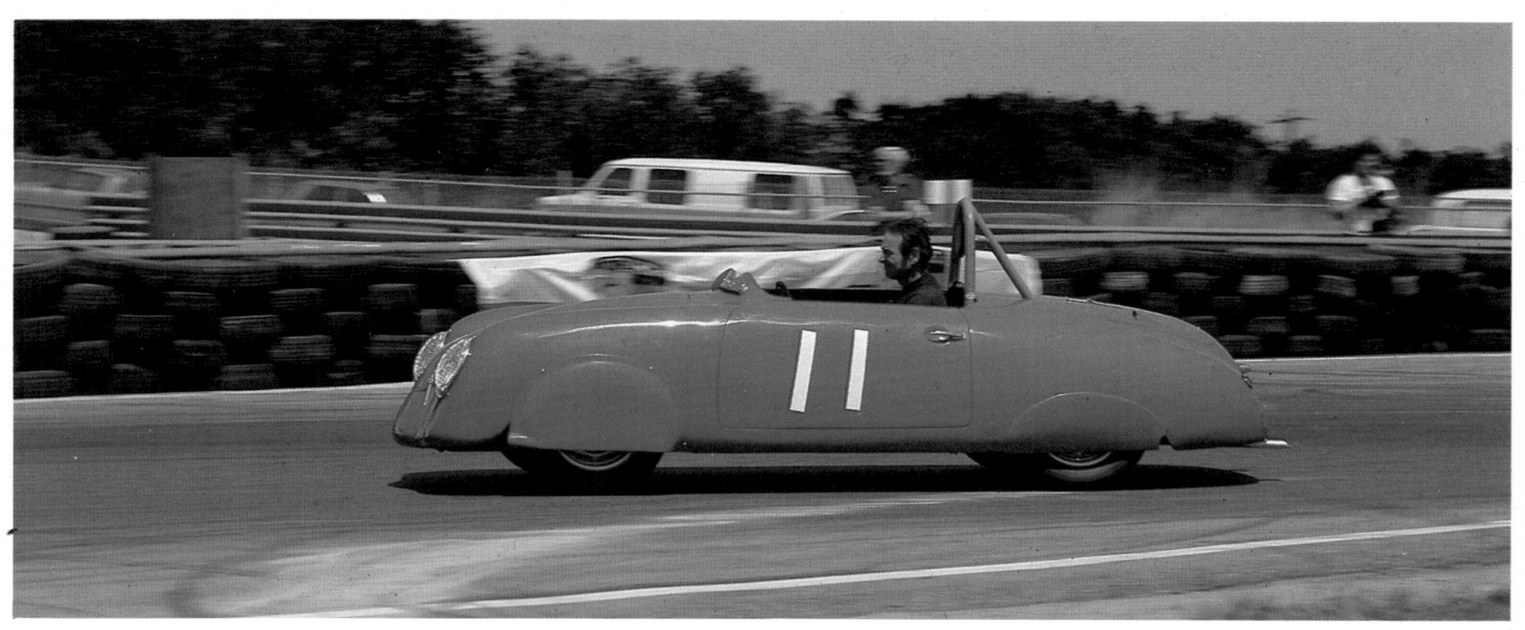

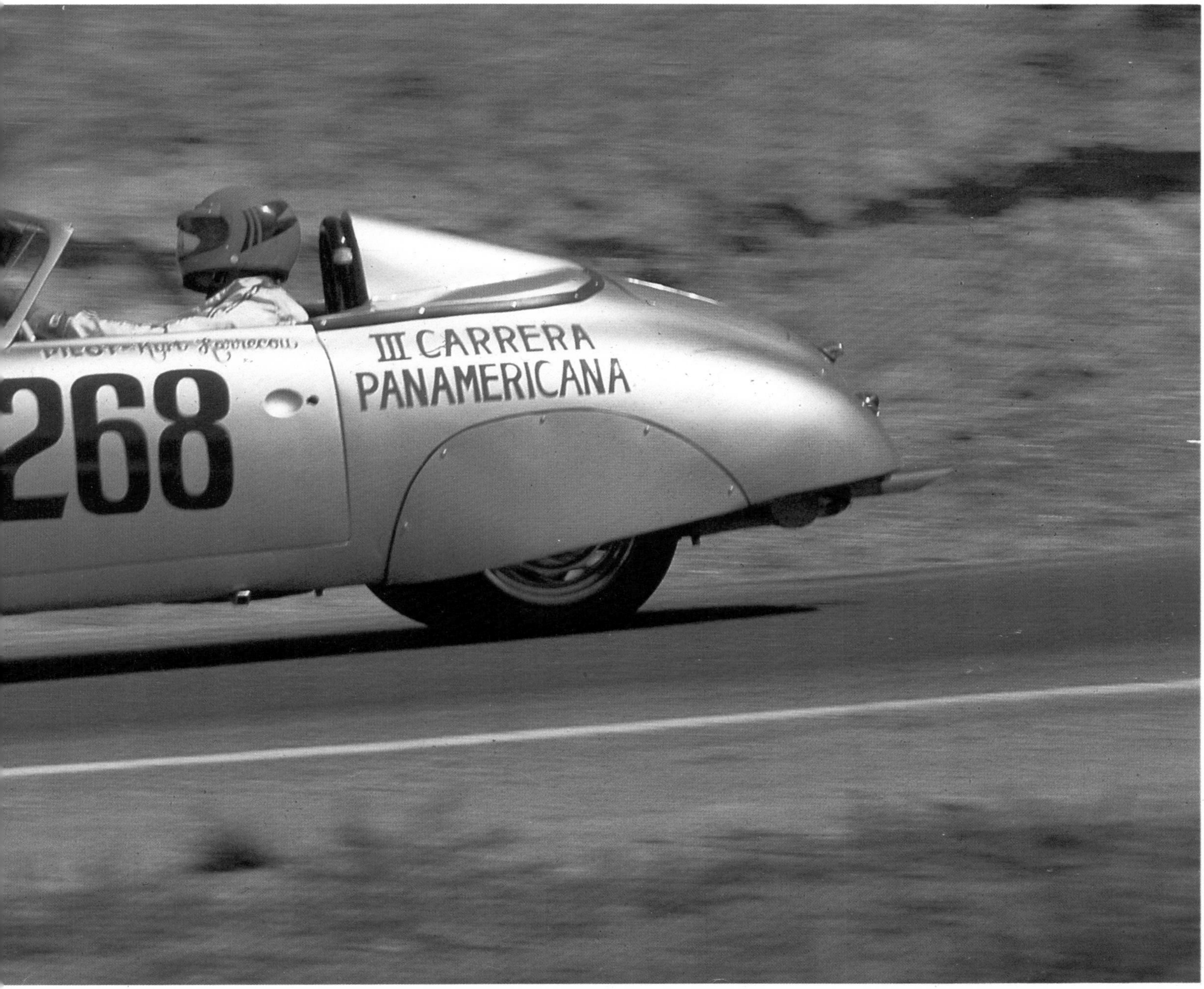
III CARRERA
PANAMERICANA
268

UW 14

UUW14

It had perhaps been expected that the younger generation of Porsches and Piëchs would take over the running of the company, but this was not to be. Ferry's oldest son, Ferdinand Alexander (known as "Butzi"), was for a number of years in charge of the styling studio and produced the shape of the 911 model; his younger brother Peter became director of production, but the two other Porsche sons did not work for the family company. Of their four Piëch cousins, Ferdinand Piëch worked on engine design and developed the 911 engine before becoming head of Porsche research and as such, responsible for the 917 racing car. His brother Michael was appointed as general manager

of Porsche's Zuffenhausen factory in 1971. But all the younger members of the family left the company at the time of the 1972 reorganization—Butzi eventually started his own Porsche industrial design bureau in Austria, and Ferdinand Piëch became head of research and development for Audi where he later produced an obvious Porsche competitor in the shape of the Audi Quattro Coupé.

Below: Ferry Porsche still lives in the house at Feuerbacherweg. In this photograph he poses with the two fastest Porsches of today: the 911 Turbo and the 928 S.

The man who took over the day-to-day running of the Porsche company in 1972 was Dr Ernst Fuhrmann, who as a young engineer had designed the Porsche Carrera engine in the 1950s but had later spent many years with other German companies. During his tenure the new generation of Porsche cars was developed—the 924, 928 and 944 models. When he retired at the end of 1980, there were rumors that Ferdinand Piëch would be brought back into the Porsche fold as his successor; instead the choice fell on a German-born American citizen who had previously worked mainly in the commercial vehicle industry: Peter Schutz who at 50 years of age at the time of his appointment, can still look forward to 12 years in the Porsche top job. With his appointment, another family tradition was broken, as Schutz was given a five percent stock holding in the company. The Porsches and the Piëchs are no longer the sole owners of the Porsche company.

Obviously the real reasons behind the 1972 reorganization have never been revealed but it has been suggested that there was considerable rivalry between the two factions of the clan—Porsche on one side, Piëch on the other, and that the conflict could only be solved if all parties withdrew from the day-to-day management of the company. So far the solution seems to have worked, and any family squabbles which may have taken place have been successfully contained behind the boardroom doors. Ferry Porsche is still at the age of 74 chairman of the supervisory board of directors; but when in time, he and Louise Piëch decide to step down from the board, or if death overtakes either of them before, there may be another conflict between the two branches of the family which can hopefully be resolved in the interest of the company.

Over the past 30 years the Porsche company has pursued many other interests apart from building cars. Soon after the return to Stuttgart, Porsche entered into an agreement with the Allgaier company which then started to make Porsche-designed tractors under license. Porsche's design consultancy business has never been short of customers although many of its activities in this field have not been subject to public scrutiny; one example of a Porsche-designed car which has been revealed was a project for Studebaker undertaken in 1953. During the 1970s, much publicity was given to the Austrian Chancellor Bruno Kreisky's project to set up a native motor industry; he sought Porsche's assistance for the design, and the resulting car, a medium-sized family saloon inevitably nicknamed the Austro-Porsche, all but went into production, but the project faltered on the difficulty of finding a suitable distribution network.

It has been claimed that there are few, if any, car manufacturers who have not sought Porsche's advice or assistance on this or that. The Porsche baulk-ring synchromesh is a famous example; this is found in many gearbox designs, and has been adopted by both Mercedes-Benz and BMW. Porsche even designed the gearbox for the abortive Bugatti type 251 Grand Prix car of 1955. Porsche's commitment to Volkswagen was strong for many years—the VW-Porsche car was an example, but it is less well known that the Porsche 924 was originally designed to a brief from VW-Audi for a sports car project, or that Porsche in the early 1970s designed a completely new small car for VW. But with the appointment of another headstrong Austrian, Professor Dr Ernst Fiala, as head of Volkswagen's own impressive research and development section, Porsche's role in VW projects has become less important. Now the mutual assistance is sometimes reversed and Porsche can for instance share the benefit of Volkswagen facilities such as the famous wind tunnel at Wolfsburg which played its part in the development of the shape of the 928.

Apart from the dual activities of manufacturing sports cars, and acting as design and engineering consultants to other companies, Porsche has from time to time explored other areas of activity, without ever going in for any large-scale diversification. Porsche car engines—especially the original flat-four from the type 356—have been successfully modified for use in aircraft, and for marine and industrial purposes. One particularly interesting vehicle made by Porsche also deserves mention—the type 597, the *Jagdwagen* or Hunter. This was developed in 1954–55 as Porsche's bid to secure a contract to supply the West German army, the Bundeswehr, with a new type of Jeep vehicle. It used a detuned type 356 engine and the stark bodywork was reminiscent of the wartime VW Kübelwagen. When the Bundeswehr preferred the Auto-Union "Munga" design instead, Porsche briefly offered the Jagdwagen for sale in a civilian version but only 71 had been made by the time Porsche dropped the project in 1958. The Jagdwagen incorporated optional four-wheel drive while the engine was of course still in the rear; an idea that may yet influence Porsche cars of the future.

Porsche's development over the years has naturally made expansion inevitable. By the time the company was given its old prewar factory back—which did not finally happen until 1955—work had already started on additional buildings near the Reutter factory. Then Porsche suddenly had two factories in Zuffenhausen, and both are still in use today. The Reutter company was taken over by Porsche in 1963, when the 911 was going into production; Reutter had been reluctant to make the investment necessary to build 911 bodies and by buying the company Porsche secured their body supply. Then when Volkswagen and Porsche joined forces to produce and sell the 914 model in 1969, a new company—the VW-Porsche sales corporation—was set up with new headquarters at Ludwigsburg just north of Stuttgart, which since 1974 (the year the VW-Porsche sales corporation was liquidated when Porsche bought out VW's half share) has served as the sales, service and parts department for Porsche alone. The 914 four-cylinder models were incidentally assembled in the Karmann factory at Osnabrück, while the 914/6 was built at Zuffenhausen.

As early as 1960, Porsche had bought a large parcel of land in the countryside near Weissach west of Stuttgart, and during the 1960s construction began of a proving ground and test track, and of what was to become a completely self-contained research and development center. This has by now grown into what must be the largest facility of its kind in the world, relative to the overall size of the Porsche company, but this is entirely justified in view of the consultancy work which Porsche undertakes for so many clients. The staff at Weissach number more than 1500—almost 30 percent of the total number of 5500 Porsche employees—from all of the specialized professions that contribute to the design and development of a new car. Porsche's racing department has also found a new home here.

Apart from the three main sites of the company—Zuffenhausen (where the 911 and 928 models are assembled), Ludwigsburg and Weissach—Porsche also leases the former NSU factory at Neckarsulm from VW-Audi. This plant was scheduled for closure when the NSU Ro 80 went out of production but by leasing it Porsche gained the production capacity to build the 20,000 924 and 944 models per year which would take the company into the big league among sports car producers in the 1970s and 1980s. The workers at Neckarsulm are

Above: The 1955 Jagdwagen, *a latter-day successor to the wartime* Kübelwagen *which was rejected by the German Army.*

still employed by Audi and are therefore not counted toward Porsche's staff; the only workers at Neckarsulm directly employed by Porsche are, significantly enough, the quality control inspectors.

From the dilapidated former sawmill at Gmünd to the laboratories of Weissach in 30 years is a magnificent achievement, even by fast-moving motor industry standards. There is however an obvious parallel to the development of the Porsche company—the development of Porsche cars, from special-bodied Volkswagens to a complete range of the most desirable sports cars in the world. In the following chapters, we will consider the Porsche cars in detail.

4: FROM LITTLE ACORNS

PORSCHE
697 UVX

Previous page: The purposeful-looking Speedster is even more functional in racing trim. This one is a 356 A model.

The birth of the Porsche car can be said to date from 11 June 1947; this was the day when design work on project 356 was officially begun by the men at Gmünd. At first, project 356 was conceived as an open two-seater roadster, built on a tubular chassis with a wheelbase of 2150mm (83.9in) and with extensive use of Volkswagen components including engine and gearbox, torsion bar suspension, steering and brakes. There was however one important difference. Where the VW had a proper rear engine, the engine of the type 356 was turned around through 180° making the car what we now call mid-engined; the layout was of course inherited from the Auto-Union racers via the prewar project 114 sports car. The engine was basically stock Volkswagen, in those days of 1131cc (69cu in), but mildly tuned with larger valves and a higher compression ratio. Later on, two carburetors would be fitted, giving a power output of approximately 40bhp. The repositioning of the engine meant that it was also necessary to turn the VW rear suspension around, so the trailing arms were converted to leading arms and the torsion bars were at the extreme rear end of the chassis.

Body design was naturally the work of Komenda. It was really a simple and unpretentious styling job, already showing many of the traits that would become so familiar on countless Porsches to follow. To enable spats to be fitted over the front wheels the body was deliberately wide at the front, tapered in plan view toward the back of the car. Body sides were flat and unadorned, with a straight-through wing line which was as yet extremely unusual on production cars. Both front and rear ends fell away in graceful curves; those at the front undoubtedly chosen to permit the fitting of the sloping VW headlamps! The whole shape was remarkably smooth with not even an air intake to scar the surface, only a line of narrow slots down each side of the engine lid. Bumpers were virtually integral with a rather symbolic rubbing strip, while even the doorhandles were of the flush-mounted pop-out type once favored by Fiat.

The front "hood" gave access to the luggage space and the fuel tank; spare wheel and battery were housed behind the engine at the rear of the car. The windshield consisted of two frameless flat panes, meeting in a V and supported only by a central pillar. The seat was of the bench type but with a shaped backrest giving some lateral support, while the simple dashboard was dominated by a large speedometer in front of the driver. The folding top was—to put it mildly—flimsy, and strictly for emergency use. In common with all Porsches built at Gmünd, the body was handbeaten from aluminum sheets.

This was the first Porsche, proclaiming its identity in bold capital letters across the nose of the car. It ran in chassis form in March 1948, and was completed at the end of May, receiving its roadworthiness certificate from the Austrian authorities on 8 June 1948—exactly three days short of a year after the design had been started. Even allowing for the fact that so many of the components were well-tried existing units, this was quite an achievement for a small company with modest facilities; and even as the first 356 was being completed, the next car, type 356/2, was already well advanced in the workshops at Gmünd. The story of Porsche number one is however worth recounting: the car was sold almost immediately, to a Swiss from Zürich, Herr von Senger—he took delivery in September 1948. He had the car somewhat modified for racing, and sold it back to Porsche in 1953. Today it occupies the place of honor in the Porsche museum; it has recently been restored and has now been fitted with the original type of bumpers which for many years it lacked, but bucket seats and more elaborate instrumentation are still reminders of the car's racing career.

Von Senger did a lot more than just buy the first Porsche. Together with his

Above: Ferry and the Professor with the Porsche number one at Gmünd in the summer of 1948. The "K" on the numberplate stands for the Austrian province of Kärnten.

associate Blank he placed an order for further cars as early as March 1948, when the revised model 356/2 was still only in mock-up form. Ferry Porsche planned the 356/2 as the actual production car which would incorporate vital modifications compared to the 356/1 roadster. The mid-engine was abandoned in favor of a Volkswagen-style overhung rear engine which gave some interior space for luggage or children's seats, and also permitted the rear suspension to revert to the standard VW layout. The tubular space-frame chassis was scrapped as unsuitable for series production and a new pressed steel platform chassis with integral scuttle, door pillars and inner wings was developed. The wheelbase was shortened to 2100mm (82in). Finally, Komenda designed a fastback coupé body in place of the roadster, although a cabriolet version of the 356/2 was always planned. The first prototype coupé was ready in July 1948.

To the uninitiated it can be difficult to distinguish this car, or any of the other Porsche coupés built at Gmünd, from the later models. Apart from the

Left: Porsche's debut at Le Mans came when Veuillet and Mouche won the 1100cc Class in the 1951 race.

Right: This is the 1951 Le Mans car in the somewhat modified form in which it can be seen today in the Porsche Museum.

Below right: The first two Porsches near Gmünd in 1948. The first coupé is followed by the original mid-engined roadster.

Below: The original drawing for the first 356.

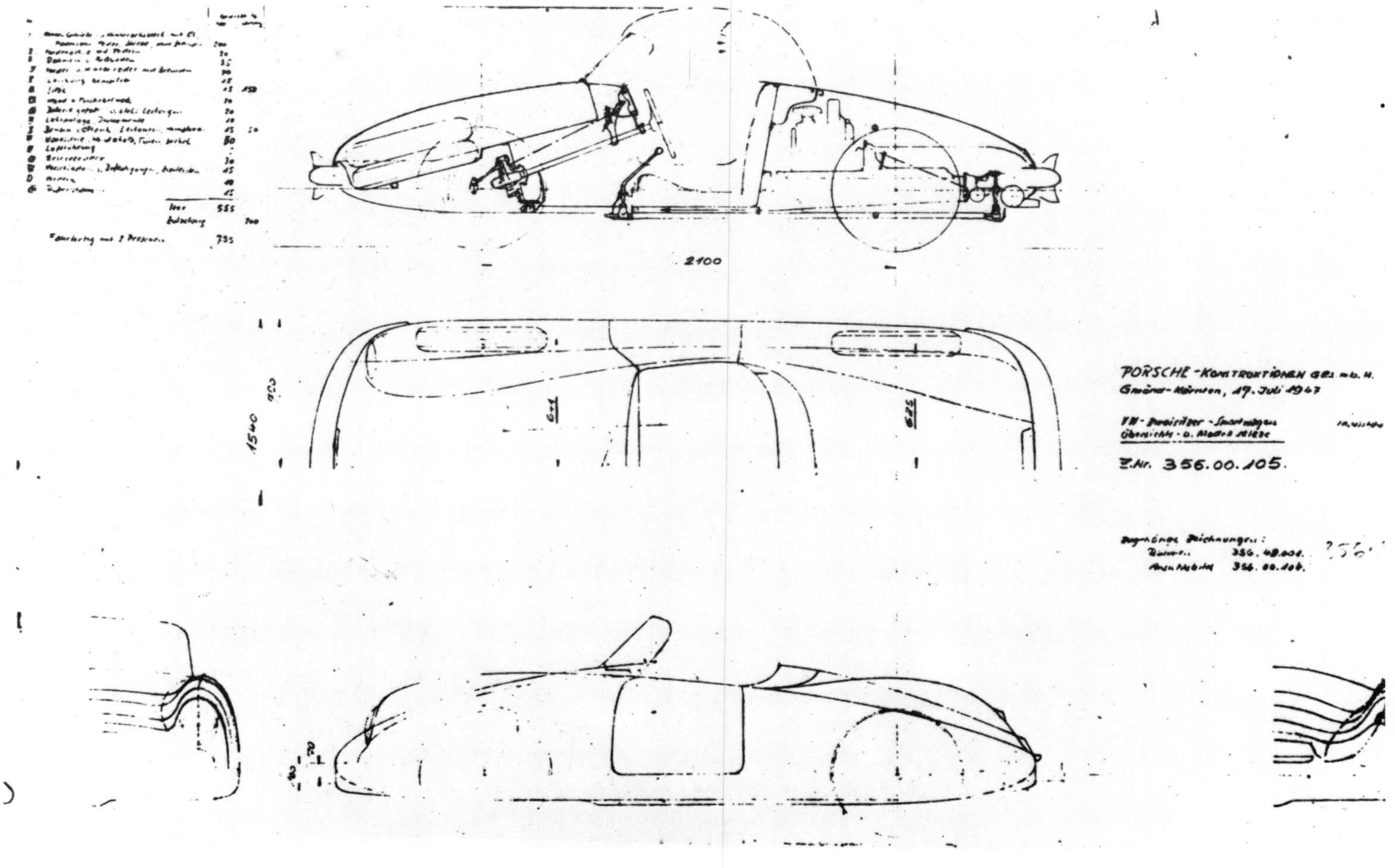

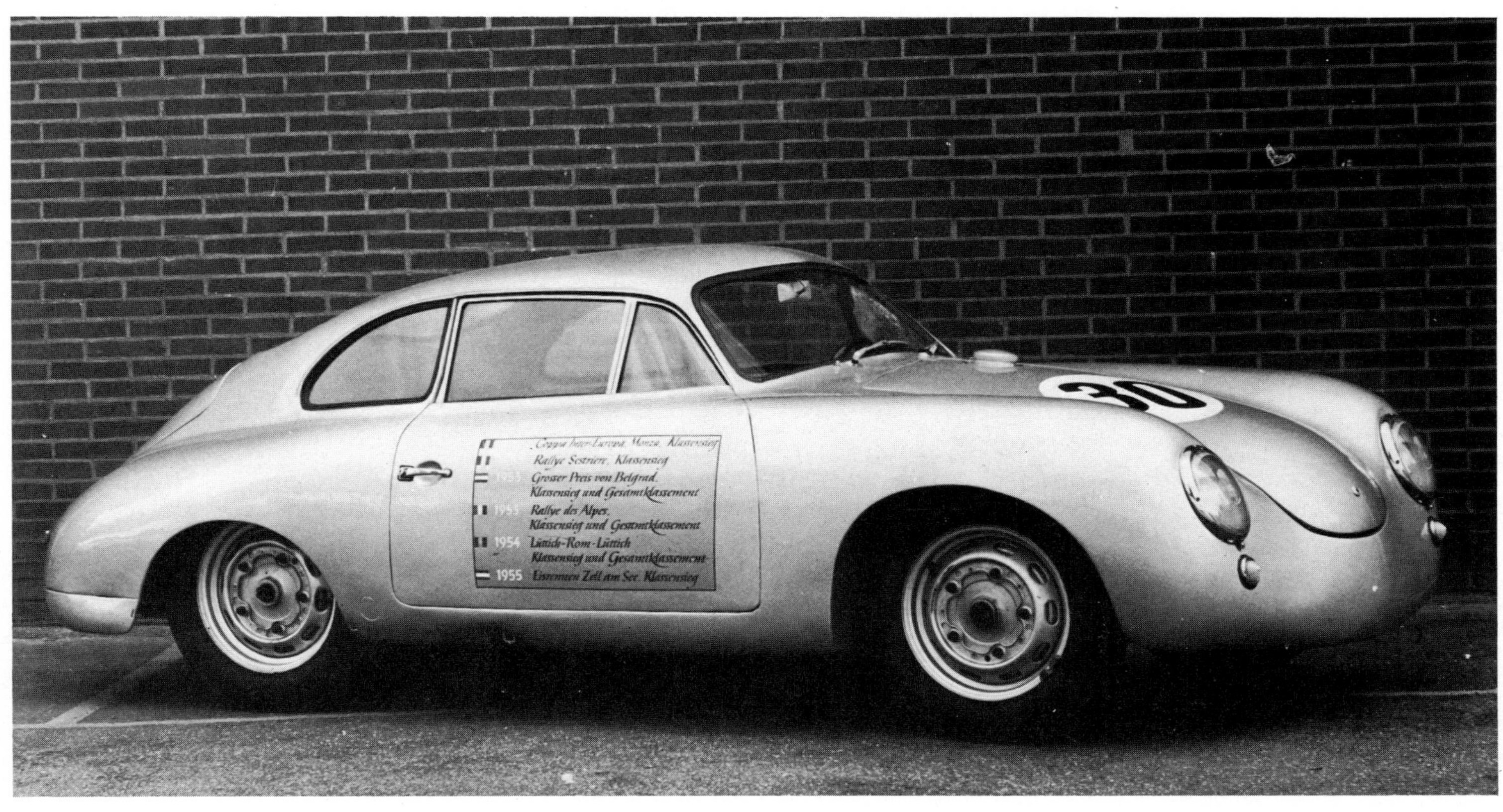

30
Rallye Sestriere, Klassensieg
Grosser Preis von Belgrad,
Klassensieg und Gesamtklassement
Rallye des Alpes,
Klassensieg und Gesamtklassement
1954 Lüttich-Rom-Lüttich
Klassensieg und Gesamtklassement
1955 Eisrennen Zell am See, Klassensieg

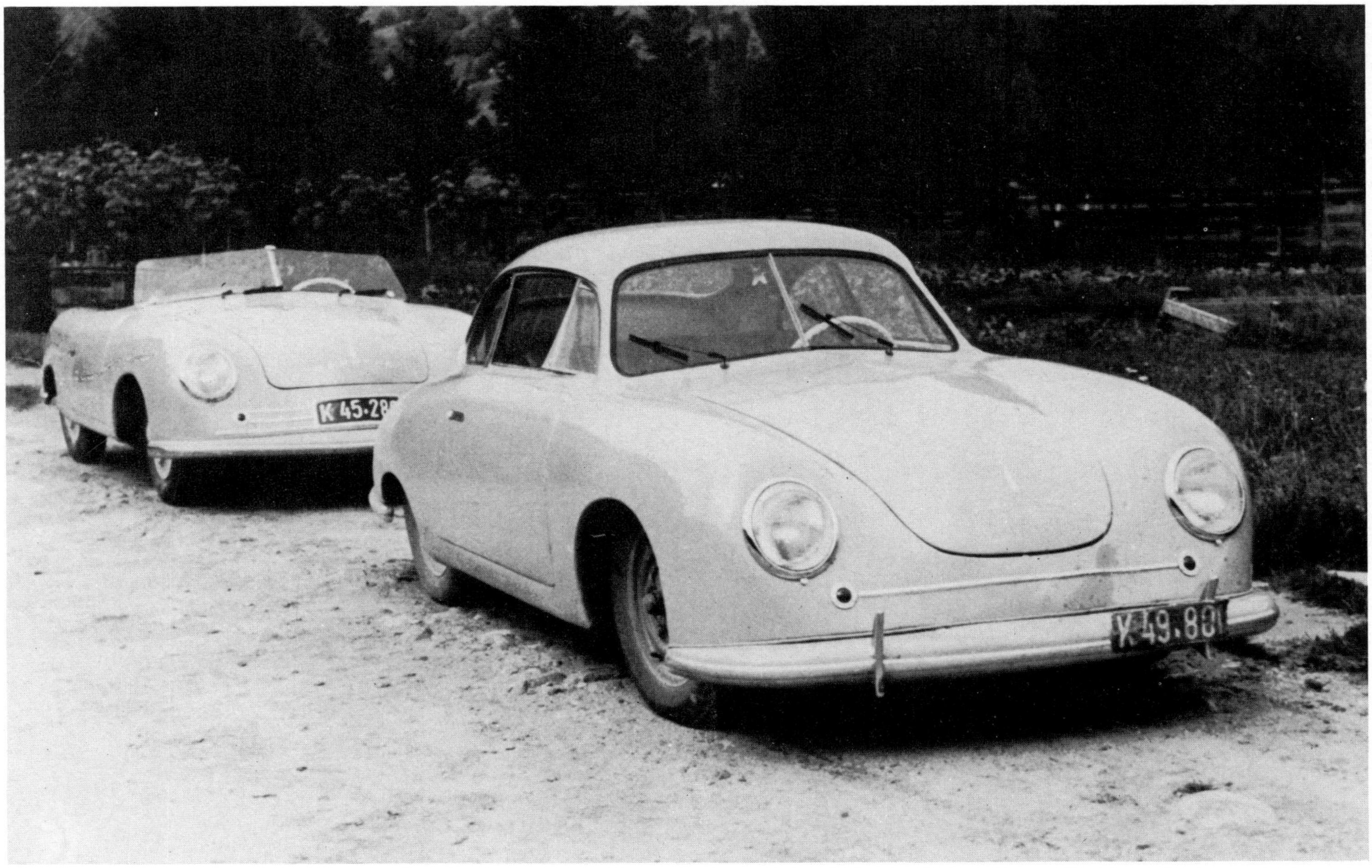
K 45-28
Y 49.801

50

Left: The original Reutter body factory at Zuffenhausen, where Porsche moved to in 1950.

Top right: The "America" roadster, from a painting by Ken Rush.

Center right: Müller and von Hanstein were not as lucky in the 1952 Le Mans—they were forced to retire with gearbox trouble.

Below: Veuillet and Mouche repeated the class win in the 1952 Le Mans, still using the Gmünd-built aluminum coupé.

fact that the Gmünd cars had aluminum bodies—handbeaten over wooden formers by a superb craftsman whose only weakness was erratic timekeeping owing to his fondness for good Austrian wine—there were few identification features on these early cars. The split V-windshield of the original roadster was retained but curved quarterlights in the front doors were added to ease the airflow round the corner of the greenhouse. Most of the Gmünd cars also had trafficators mounted in the front wings, and one or two trim strips running across the front of the car below the trunk lid. The air intake in the engine cover at the back, a typical 356 feature, was already in evidence on the Gmünd cars.

Just over 50 cars were built at Gmünd, equally split between coupés and cabriolets; of the latter, only a few had Porsche's own cabriolet body, the

Below: An early 356 Cabriolet of 1952.

majority were bodied by the Swiss coachbuilder Beutler. The records also reveal that a number of cars were assembled in the Tatra works at Vienna. Von Senger in Zürich only took delivery of another five cars after the first roadster; the biggest single customer was the Swedish truck manufacturer Scania-Vabis which took 15 cars. Scania had already secured the Volkswagen agency for Sweden, and these 15 Porsches which were all cabriolets were delivered in 1950–51. It will be appreciated that car production at Gmünd was on a very small scale indeed, with only four cars being finished during 1948. But even after production had started at Zuffenhausen, Gmünd was kept going with the last Austrian car being delivered in March 1951. After that time the Austrian Porsche activities were centered at Salzburg, and the last few aluminum-bodied Gmünd coupés were retained by the Porsche company for racing—the famous light-alloy cars were the first Porsches seen in competition, apart from the original roadster raced by von Senger in Switzerland.

Porsche's competition debut came about in a slightly casual way. During a visit to the Paris Motor Show in October 1950, Professor Porsche ran into an old friend, the French motoring journalist Charles Faroux. Faroux had been intimately connected with the 24-hour race at Le Mans since its inception in 1923, so it was natural that he should suggest to the Professor that Porsche cars should be entered in the 1951 Le Mans race. Porsche grunted his assent, and the company subsequently obtained an entry for two cars. In the event only one ran, a Gmünd light-alloy coupé with a small-bore 1086cc (66.2cu in) engine to bring it into the 1100cc class and fitted with wheel spats both front and rear. The drivers were French—Mouche and Veuillet, the latter an experienced Le Mans campaigner who had obtained the Porsche agency for France. They had the cheek to win their class, in 20th place overall (admittedly there was only one other car in the 1100cc class, a D.B. which finished 21st) but by all accounts the French took it well. The same car went on to score class wins in several rallies, in the Mille Miglia and in the 1952 Le Mans again, and is now in the Porsche museum albeit with some bodywork modifications, including a lowered roof.

Meanwhile, production at Zuffenhausen was in full swing. Reutter tooled up for all-steel bodywork, and made some retouches to the styling—notably a slightly lower and wider windshield still with the split V shape but also with the outer ends of the two glass panes curving slightly round toward the doors. This obviated the need for the complex curved quarterlights on the Gmünd cars, and front quarterlights did not appear on Zuffenhausen coupés before the 356 B in 1959. Trafficators were replaced by flashing direction indicators, those at the front mounted inboard and below the headlamps, and the nose was unadorned, save for the trunk lid handle and the Porsche script, now below rather than on the trunk lid itself. Doorhandles were of the VW type. The first coupé was ready for Easter 1950, and toward the end of the year the cabriolet was in production as well—both models were displayed at the Paris Motor Show. A few of the early Zuffenhausen-built cabriolets had bodywork by the respected German coachbuilder and cabriolet specialist Gläser.

Incidentally in spite of the fact that the bodywork was made of steel rather than aluminum, the first Zuffenhausen cars still weighed only 780kg (1716lb), the same as the Gmünd cars—later they put on rather more weight. In mechanical terms, the main difference was that the engine was now of 1086cc (66.2cu in) rather than 1131cc (69cu in), achieved by reducing the bore from the standard VW dimension of 75mm (2.9in) to 73.5mm (2.86in) while the stroke was unaltered at 64mm (2.5in). With two Solex carburetors and a 7:1 compression ratio, output was a modest 40bhp at 4200rpm. The cylinder heads were now of a design unique to Porsche and were cast in aluminum, but the cylinders were still the cast-iron Volkswagen type.

Other Volkswagen components used included the gearbox, as yet innocent of synchromesh, the brakes—Volkswagen's recently introduced ATE-Lockheed hydraulics—steering and the torsion bar suspension. The finished product sold in the German home market for DM9850 which to put it in perspective was also the price of the Opel Kapitän 2.5-liter (152.5cu in) six cylinder saloon, or just over twice the cost of the Volkswagen standard model. A Porsche has never been a cheap car . . . still, over 400 had found customers before the end of 1950, and in March 1951 the factory celebrated the 500th German-built Porsche. In one year, Zuffenhausen had built 10 times as many cars as Gmünd managed in three years. Porsche had arrived.

From then on, the 356 story is one of careful development and attention to detail—in much the same way that big brother at Wolfsburg improved and refined the Beetle. The year 1951 saw two new Porsche engines, in the spring the bore was increased to 80mm (3.1in) for 1286cc (78.45cu in) and 44bhp, and in the autumn 10mm (.39in) was added to the stroke to give Porsche their first 1.5-liter engine—of 1488cc (90.77cu in) to be exact, and giving 60bhp. Comparative top speeds for the three models of 356 were: 1100, 87mph (140km/h); 1300, 90mph (145km/h); and 1500, 104mph (167km/h). The new engines had aluminum cylinders with chrome-plated bores produced by Mahle, and the crankshafts used roller bearings for the big ends. From now on Porsche engines would develop completely independently of the Volkswagen units, although the basic layout of the air-cooled flat-four was retained until 1976 when the final version of the four cylinder 912 model was discontinued.

The original 356 series lasted until 1955 but underwent some further notable improvements. The 1952 cars had brakes with two leading shoes operating in finned drums and from mid-1952, the windshield was in one piece although it still retained the V-shape. For the 1953 model year, the original 1500 engine was replaced by a detuned 55bhp version with a plain bearing crankshaft—this engine was nicknamed the "Dame" as it was far more quiet and refined than the previous version. A new 70bhp 1500 Super engine with roller bearings was soon introduced alongside the "lady". At the same time, Porsche's own gearbox was introduced, with baulk-ring synchromesh on all forward ratios, and the 1953–55 models may be identified by their heftier separately-mounted bumpers with overriders, the ventilated wheels and direction indicators directly underneath the headlamps. In 1952, the Porsche emblem made its first appearance on the cars; this was a combination of the coat of arms of the city of Stuttgart (a prancing black horse) and those of the land of Baden-Württemberg, a quartered shield with three stag antlers in opposite corners. Like Alfa-Romeo, Morris and Volkswagen, Porsche demonstrated its loyalty to its home in its emblem.

During 1953, a new 1300 engine appeared, of 74.5 × 74mm (2.9in × 2.89in) and 1290cc (78.7cu in)—fitted with a roller bearing crank and developing 60 bhp this was known as the 1300 Super. A year later the original 1286cc (78.45cu in) engine disappeared in favor of the 1300 A which shared dimensions with the Super but had plain big end bearings and was detuned to give 44bhp. A new bodystyle appeared briefly in 1952–53, the "America" roadster which as the name indicates was built specially for the US market where 14 of the 15 cars made were sold. The America had a slight dip in the wingline unique to this model and with spartan equipment, weight had been pared down to 605kg (1331lb) so performance was impressive with the 1500 Super engine.

The America was only a foretaste of things to come—the Speedster, one of the most famous Porsche models, was launched in September 1954. The basic Speedster body was clearly derived from the cabriolet but the rear tonneau

The Speedster was originally introduced in 1954 but the original 356 model was only in production for a few months before being replaced by the 356 A. From the outside it is difficult to spot the differences between the 356 and the 356 A Speedster. Only the absence of the Porsche badge in the trunk lid handle shows this to be the original 356 model. Note the "1500" badge on the rear of the car; the steering wheel fitted is not the original, but the fascia is the classically simple and functional type which was used only on the Speedster model.

XYE84

XYE84
PORSCHE
HISTORIC
SPORTS CAR
CLUB

The absence of bumpers and hub caps is natural on a Speedster, which is still pursuing a racing career. The headlamps may appear unoriginal but this type of recessed vertical lamp with a smooth outer cover was seen on many Porsches of the 1950s.

panel was extended forward encroaching on the passenger space and the car was strictly a two-seater, with proper bucket seats. The one-piece wraparound windshield was lowered and had a simple chrome surround, and the top was a very sketchy affair—completely unlike the superbly constructed cabriolet top, the speedster top was more reminiscent of tops fitted to British sports cars at the time and so were the loose sidescreens. A Speedster with the top up is not a pretty sight and entry and exit is undignified in the extreme! The Speedster owner had to put up with a much more spartan dashboard and interior but it is unlikely that he complained, as he had saved DM500 compared to the coupé, or a whacking DM2500 over the cabriolet. At first however the Speedster was exported exclusively to the USA where it sold for less than $3000 and was intended to take Porsche into competition with the cheaper British sports cars such as Austin-Healey, Triumph and MG. The model was normally only available with either of the two 1500cc engines, the Dame or the Super, although at least one German home market brochure describing the 356 A in October 1955 mentions Speedsters with 1300 engines as well.

The 356 went into its final production year with a few more modifications—an anti-roll bar was added to the front suspension, and the original VW crankcase was replaced by a new three-piece crankcase. Externally, small horn grilles appeared by the front direction indicator lamps. For 1955, only the 1300 and 1500 engines were quoted, as the original 1100 model was discontinued.

The original 356 notched up some useful competition results for Porsche—notably class wins at Le Mans every year from 1951 to 1955, but also class wins in several of the important international rallies, such as the Alpine Rally, the Tour de France and—most impressive of all—outright victory in the 1952 Liège-Rome-Liège Marathon. In the 1952 Mille Miglia road race Porsche won both the 1100 and the 1500cc classes—the latter car was co-driven by that seasoned Mille Miglia veteran, Count Lurani. Many of these successes fell to the original light-alloy bodied cars built at Gmünd. But gradually, Porsche's sporting efforts became centered on the real racers, the Spyders which will be considered in a following chapter, and the limelight passed away from the 356 models which however were a force to be reckoned with in club racing for a good many years to come. Not least of course in Britain where 356 drivers included such different personalities as a very young Jim Clark, and Denis Jenkinson, roving correspondent of *Motor Sport*. The latter took delivery of a 356 in 1955, became firmly addicted to the marque and has written two entertaining books about his Porsche experiences.

Porsche in Britain had a very inauspicious start. Three cars were exhibited at the 1951 London Motor Show; a special permit had to be obtained to import these cars as Britain was effectively closed to all car imports until 1953. The Porsche display at Earls Court had been organized on the initiative of Czech-born Charles Meisl, who was then working for Connaught Engineering Limited. This company held the Porsche agency for a brief period, but passed it on to John Colborne-Baber who had been the patron saint for Volkswagen in this country when the first VWs started to appear soon after the war, brought back by British servicemen returning from Germany.

In 1954 A.F.N. Limited at Isleworth took over—founded by the three Aldington brothers in the 1930s, A.F.N. had taken over production of the Frazer-Nash car which was still being made in small numbers, but had also been associated with BMW before the war when these were sold as Frazer-Nash-BMW in Britain. During the 1950s they imported a range of German cars, including BMW, DKW and Porsche. One of the later Frazer-Nash cars, the Continental GT coupé of the late 1950s, used a BMW engine and incor-

Above: The 356 Cabriolet was a favorite with the German police. In this photograph the Stuttgart police pick up their new 356 Bs from the factory in 1962.

porated several Porsche 356 body panels! A.F.N. were the Porsche agents until 1977 when a new company, Porsche Cars Great Britain Ltd, was set up; this is 60 percent owned by Porsche in Germany, and new headquarters at Reading were opened by Ferry Porsche. There is still a close link with A.F.N. at Isleworth whose premises are an important sales outlet, and the managing director of Porsche in Britain is John Aldington, the son of one of the three A.F.N. founders. Over the past few years, Porsche has enjoyed a spectacular increase in sales in Britain, which is now the company's third biggest market, after the USA and Germany.

In many other countries, Porsches were imported and sold by the Volkswagen agents—we have mentioned Scania-Vabis in Sweden but there were also AMAG in Switzerland, Ben Pon in Holland, the coachbuilder D'Ieteren in Belgium and SMC in Denmark. The most important market was the USA, where the first Porsches were imported in 1950, by one Max Hoffman, an Austrian-born foreign car dealer in New York who in 1947 had launched Jaguar in the USA and in 1950 had been appointed exclusive VW importer for the Eastern States. Eventually Porsche set up its own importing company in the USA, and much later, when the VW-Porsche was launched at the end of the 1960s, VW and Porsche interests in the States were merged and a special division was set up to handle Porsche as well as Audi. That explains the perhaps confusing "Porsche--Audi" name sometimes seen on Porsche racing cars in the USA. This market alone absorbs virtually half of Porsche's entire production, although at the time of writing neither the 924, nor the 911 Turbo are sold in the USA.

5: DRIVING IN ITS FINEST FORM

LUK 99

Previous page: The final form of the 356: the disk-braked 356 C of 1963–65. Bodywork was identical to its immediate predecessor the 356 B T-6, but the new wheels and hubcaps were an immediate identification point.

The Porsche company had reached maturity when the 356 A was introduced at the Frankfurt Motor Show in September 1955. The new model was immediately identifiable by its new curved windshield and rubbing strips underneath the doors. It also had wheels of 15in diameter replacing the 17in wheels used on the 356. Inside, there was a new instrument panel and the equipment was on a rather more lavish scale than had hitherto been normal on a Porsche. Coupé, cabriolet and Speedster bodies were available as before.

More important however was the engine. The 1300 and 1300 S engines were continued but the 1500 engines were dropped in favor of a new pair of 1600 engines, of 82.5×74mm (3.2×2.9in) and 1582cc (96.5cu in). The "Dame" with plain big end bearings developed some 60bhp, while the S with roller bearings gave another 15bhp. But even this paled in comparison with the new 1500 GS model, also referred to as the "Carrera" (following a Porsche Spyder's 3rd place and class win in the last of the Mexican Carrera Panamericana road races in 1954). The Carrera formula was simple, consisting of a basically standard 356 fitted with the type 547 engine from the Spyder. This was inevitably an air-cooled flat-four, of 85×66mm (3.3×2.6in) and 1498cc (91.4cu in), but had four overhead camshafts driven by a complicated system of shafts. This jewel of an engine was designed by Ernst Fuhrmann and had first appeared in the type 550 Spyder in 1953–4. With exactly 100bhp available, it pushed the top speed of the 356 A Carrera up to almost 200km/h (125mph).

Price was prohibitive, at DM18,500 for the coupé which was more than a Mercedes-Benz 190 SL—one of few other sports cars Germany had to offer. It is even more illuminating to consider Porsche prices in Switzerland, where the Carreras cost more than the Jaguar XK 140 and even the cheapest 1300 model was on par with an Austin-Healey 100. This helps to explain why Porsche only made some 700 Carreras of the original type. Nevertheless, Porsche was an established commercial success when the 10,000th car was delivered in early 1956, driven off the assembly line by a very young Butzi Porsche and timed to coincide with the 25th anniversary of the founding of Dr Porsche's original design bureau.

For 1958 there was an additional body style: the Hardtop, a cabriolet fitted with a detachable hardtop in a contrasting color. On some later Karmann-bodied cars the hardtop was welded permanently in place and was then normally painted in the same color as the main bodywork. Small detail changes that year included quarterlights fitted to the cabriolet doors, and on 1600 models the exhaust pipes were taken through the bumper overriders—not a very clever idea, and soon dropped. The 1300 models were phased out, and the 1600 S was now fitted with a plain bearing crankshaft. There were two versions of the Carrera, the 100bhp De-Luxe and the 110bhp GT.

A year later the Carrera engine had an increased bore of 87.5mm (3.4in) and capacity went up to 1588cc (96.9cu in), with outputs of 105 and 115bhp respectively for the De-Luxe and the GT models. The Speedster model was dropped—it never sold as well as had originally been hoped, and only later became appreciated as a collector's piece. In its place came the Convertible D which featured ordinary Porsche seats instead of bucket seats, a higher windshield, winding windows in the doors and a better top. The D indicated that this body was built by Drauz at Heilbronn rather than Reutter, although some of these bodies were later supplied by the Belgian coachbuilder and Porsche importer D'Ieteren. Just to add to the confusion, the Convertible D later changed its name to Roadster.

The 356 range underwent two further rejuvenations. After a four-year run

Right: The 356 B of 1959–61 in coupé (top) and cabriolet forms.

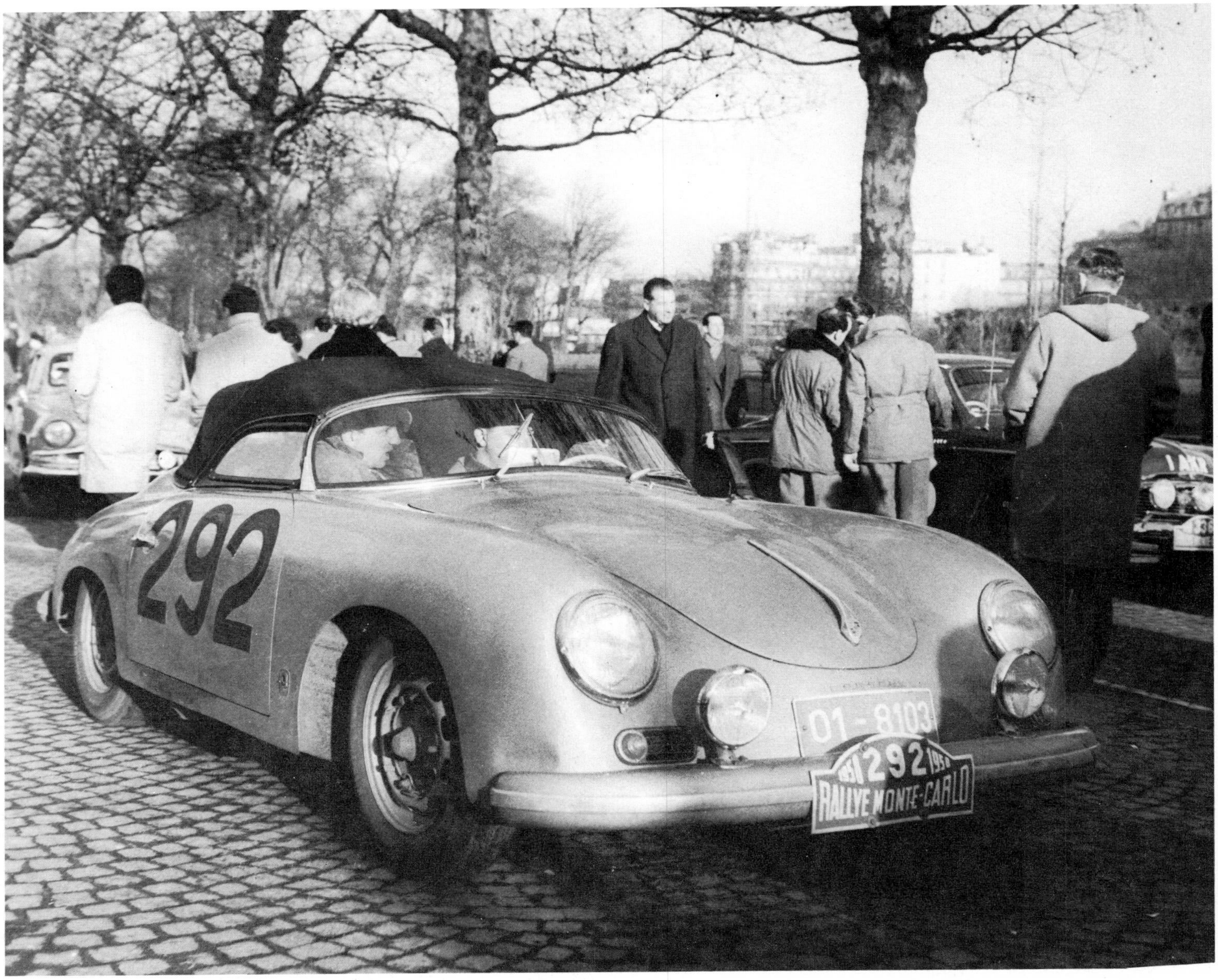
292
01-8103
292
RALLYE MONTE-CARLO

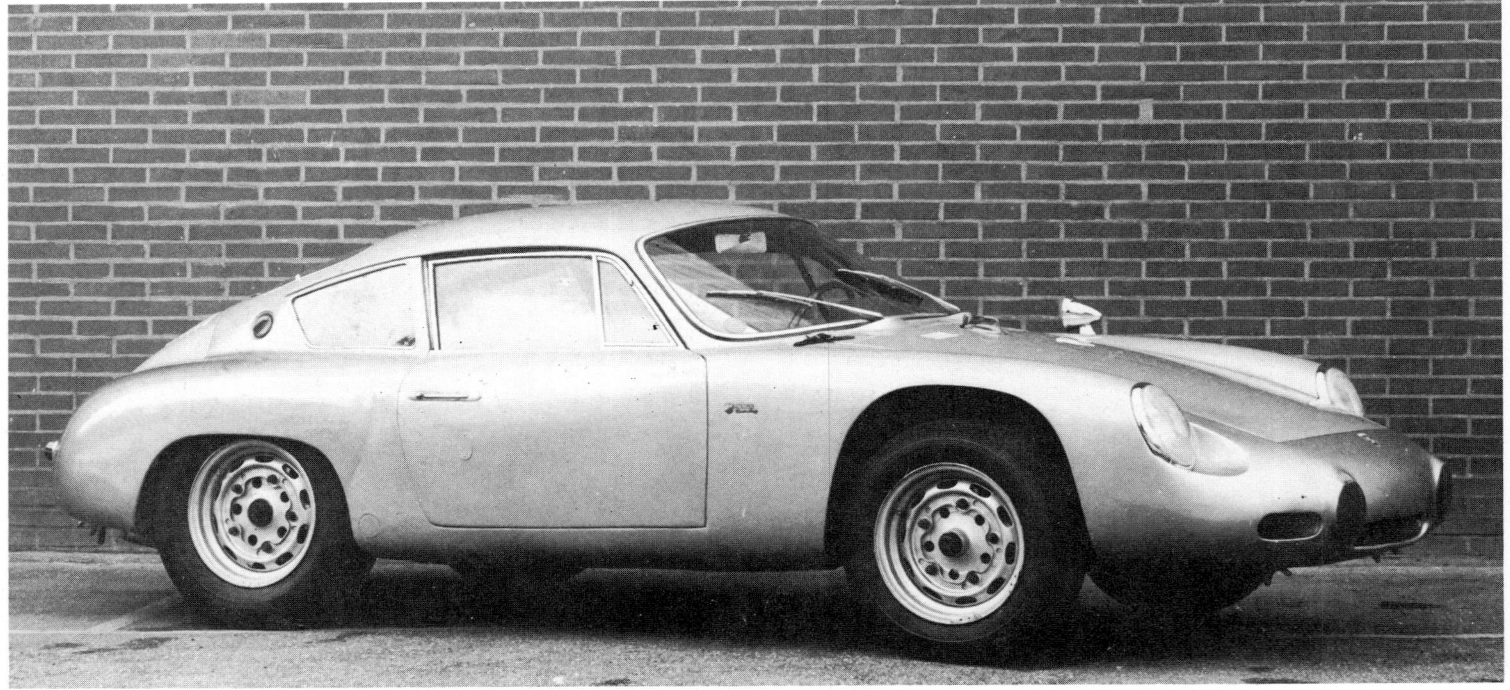

the 356 A gave way to the 356 B in 1959. Again there were both external and internal modifications. The 356 B body had a higher front wing line which raised the headlamps, there were heftier bumpers front and rear which were also mounted higher than previously—obviously in an effort to defend the poor Porsches from car parking attacks by US monsters. The horn grilles by the front indicators were redesigned, and the 356 B sported unmistakeable "nippled" hubcaps which featured the Porsche emblem prominently. Also on the 356 B, quarterlights appeared on the Coupé body for the first time since the Gmünd cars.

A choice of three push-rod 1582cc (96.5cu in) engines was now offered. In addition to the standard "Dame" of 60bhp, the 75bhp S was re-named Super 75 and another famous Porsche type designation appeared for the first time: the Super 90 with as one might guess 90bhp. The 1588cc (96.9cu in) Carrera engine was initially continued in the 356 B range. The rear suspension of the Super 90 and Carrera models included a transverse leaf spring fitted underneath the gearbox, which went some way toward compensating for the unavoidable oversteering tendencies. A particularly interesting model was made available in 1960: the Abarth-Carrera GTL, with an aluminum body built by Zagato and put together by Abarth in Italy on the Porsche chassis. It will be remembered that Porsche and Abarth had had dealings previously, when Carlo Abarth was the agent who helped to secure the Cisitalia contract for Porsche in 1947. Only about 20 of these Abarth-Carreras were made, and

Left: The Speedster is not a pretty sight with the hood up. This 1958 Monte Carlo Rally entrant would also find it difficult to get in and out of the car. The sidescreens were primitive.

Left, below: The rare Abarth-Carrera version of the 356 B. This car is part of the Porsche Museum's collection.

Below: Ferry Porsche, on the left, and the workforce pose around the 10,000th Porsche which left the factory in 1956.

Overleaf: A procession of 356s at Laguna Seca in 1982, led by one of the original Gmünd-built aluminum coupés.

Overleaf, inset: The 356 B Roadster was developed from the Speedster but had a more substantial screen and hood (removed for racing on this car) and wind-up windows.

LAGUNA SECA
CHAMPION
LAGUNA SECA

RADSON
10

The Carrera was the rarest and most desirable of the 356 C range, with the two-liter four cam engine. Other than the badge on the rear of the car, there are few external clues to the identity of the Carrera, although the absence of bars in the horn openings by the front indicator lights may be noted. The bodywork, wheels and hubcaps on this immaculate British-owned 1964 car are the same as on all 356 Cs.

EMD 932B
GB

the model was chiefly intended as a competition car although it remained perfectly usable on the road; in the interests of weight-saving it was however rather more spartanly equipped than the Reutter-bodied cars. There was also a special lightweight Reutter Carrera GT coupé around this time.

In 1961 the bodywork was partially redesigned although the model designation was still 356 B. The new body which is known as the T-6 had enlarged front and rear screens, a bigger front luggage lid with a more square outline, and there were now two air intake grilles in the engine lid. By redesigning the fuel tank, much more luggage space was gained, and the fuel filler cap now lived under a separate flap in the front wing, rather than in the luggage compartment. Also in 1961, the 1600 Carrera was replaced by the 2000 GS Carrera 2, with a 1966cc (119.9cu in) engine of 92 × 74mm (3.6 × 2.9in) and no less than 130bhp.

Porsche themselves have never produced a true four-seater model—even today's 928 can only be called a two-plus-two—although it is known that such models have from time to time been on the drawing boards of the designers at Zuffenhausen or Weissach. For a short while in 1962, the Swiss coachbuilder Beutler stepped into this breach by offering a four seater two-door saloon based on the 356 B chassis with the wheelbase lengthened to 2300mm (89.7in), or 2350mm (91.7in) depending on model. It was not an unattractive car, but the shape was much more conventional by contemporary standards and despite the use of Porsche bumpers, rear lamps, air intakes and other identification features, the Beutler four-seater was still not readily identifiable as a

Below, left and right: One of the Beutler-bodied 356 Bs with the lengthened wheelbase and proper rear seats. The interior was well-appointed but the car looked very conventional, even down to the simulated radiator grille on this example.

Porsche to the casual uninformed observer, and this was probably its greatest failing. The Beutler car was available with either the 68 or the 75bhp engines, and performance must have compared favorably with the standard Porsches as dry weight was quoted at 885kg (194lb)—amazingly, 40kg (88lb) *less* than the Reutter coupé.

In 1962 Porsche for the first time offered disk brakes which became an option on the Carrera models. These were Porsche's own design which had been under development since 1958—the caliper was mounted on the inside of the disk to suit the Volkswagen-type open center wheels. Also in 1962 there was a further variation on the Carrera theme—the 2000 GS-GT with a special lightweight body, styled by Ferry's son Butzi and looking rather like the type 718 racing coupé; but where the type 718 used the mid-engined Spyder chassis, the 2000 GS-GT had the normal chassis with the rear-mounted engine and thus retained the two-plus-two seating package of the type 356. The result was an attractive and very fast motorcar suitable for a wide range of competition activities. It was not distinguished by a special type number or model name but was nicknamed the "Wedge" or even the "Rasp" (in German: *Dreikant-schaber*), because of its distinctive almost triangular profile.

The final 356 model was the 356 C which was produced from 1963 to 1965. The bodywork was carried over from the 356 B T-6 without change, and the most important modification was the use of disk brakes as standard equipment on all four wheels. Not Porsche's own disk brakes this time, but made by ATE to Dunlop designs. These brakes were not suitable for use with Porsche's

traditional wheels, so the 356 C had new wheels with only a small hole in the center, and hubs with the wheel studs mounted closer together. These wheels, with a new plain hubcap design, were the most prominent identification points of the 356 C which is otherwise indistinguishable from the late 356 B.

The 60bhp push-rod engine was no longer produced, and the 75hp and 90bhp models were renamed 1600 C and 1600 SC; the 130bhp 2000 GS Carrera 2 continued in limited production, but only 126 356 C Carreras were built. The coupé and cabriolet body types were available, and the removable hardtop could still be specified for the latter; but the roadster (ex-convertible D) and the Karmann fixed hardtop model had disappeared, with Porsche's production planners undoubtedly heaving a collective sigh of relief. When in 1963 Porsche took over the Reutter company, Porsche at last had control over the body supply problems, and would never again be dependent on three or four different coach builders.

Production of the 356 C came to an end in September 1965, with a grand total of more than 76,000 cars of all models having been made since 1948. Even allowing for the length of the production run it is an impressive figure for a small company which started from scratch; we may compare it to the total of approximately 150,000 MG sports cars made from 1945 to 1962 (TC to MGA), remembering that MG was a well-established concern, part of a large manufacturing group and whose products normally cost a great deal less than the typical Porsche. The 356 C was replaced by the 912 which used the 356 C engine in the chassis and body of the new 911 six-cylinder model which had first been shown in 1963.

Did the 356 really represent "Driving in its Finest Form"—*Fahren in seiner Schönster Form*—as Porsche's advertising slogan even then would have us believe? In terms of pure performance, the 356 in almost any of its many derivatives was streets ahead of any of the opposition of similar engine size—even if the high prices meant that the 356s would occasionally compare unfavorably in performance terms with other sports cars of similar price. Apart from top speed and acceleration, the 356s also scored on fuel consumption which thanks to low weight and efficiently streamlined bodywork was almost always reasonable for cars of this type. The exception was the Carrera models which were always rather heavy on fuel.

Although no one would surely call the air-cooled flat-four engines quiet in absolute terms, the engine position at the rear of the car means that noise is left behind and this helped to create the impression of effortless motoring in a 356. The aerodynamic qualities of the bodywork helped to keep wind noise down, although the price for the low drag coefficient was paid in terms of side-wind sensitivity, common to so many rear-engined streamlined motorcars. The rearward weight bias, and the swing axle rear suspension, also contributed to the Porsche handling with all its good and bad points. We cannot get away from the fact that a Porsche 356 would ultimately oversteer, whatever the development engineers did to the suspension. True, the experienced driver knew how to put oversteering tendencies to good use but one would not call the 356—or for that matter any rear-engined Porsche—a forgiving car, particularly not in the hands of a novice who had yet to be initiated in how to get the best from a Porsche.

This includes the cornering technique which the Germans call "Wischen"—one is tempted to translate this punningly into English as "Wishing" but it actually means "Wiping". The technique was to provoke a tail-sliding oversteer, which was then instantly corrected by steering, provoked again and corrected, and so on, until one was through the curve—all the time driving on the limit, on the brink of a total skid and a very possible major disaster. Well,

Above: End of an illustrious line: the final 356 C carries a wreath on its journey along the Zuffenhausen assembly line in 1965.

enough people lived to tell the tale, so there was something in it . . . although most Porsche drivers have probably never taken their cars quite as far out as that. Another interesting phenomenon which the driver however experienced could do little about except trust to luck was the tendency of the swing axles to tuck under if the car inadvertently took off after hitting a bump in the road at high speed. Let us not forget that the behavior of another high-performance rear-engine swing axle suspended car a few years later was to cause a major upset in the US automotive industry—the Chevrolet Corvair about which Ralph Nader wrote his book *Unsafe at Any Speed*—though in all fairness, this reflected as much on the lack of handling expertise of the average American motorist as on the dangers of the basic Volkswagen/Porsche/Corvair type of design.

The 356 has its ardent followers and there is no doubt that it is a particularly exhilarating motorcar; but the German road tester who in 1955 wrote in his magazine that "one would not know from the handling that this is a rear-engined car" was perhaps as naive as his British colleagues who 20 years before were apt to remark that one would not know that the Citroën Light Fifteen had front-wheel drive. . . .

Apart from anything else, the 356 established Porsche's reputation, by its performance and behavior, and by the care and attention to detail and quality which went into the design and construction of the car. It is tempting to describe the 356 as a super car, but not a supercar. This was yet to come from the house of Porsche.

6: SUCCESS AND SIDELINES

Porsche's commitment to motor racing is virtually unique. Almost without interruption, the company has been on the racetrack for 30 years, concentrating on sports car racing, but with an interest in rallying as well. There was even a short—and as we shall see, less successful—involvement in single-seater formula racing. What sets Porsche's racing career apart from most other car manufacturers is not just its constant devotion to the sport, but the fact that Porsches, in one form or another, have been almost invariably successful in their undertakings.

Given the pedigree of the Porsche company, it is not surprising that the men from Zuffenhausen are so keen on racing; the old Professor was a firm believer in racing, as a means of improving the breed as well as for the undoubted publicity benefits. Porsche has reaped an enormous amount of publicity from its racing victories over the years, and much of their engineering has been proven on the race track before being passed on to the road cars—the turbocharger is an outstanding example of this. Also many of the Porsche racing models—from the Spyder of the 1950s to today's 956 Group C car—have been available over the counter, at least to selected customers, and no doubt the sale of such production racing cars has been profitable.

While the early 356 models, especially the aluminum-bodied cars, were raced as well as rallied, scoring some notable successes, the development of a separate strain of racing cars did not begin in earnest before 1952. It is interesting to record that the impetus came from outside the Porsche company—from one Walter Glöckler, a Frankfurt-based Volkswagen dealer, who as early as 1949 began to build a special racing sports car based on VW and Porsche components. This first car, with a 1086cc (66.2cu in) engine, gave Glöckler a German sports car championship title in 1950; he was equally successful with a later 1500cc (91.5cu in) car, and his cars, universally referred to as the Glöckler-Porsches, received much attention from both Porsche and the German public.

In 1952 Porsche took up the challenge and began the design of a tubular-framed mid-engined racing sports car, based on the Glöckler car but perhaps also drawing inspiration from the very first Porsche 356 of 1948. It also initiated the design of a completely new engine to power the car, with Ernst Fuhrmann in charge of the engine project—who many years later became

Previous page: This could, almost, be a period photograph: two Porsche Spyders battling it out on a 1950s race track. In fact this is the Laguna Seca and the year is 1982.

Right: The car that started something: the innocent looking Glöckler-Porsche of 1950–52.

Right, below: As first raced at the Le Mans in 1953, the 550s were fitted with this type of streamlined hardtop.

Left: The Glöckler-Juhan type 550 which finished 6th in the 1955 Le Mans.

Above: The Spyders are also still active in racing. This car took part in the race at Thruxton, England, in 1975.

Left: Another Spyder in modern-day racing. However, the full-width windshield, even if supplied by Porsche, looks strange on a racing car.

MARTINI
RACING
39
MARTINI INTERNATIONAL CLUB
MARTINI

Left: Jean Behra in a type 550 at Rouen in 1958, the year before his death.

chairman of the Porsche company. While he stuck to the air-cooled flat-four layout, he evolved cylinder heads with two overhead camshafts in each, driven by shafts from the crankshaft. The car was ready before the engine so a mid-engined Porsche was first raced in early 1953, with the 1500 S push-rod engine, and two such cars were entered for the 24-hour race at Le Mans. The Le Mans cars were fitted with aerodynamic hardtops, made from aluminum as was the rest of the body, and even with engines developing little more than 80bhp they were capable of some 125mph (201km/h). Drivers for Le Mans included Richard von Frankenberg, Paul Frere, Hans Herrmann and Helm Glöckler, a cousin of Walter. Von Frankenberg/Frere came 15th and won the 1500cc class, with Herrmann/Glöckler following them home, giving less than a mile away on total distance.

Shipped out to Mexico for the spectacular and gruelling Carrera Panamericana 2000-mile road race later in the year, one of these Le Mans cars took the 1500cc class in this event, and other similar cars made further race appearances in 1953. On at least one occasion the public was given a preview of the four-cam car, driven in a German hill-climb by no less than Hans Stuck, the prewar Auto-Union ace. The first appearance of the definitive type 550 with the type 547 engine, the 1500 RS Spyder with the 1498cc (91.4cu in) four-cam engine, did not come before the 1954 Mille Miglia, where Herrmann and Herbert Linge finished sixth. The Spyder designation has become almost universal for these cars, despite the fact that the Porsches of the 550/718 family were often raced with closed bodywork. Three type 550s were entered for the 1954 Le Mans, and Claes/Stasse romped home in 12th position to score another 1500cc class victory, although the two other cars—one a 1300cc version—retired. The year 1954 saw the fifth and last Carrera Panamericana, but for Porsche the event went out with a flourish—Herrmann, driving solo in a 550 Spyder, came third and won his class, while other Spyders were 4th and 9th. Apart from anything else, Porsche had discovered the name for some of their most exciting cars—Carrera.

Left: This center-seat development of the Spyder appeared in Formula 2 racing in 1958.

Bottom left: The development of the original Spyder—a type 718 at Laguna Seca in 1982.

Before 1954 was out, Porsche had started to supply private customers with type 550 Spyders, at DM24,600 for each. These production models had 110bhp engines and were normally sold with hubcaps and a full-width windshield—most serious-minded owners discarded these and installed a small aeroscreen similar to the works cars. One unfortunate customer was the actor James Dean who was killed driving his Spyder in California in 1955. While Zuffenhausen was to turn out more than 100 of the cataloged Spyder models, development of the works racers was not allowed to stand still, and by 1956 Porsche had come up with type 550 A, which had a complete space-frame, a five-speed gearbox with baulk-ring synchromesh and a 130bhp engine. The revised car gained Porsche their most outstanding victory so far—an overall win in the 1956 Targa Florio, with Italian driver Maglioli at the wheel.

Further development resulted in the type 718 RS-K model for 1958 with revised rear suspension using coil springs instead of torsion bars, and at Le Mans that year, one of these cars with a 1588cc (96.9cu in) engine and driven by Herrmann and Jean Behra produced an almost miraculous performance, finishing in third place at an average of over 161km/h (101mph). This won them the two-liter class, but more remarkable was the fact that the two cars in front—the winning Ferrari, and an Aston Martin—were three-liter cars, yet the winner's average was only 8km/h (5mph) more than that of the Porsche. Other Porsches, with 1500cc engines, followed in 4th, 5th and 10th places. This and other results gained for Porsche a second place in the 1958 World Championship for makes in sports car racing.

By then however, Porsche was well into a completely new field. Modified

Left: Richard von Frankenberg, the Porsche driver, historian, author and public relations man, in a type 550 during the 1000-kilometer race at the Nürburgring in 1956.

Left: Van Hanstein, Kling and Herrmann with the 1953 Carrera Panamericana car.

Left: Hans Herrmann in the Formula 2 Porsche at Solitude in 1960.

Above: Pitstop for a Spyder in the 1958 Le Mans race.

Spyders with central steering and without headlamps had begun to appear in Formula 2 racing; Edgar Barth drove such a car to victory in a 1957 Formula 2 race at the Nürburgring, and Jean Behra repeated this in a similar car entered for a Formula 2 race held at the Rheims circuit before the French Grand Prix of 1958. For 1959 Porsche developed a proper open-wheeled Formula 2 single-seater racing car; but under the new skin, the car was almost identical to the type 718 1500 RS-K Spyder. Jean Behra (who was tragically killed while racing a Porsche Spyder at Avus in 1959) had his own ideas about the design of a single-seater Porsche, and had the Behra-Porsche built in Italy using all vital components from a type 718. Initially, his car—in the hands of Hans Herrmann—proved more successful than Porsche's works F.2 racers.

After Behra's death, and with further development of the works cars, 1960 brought success. Works drivers that season included Jo Bonnier, Graham Hill and Dan Gurney, while Stirling Moss drove a similar car entered by Rob Walker. Moss won at Aintree and Zeltweg, while Jo Bonnier was first at Modena and in the German Formula 2 Grand Prix at the Nürburgring. The season's results were sufficient for Porsche to share the honors with Cooper in the Formula 2 Manufacturers' Championship.

For 1961, the racing formulae were changed, and the maximum capacity for Formula 1 was reduced from 2.5 liters to 1.5 liters. Overnight, the previous Formula 2 cars were turned into Formula 1 cars, and Porsche was suddenly in the middle of the most prestigious type of motor racing. The reduction in Formula 1 capacity was brought about for the usual reasons—concern about the increasing speeds and racing safety—but the 1.5-liter formula which incidentally brought with it a complete ban on forced induction, was unpopular and only lasted five seasons. Historically, we may remember the 1.5-liter formula for bringing about the end of front-engined Grand Prix cars; a development already hastened by the championship-winning Coopers in 1959 and 1960, and henceforth Porsche no longer had a monopoly on the mid-engined racing car.

A new design would be necessary to make Porsche competitive in Formula 1.

Above and left: Studies of Porsche's Formula 1 car with the flat-eight engine at Laguna Seca 1982.

Right: The same car 20 years before, piloted by Dan Gurney in the 1962 Grand Prix season.

At first the well-tried Formula 2 cars were entered, for instance in the Brussels Grand Prix, but a new chassis was ready for the Monaco Grand Prix, if still fitted with the four-cylinder engine. The new engine, a 180bhp flat-eight still with four overhead camshafts, was not yet ready, and did not make its first public appearance until the Dutch Grand Prix in 1962. The chassis design incorporated front wishbone suspension initially with coil springs but for 1962 a reversion was made to Porsche's traditional torsion bars. For 1961, the four-cylinder car had retained drum brakes, but Porsche were developing their own disk brakes which appeared on the eight-cylinder car in 1962.

Throughout 1961, Porsche was up against the might of Ferrari, and the best places were all seconds, in the French, Italian and US Grand Prix races all taken by Dan Gurney who clinched a second place in the drivers' championship. Gurney was also Porsche's star in the eight-cylinder car the following year; although it was generally conceded that the Porsche was as yet not fully competitive against the British Formula 1 cars, Gurney won the French Grand Prix held that year at Rouen. But apart from a win (also by Gurney) in the non-championship Solitude Grand Prix on Porsche's own doorstep in Stuttgart, this was to be Porsche's only Formula 1 victory.

Gurney could do not better than a third place in the German Grand Prix, and after the US Grand Prix at the end of the season, Porsche threw in the towel and withdrew from Formula 1 racing. Undoubtedly the car could have been developed to a fully competitive stage, but the cost and complications of Grand Prix racing must have been too great for the Porsche company, compared to the relatively modest gains in terms of publicity. From then on, Porsche stuck to what it knew best—sports car racing. The single-seaters had never been more than an unprofitable sideline to Porsche's main business in the racing world, and 20 years on, Porsche has yet to make a return to the Grand Prix circus, although this possibility has been the subject of frequent—and usually uninformed—speculation.

In sports car racing, Porsche's triumphs continued. The marque's second victory in the Targa Florio came in 1959, and was backed up by other Porsches in 2nd, 3rd and 4th places. By contrast, Le Mans was a fiasco; six Porsches were entered, and all retired with broken crankshafts. While still in the running however, Porsches had managed to hold on to fourth position. The type 718 was developed into the RS 60 for the 1960 season, featuring wishbone rear suspension with coil springs but still with trailing links and torsion bars at the front. The important victories of this season came in the Targa Florio again, but also in the 12-hour race at Sebring in the USA. Le Mans did not add much to Porsche's laurels; four Spyders retired, and the only RS to finish was the Barth/Seidel car in 11th place which conceded the 1600cc class win to the Porsche Abarth-Carrera of Linge/Walter which finished 10th.

For 1961 the Spyder became the RS 61 and a new engine size appeared—a full two-liter unit of 1967cc (120cu in). Porsche had already tried their luck in the two-liter class with engines of "odd" capacities such as 1606cc (98cu in)

Overleaf:
The RS 60 was run during the 1960 racing season and was developed from the type 718 but featured wishbone rear suspension. The engine was still the four-cylinder, four cam type 547 but it was nearing the limit of its potential.

GAS
OPEN
CALIFORNIA
UTV 636

and 1679cc (102.4cu in) seen in some races during 1960. The first outing for the real two-liter car came in the Targa Florio, where Bonnier and Gurney scored a 2nd place. At Le Mans, a two-liter RS 61 coupé in the hands of Masten Gregory and Al Holbert came 5th overall, winning its class and again only giving way to cars of three-liter capacity. The basic design of the Porsche four-cylinder engine was by now getting a little dated, having been around since 1953, and although the two-liter version was still competitive in its class, no doubt the Porsche sports car racers were looking with some envy at the completely new flat-eight engine which was being prepared for the Formula 1 car.

The marriage of the flat-eight engine—type 771 derived from the Formula 1 design but opened up to 1981cc (121cu in) and developing 210bhp—and the RS 61 Spyder happened for the 1962 Targa Florio, which also became the first outing for the Porsche disk brakes on a racing sports car. Two eight-cylinder cars were entered, a Spyder and a Coupé similar to the 1961 Le Mans car—the latter finished third after some problems with the brakes. The eight was also seen in the 1000km race at the Nürburgring in which it was placed 3rd again. A change in the regulations at Le Mans meant that Porsche did not enter any cars in the new "experimental" class, preferring instead to concentrate on the GT class in which they ran three 1600cc Carreras. The only one to finish was the Barth/Herrmann car in 7th place, winning the 1.6-liter GT class.

With the end of the Grand Prix racing program in 1962, Porsche could once again devote all its efforts to sports car racing, as the yet-to-be-revealed type 904 would demonstrate. Meanwhile, the aging Spyder design which would celebrate its 10th anniversary in 1963, kept the Porsche flag flying. An eight-cylinder 718 RS 61 won the Targa Florio—Porsche's 4th victory in the classic Sicilian road race—and two similar cars were entered for Le Mans. One of these retired after an accident but Barth and Linge kept going to finish in 8th place, taking the two-liter honors. While the type 718s were to keep racing for some time, especially in hill-climbs, the spotlight now moved on to the new type 904 which heralded a new era in Porsche history and in many ways, was a complete break with the engineering traditions of the company.

The 904—also known as the Carrera GTS—conformed to Porsche practice by being a mid-engined car, and in its original form it still featured the 1967cc (120cu in) version of the type 587 four cylinder, four-cam engine. Apart from this, the whole concept was distinctly novel by Porsche standards. The chassis was built up from impressively dimensioned and extremely rigid pressed-steel box sections, and the coupé bodywork was made from fiberglass. Chassis and bodywork were both contracted out and were supplied by Heinkel, the erstwhile aircraft manufacturer who turned to bubble cars in the 1950s. The 904 was very low—the overall height was a mere 1065mm (41.5in)—and was possibly the most attractive Porsche car ever made. In a way, its styling was an even bigger break with Porsche tradition than the 901/911 road sports car which appeared at the same time. The 904 completely eschewed the use of torsion bars for its suspension and instead featured double wishbones and coil springs front and rear, while ATE-Dunlop disks—similar to those used on the 356 C and the 911—looked after the braking.

The idea behind the 904 project was to make a fairly simple and low-cost car which could be built, and sold, in sufficient numbers to achieve homologation in the GT class. A price of DM29,700 was quoted—which we may compare to the DM21,900 asked for the basic 911 model in 1964—and Porsche's ploy succeeded brilliantly as the total production run of the 904 approached 120, well in excess of the 100 cars required for homologation. Nor did all customers use their 904s exclusively for racing; the author remembers encountering one in a Paris street in 1964, and the first 904 to come to Britain was used by

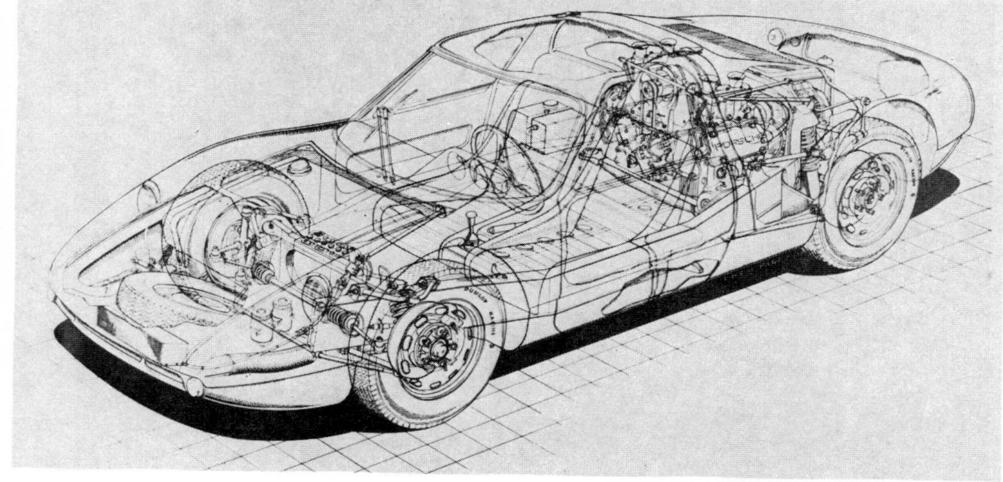

Above: The line-up of five 904s which marked this model's debut at Le Mans in 1964. All of them finished, in 7th, 8th, 10th, 11th and 12th places. They all had two-liter four-cylinder engines.

Above right: The 904 reveals all, including its substantial box section frame, in this ghosted drawing.

Dickie Stoop for shopping . . . among other things. While the 904 was rather noisy and cramped as a runabout, its attractions included a 160mph (258km/h) top speed. Of the production road cars, many inevitably went to the USA, and most of the rest were sold in Germany and France. Those that found their way into the hands of private customers had the four-cylinder engine, but of the works racing cars many were fitted with the type 771 flat-eight two-liter engine which we have already encountered in the type 718 RS 61, or with the new flat-six type 901 engine which was fitted to the 911 model.

Success came the way of the 904 almost immediately. One of its first races was the Sebring 12 hour in March 1964, when Briggs Cunningham took his brand-new 904 to a win in the under-3 liter prototype class. This was quickly followed up by 1st and 2nd places in the Targa Florio, and at Le Mans, five four-cylinder 904s were entered and five finished, taking 7th, 8th, 10th, 11th and 12th places. By contrast two eight-cylinder 904s also entered in the 24-hour race both retired with clutch failure. There were plenty of class wins in other important sports car races, and 904 successes were not restricted to track racing either; a 904 came 2nd in the 1965 Monte Carlo rally, and another won the Spanish rally outright in the same year. During 1965, a number of variations on the 904 theme were tried out, including a Spyder-bodied car, and a six-cylinder 904 coupé was 3rd in the Targa Florio. Linge and Nocker took a similar car to 4th place at Le Mans, followed home by a four-cylinder 904. A four-cylinder car won the GT class in the Marathon de la Route, the 84-hour event held on the Nürburgring, for the first time that year instead of over the classic Liège-Rome-Liège course.

A production version of the 904 with the six-cylinder engine, tentatively called the 906 GTS (a type number we shall meet again later) almost happened for 1965, but was abandoned in favor of further development of the 911 as a road car with a more general appeal, and by a new design for a racing car which returned to the tubular frame construction. The change in policy was decided when the CSI (Commission Sportive Internationale, the governing body of motor sport) introduced the new Sports Car category for 1966 which reduced the number of cars required for homologation to 50 built in a period of 12 months. A tubular-framed car with the eight-cylinder engine was seen in hill-climbs during 1965, and this led directly to the next generation of Porsche racing cars—the 906 "Carrera 6" and the 910. The 904 was left behind; it had marked the beginning of a new era for Porsche racing cars, yet with the four-cylinder engine, its abilities as a road car as well as a racer, and its supremely good looks, it was also in its way the last of the line which had begun with the Glöckler-Porsche and the type 550 Spyder.

7: THEMES AND VARIATIONS

Previous page: *A beautiful car in a beautiful setting: the original 911 shape with well-integrated bumpers. This example sports forged five-spoke alloy wheels.*

The 1950s and 1960s were the era of the German economic miracle, the *Wirtschaftwunder* achieved under Chancellors Adenauer and Erhard. The motor industry both contributed to and benefited from this unprecedented boom. Already by 1952, the West German motor industry on its own had exceeded the best prewar production total achieved by the motor industry of the entire German Reich; in 1956, West Germany rivaled Britain as the biggest European motor vehicle producer and by 1960 had firmly overtaken the rival. Germany was also by then the world's biggest exporter of motor vehicles.

While the German motor industry in the postwar period was never as compact as for instance the French or Italian industries, it still did not number more than 10 manufacturers of any size or importance. The war, and the division of Germany, had pruned the industry which lost Adler, Stoewer and most of the Auto-Union makes. The majority of surviving German car makers were in a position to make the most of the nation's economic recovery, and while there were some casualties and mergers, they were not as frequent as those seen in Britain. The most spectacular failure was that of the Bremen-based Borgward group in 1961. Glas and NSU disappeared, after having been taken over by BMW and VW-Audi respectively; DKW changed into Auto-Union, was taken over by Mercedes and re-emerged as Audi, eventually to be passed on to Volkswagen.

Porsche, the smallest company, thrived, and stayed contentedly independent and successful. Their role as the only German manufacturer of specialist sports cars was largely unchallenged. From time to time, Mercedes, BMW or even Glas might launch would-be Porsche competitors, not all of them successful and those that were, were usually so different from the sort of cars Porsche were building as not to make the Porsche men worry unduly.

However it did become apparent to the Zuffenhausen team that the days of the 356 were numbered as the 1950s drew to a close. Following a success is never easy, and there was some soul-searching in the boardroom and design departments in deciding which way Porsche should go in the future. At first the intention was to develop a four-seater car, the type 695 for which Butzi Porsche designed a new body in 1959. The proposed design had a typical Porsche front, with a sloping trunk lid and the headlamps raked backward. But to give sufficient rear seat headroom, the roofline was higher and longer than the 356, and the windows were very deep. The rear end had a semi-fast-back line. The proposed car had a wheelbase of 2400mm (93.6in); curiously enough exactly the same as a VW Beetle.

With project 695, Porsche would be moving up-market, and there would have to be a new engine for the new car. This became the responsibility of Butzi's cousin, Ferdinand Piëch. It was taken for granted that it should be a light-alloy air-cooled horizontally opposed unit mounted in the rear, and the decision was soon made to have six cylinders. The engine dimensions were 80 × 66mm (3.1 × 2.6in) bore and stroke, giving a capacity of 1991cc (121.5cu in). A number of experimental engines were made, starting with a design incorporating push-rod overhead valves and a wet sump in the manner of the 356 engine, but the final version had a single chain-driven overhead camshaft for each bank of cylinders, and a dry-sump lubrication system. The original production version developed 130bhp.

In 1962 Porsche began to have second thoughts about the wisdom of type 695. Porsche's renown was in the field of sports and racing cars. The four-seater was a departure from this and might possibly lead to close competition with Mercedes-Benz which had a line of sporting four-seater coupés and cabriolets based on their saloon models. So the wheelbase of the type 695 was

Above: The type 695 as originally conceived, with a longer wheelbase than the 911, permitting four seats, and with its own distinctive roof line.

shortened to 2211mm (86.2in), and while Butzi's original front end styling was kept, he developed a new rear end with a smooth fastback line running directly down from a lowered roof. While the new shape only offered room for children in the emasculated rear seat, it was more in the Porsche tradition. The flat-six engine was carried over into the revised car, for which a new type number signifying the beginning of a new series was chosen: 901.

The 901 was first shown to the public at the Frankfurt Motor Show in September 1963 and although a catalog was issued and a price of DM23,900 was quoted, Porsche did not hide the fact that the car was not yet ready for production and would not be available for another year. The specifications of the new Porsche were mouth-watering enough, both for enthusiasts of the marque and for writers for the motoring press. Not only did the new car have the all-new engine and body—which incidentally was Porsche's first true unitary construction body—but there was a new five-speed gearbox, fully synchronized naturally, the four-wheel disk brakes pioneered on the 356 C, and new suspension which incorporated McPherson-like shock absorber struts at the front but also lower wishbones acting on forward-running torsion bars, while at the back there were semi-trailing arms and transverse torsion bars. This new layout was an effective guarantee against the vices of swing axle handling! Another intriguing feature was the rack-and-pinion steering, with

Left: It is a credit to "Butzi" Porsche that his 911 shape, although 20 years old, still looks so good today.

Above: The Original 901 prototype of 1963 only differed from the 911 in a few small details, such as the shape of the fuel filler flap.

Below: The 911 Targa eventually succeeded the 356 Cabriolet as the German police's favorite for highway work, but has been replaced by 924s.

The standard road-going 911 has never been a great force in sports car racing, which requires rather more specialized machinery, but it is nevertheless popular in smaller events and clubman's racing. On the left is one of the early 1964 models, while on the right a 911 L shows a typical Porsche cornering attitude with the rear wheels hanging well out.

the pinion housing centrally mounted so the steering column had to incorporate two cardan joints; this facilitated construction of both left- and right-hand drive cars and the joints were also a valuable safety feature.

The German magazine *Auto Motor und Sport* tested a 901 pre-production car in the spring of 1964, and measured a top speed of 210km/h (131mph) together with an acceleration from 0 to 100km/h (0 to 62mph) of 8.7 seconds. The car was found to possess a performance equivalent to the two-liter Carrera version of the 356 and the new Mercedes-Benz 230 SL. The 901 was summed up as possessing all the functional characteristics of previous Porsche sports cars but with the added attraction of more civilized behavior and luxurious equipment. Everything was set fair for the new Porsche except for one thing: the Peugeot company objected to the 901 type designation, claiming they had the sole right to all three-digit type numbers with an 0 in the middle used on road cars. Porsche complied with the French request rather than contest the issue, and henceforth the new model became the 911. At least Porsche could retain other similar numbers for their racing models.

Production 911s started to appear in late 1964, and by deleting some items of equipment the price was cut to DM21,900 for the basic model; customers could then take their pick from the company's list of extras and accessories, comprehensive as ever. In the spring of 1965 an additional model was offered: the 912 which was a 911 with the 90bhp 1582cc (96.5cu in) engine from the 356, and slightly less well equipped than the six-cylinder car. At DM16,250 this was priced between the 356 C and SC coupé models which it replaced, and it had a four-speed gearbox as standard with the five-speed box as an option. The original 912 series lasted until 1968 and permitted Porsche to keep a foothold in the lower end of the market. The model disappeared with the advent of the VW-Porsche 914 (see chapter 10) but was briefly reintroduced for the US market in 1975–6 with a two-liter engine, bridging the gap between the discontinuation of the 914 and the introduction of the 924.

With a choice of two new cars, virtually identical but with either a four- or a six-cylinder engine, the Porsche customer might have been satisfied. However, there was one noticeable gap in the Porsche range of 1965–66 — there was no open car to please the minority who wanted wind in the hair. Porsche had no plans to stop catering for this clientele, and their requirements were amply met when the Targa model was introduced. It was first unveiled in 1965

although production models only became available in 1967. The Targa body style was available in both 911 and 912 forms, at an extra cost of DM1400 compared to the coupés. It was not a completely open car in the way the old cabriolet or Speedster had been, as the hallmark of the Targa was a substantial roll-over bar behind the doors, made all the more prominent by being finished in polished metal. Experiments with different types of roof panel resulted in the use of a collapsible cross-braced fabric panel which could be stowed in the front luggage compartment, and the rear window made from plastic could be unzipped and stowed away as well. However, from 1968 this was replaced by a glass rear window fixed in place. A very similar roof solution had been tried by Triumph on the TR 4 model four years before Porsche, but the infelicitously-named "Surrey top" did not catch on and it was left to Porsche to add the word Targa to the sports car vocabulary.

It must be said that the 911 initially did not live up to the standards of quality expected from a Porsche, and in particular it took some time before the finish of the coachwork was beyond criticism. Although Porsche had recently bought the Reutter body factory, the production capacity of this plant still failed to keep up with the demand for the new models, and for a time Karmann became a second supplier of Porsche bodywork. The 911 had valve problems at high engine speeds which were solved by the addition of a rev-limiting governor, and carburation flat spots were dealt with by adopting Weber instead of Solex carburetors. On the original narrow rims and tires, the 911 was found to be somewhat deficient in straight-line stability and it was particularly sensitive to sidewinds, while the ultimate oversteer was inevitably present. As suspension development continued and wider tires were fitted, the handling improved out of all recognition; but one of the remedies adopted in the early days was simple and effective if old-fashioned: a 24lb (11kg) lump of lead was inserted behind each corner of the front bumper!

The 911 range began to multiply with the introduction of the 911 S in 1966. This had the engine output increased to 160bhp, the disk brakes were ventilated and for the first time, Porsche fitted the famous forged magnesium wheels with their characteristic five-spoke pattern. In the following year, an additional model was the 911 T with a detuned 110bhp engine, less equipment and a four-speed gearbox as standard. The original 911 model was now known as the 911 L. All models had dual circuit brakes, and the semi-automatic

HOMETUNE
35
Wild Rose Caravan Park
HISTORIC SPECIAL G.T. CHAMPIONSHIP

The 911 R of the 1967–69 period was a rather different animal. The much lightened bodywork was the work of Stuttgart coachbuilder Baur and incorporated several fiberglass panels. The two-liter engine was tuned to give 210bhp and was rather similar to the 906 racing engine.

Above: A Porsche 911 first took part in the Monte Carlo Rally in 1965 and finished 5th. The 1967 Rally was however not a success, as may be judged from the mangled front end of the 911 above.

Sportomatic transmission was offered as an option. This combined a torque converter, an automatic clutch and a four-speed gearbox; it offered two-pedal control, but still with the full flexibility of an ordinary gearbox. Just to prove their point that automatic transmissions were compatible with sports motoring, Porsche entered a racing version of the 911 with Sportomatic transmission in the 1967 84-hour Marathon de la Route at the Nürburgring . . . and won.

The years 1967–68 also saw more serious development of the 911 model for both racing and rallying. The 911 had made an impressive debut by coming fifth in the 1965 Monte Carlo rally, and 911 S drivers Elford and Stone were European rally champions in 1967. They won the 1968 Monte Carlo, and Finnish driver Toivonen in a 911 T was that year's rally champion. The Monte Carlo win was repeated in 1969 and again in 1970, with Swede Björn Waldegaard driving on both occasions. A special lightweight racing version of the 911, the 911 R with most of the body panels in fiberglass bringing the weight down to 830kg (1826lb), appeared in early 1968; it was fitted with the engine from the 906 Carrera 6, and was sold to private owners as well as being raced by the factory. The model won the Tour de France in 1969, as well as the Tour de Corse, where some works cars were seen with experimental four-camshaft engines. After 1970 Porsche withdrew official works support for rallying, and although they continued to make specially-prepared 911s available to private owners for rallying as well as GT racing, the 911 S models of the 1970–72 period were closer in specification to the ordinary production cars.

In August 1968, the so-called B-series of the 911 had the wheelbase increased to 2268mm (88.5in), and the wheelarches were flared to accommodate wider wheels. The 911 T was continued without mechanical change but the 911 E (previously the L model) and the 911 S were fitted with mechanical Bosch fuel injection in place of carburetors. The injected engines produced 140bhp and 170bhp respectively but the performance was more or less unchanged as Porsche's main reason for the change to fuel injection was the necessity to meet the new American emission control legislation requirements. The fuel injected two-liter engine lasted only one year before the 911s acquired a bigger engine; bored out to 84mm (3.3in), the new engine had a capacity of 2195cc (133.9cu in), with power output improved to 125, 155 and 180bhp for the T, E and S models respectively. An interesting feature of the 911 E were self-

Right: Success came in 1968 when Vic Elford won the Monte Carlo in a 911 T and Björn Waldegaard followed this up by winning the Rally in 1969 and 1970. The top picture shows a beaming Waldegaard after his victory and the bottom picture shows him on his way in the Alpes Maritimes. A 911 won the Monte Carlo again in 1978.

Overleaf:
The 1967 911 S incorporated worthwhile improvements over the original 911, notably the 160bhp engine. The alloy wheels were still extra equipment.

37
RALLYE MONTE-CARLO

BLH7

Left, top: The 911 R had a special fiberglass bumper with neatly integrated numberplate mountings. The wheels on this car are not original but suit the shape extremely well.

Left, below: A later Model 911 with the impact-resistant bumpers introduced in 1973.

Above: Compare the original front bumper on this early 911 to the car on the opposite page. The 911 behind shows the rear bumper and the rear lamp layout used since 1973.

leveling hydro-pneumatic front suspension struts which were optional on the other models, but these were only used in the 1968–71 period.

The 1972 models had the engine further increased in size, this time the stroke was lengthened to 80.7mm (3.1in) and the capacity went up to 2341cc (142.8cu in). At the same time compression ratios were appreciably lowered so the Porsches could be run on "normal" petrol (the equivalent of regular or 2-star). The 911 T with carburetor now had 130bhp, the fuel-injection models 165bhp (911 E) and 190bhp (911 S). The top speed of the manual transmission 911 S was in the order of 145mph (234km/h). All models were now fitted with the four-speed gearbox as standard although the five-speed box was still available as an option. The S model was further distinguished by the fitment of a front air dam underneath the bumper. For a year the oil filler cap was mounted under a flap on the right-hand side of the car behind the door, but it was moved back in the engine bay after complaints were received from customers who had suffered when careless filling station attendants had poured gasoline in the oil tank. . . .

8: FROM CARRERA TO TURBO

333 RWC

Porsche celebrated the ninth birthday of the 911 by introducing a new top-line model in the autumn of 1972. This brought with it not only the return of the famous Carrera model name, but a still bigger engine which was bored out to 90mm (3.5in) for a capacity of 2687cc (163.9cu in). Originally the Carrera was intended as a homologation special for Group 4, the Special GT category, but in the end production exceeded the required number of 500 cars more than three times. Two versions were available—the specially lightened RS model which dispensed with sundry creature comforts to bring overall weight down to 900kg (1980lb), so with 210bhp available, top speed was around 150mph (240km/h); there was also a fully-equipped Carrera which was not much slower. The model was easily identified by the duck's tail spoiler integrated in the fiberglass engine lid, and large Carrera scripts along the flanks of the car.

With the absence of Porsche works entries in the World Championship for Makes in sports car racing in 1972, 911 derivatives such as the Carrera and its race-tuned RSR version were left to uphold Porsche's racing prestige. In 1973 the Carrera dominated the European GT championship as well as the hill-climb championship, and the model began to appear in rallying as well. In North America, it was victorious in both the Trans-Am series and the IMSA championship. A 2.8-liter version of the RSR appeared already in 1973, and in the following year the RS and RSR models were extended to 3.0 liters and up to 330bhp. Carreras continued to dominate GT racing on both sides of the Atlantic through 1974 and 1975, and they were also entered for the East African Safari Rally in 1973—when both Porsches retired—and in 1974, when Waldegaard and Thorszelius took second place. Undoubtedly the Carrera was a highly versatile motorcar.

In 1973 a Carrera RSR Prototype appeared to contest the World Championship, and it was successful on its first outing, the Daytona 24-hour race where Gregg and Haywood were victorious. These cars were normally run by the works-supported, Martini-sponsored team with the characteristic striped livery, and other results in the 1973 season included Gregg and Haywood's win of the Sebring 12-hour race, while Gijs van Lennep and Herbert Müller set the seal on Porsche's career in the Targa Florio by winning the last-ever race. The same drivers also came a very creditable fourth at Le Mans, although the Porsches were really outclassed by the much faster prototype cars entered by Matra, then the dominant force in endurance racing, and other manufacturers. For 1974 the Carrera racers went turbocharged, which amply compensated for their lack of ccs.

The 1974 production road-going 911 models all featured the 2.7-liter engine size, and while the 911 T was discontinued the 911 E became once again plain 911. The price of this and of the 911 S were actually reduced in the German home market. The 911s also underwent their biggest restyling job so far—the original neatly integrated bumpers with their discreet rubbing strip were replaced by impact-resistant protruding bumpers mounted on rubber bellows. Rear lamp clusters changed in shape and were connected by a reflective panel running across the back of the car proclaiming PORSCHE to the world . . . as if such identification was necessary. The duck's tail spoiler became optional equipment on all models, and the Carrera gained a longer, flatter rear spoiler. New seats were fitted with integral headrests—the so-called tombstone seats. While the Carrera continued to use mechanical fuel injection, the 911 and 911 S were now fitted with electronic Bosch K-Jetronic injection. The standard Carrera (but not the RS) was now made available also in Targa form.

In 1974 ATS cast-alloy wheels were standardized on the 911, after having first appeared two years earlier on the 911 E. During that year, Porsche cele-

Previous page: The latter-day 911, a 1980 SC model. Alloy wheels are now standard, and the tombstone seats prominent. This example features "Martini" stripes and what is probably a Turbo rear spoiler.

Above: The 911 came close to winning its 5th Monte Carlo Rally in 1981.

911 TURBO

BOUCAU PROMOTION
LA GRANDE MOTTE
kléber
MOTUL
TOUR DE CORSE
22
ESSO

Left: The "business end" of the original prototype Turbo shown in Paris in 1974.

Left, below: Ballet won his class in the 1981 Tour de Corse in this Carrera RSR with the duck's tail spoiler.

Below: Waldegaard and Thorszelius drove this 911 in the 1982 Monte Carlo Rally.

brated their 25th anniversary as car manufacturers by producing a limited edition of 500 911 anniversary models, painted silver with special black and silver trim, each car bearing a special plaque with an inscription, a facsimile of Ferry Porsche's signature and that particular car's individual number in the series. But even this exercise paled besides the real sensation of 1974: the Porsche Turbo introduced at the Paris Motor Show. The use of an exhaust-driven turbocharger to increase engine output had been tried on road-going cars by Chevrolet and Oldsmobile in the early 1960s, and in Europe BMW was the first to launch a turbo car—the unsuccessful short-lived 2002 Turbo of 1973–74. Ten years ago, turbos were neither commonplace nor wholly respectable outside racing circuits, but there is no doubt that the Porsche Turbo was the real beginning of the turbo revolution. While the Carrera had taken Porsche into the supercar class, the Turbo reinforced the company's position on this exalted level.

Porsche had begun experimenting with turbocharging in 1970, and in 1972–73 ran a turbocharged 917 in the Can-Am racing series. In 1974 a 911 Carrera Turbo had been raced throughout the season, finishing in second places at both Le Mans and in the Watkins Glen 6-hour race. This car had an engine of 2142cc (131cu in) capacity as race regulations stipulated that turbocharging, in common with supercharging, should incur the penalty of having engine capacity multiplied by 1.4, and the then maximum capacity for prototype cars was 3000cc (183cu in). No such limit was imposed on production road cars, and the Porsche engineers accordingly opted for the 95× 70.4mm (3.7×2.7in), 2993cc (182.6cu in) engine size already seen in normally aspirated Carrera racers. K-Jetronic fuel injection was fitted in addition to the turbocharger, and even with a seemingly ridiculous compression ratio of 6.5:1 power output was 260bhp—the racing Carrera Turbo had developed

Porsche's 25th anniversary as a car maker was celebrated in 1974 by making a limited edition of 500 specially finished 911s, each bearing a numbered plaque with the company motto and Ferry's signature (inset).

PORSCHE
25 Jahre Fahren
in seiner schönsten Form
Jubiläumsmodell Wagen Nr.

2 GOO

Previous page: The Turbo is the most exciting Porsche today. One hopes that the numberplate does not foretell a sticky end to this example.

Right: This is how most drivers see the Turbo on the road.

Below: The dashboard is similar to the 911 SC but incorporates a Turbo boost gauge in the impressive display of dials confronting the driver.

Below, center: Unusual but effective high pressure headlamp washers are built into the front bumper.

Far right, below: The rear end of the Turbo showing off the "tea-tray" spoiler with the built-in intercooler.

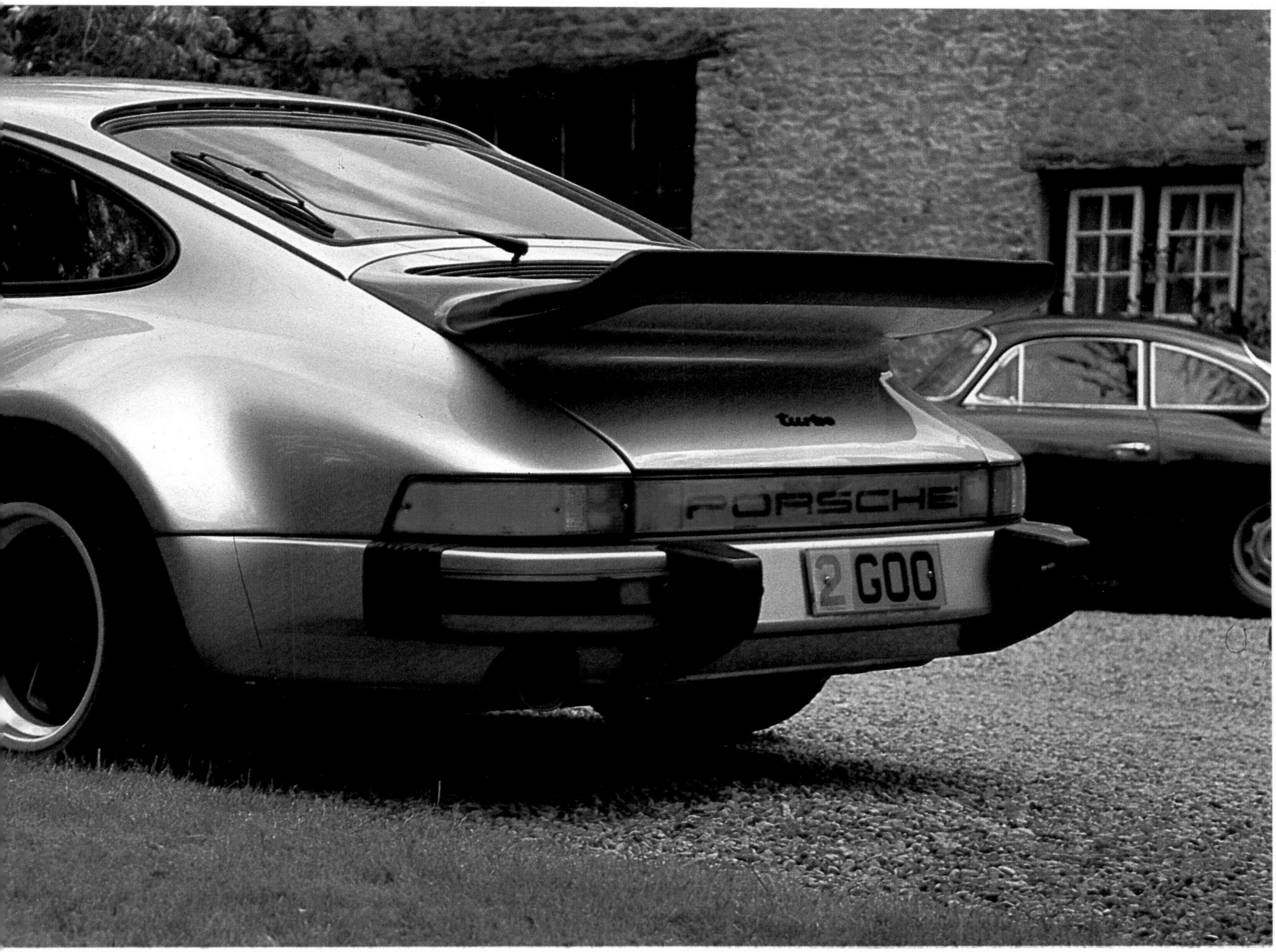
turbo
PORSCHE
2 GOO

PORSCHE

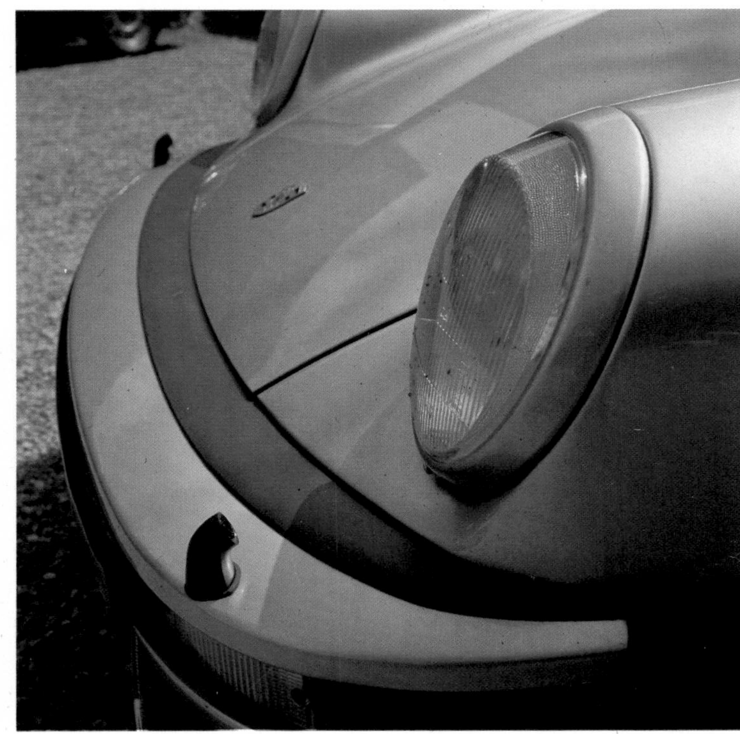

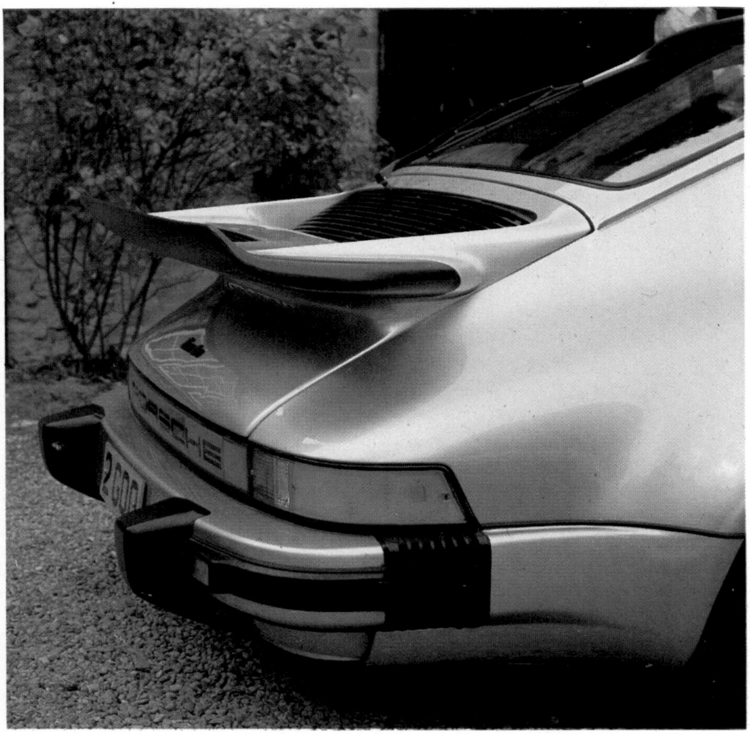

close to 500bhp. Turbo performance was, even in the "detuned" production version, quite astounding—top speed was at least 155mph (250km/h), and the Turbo had the ability to accelerate from standstill to 60mph (97km/h) in less than 6 seconds, while 100mph (161km/h) was reached in less than 15 seconds.

The Turbo was and is officially the type 930, but is still close enough to the 911 to be considered as part of the family, and is indeed sold as the 911 Turbo. Apart from the engine there were however numerous other differences, as were needed to justify the price tag in Germany of DM65,800 or just over twice the cost of the basic 911. Externally, the wheelarches were flared more than ever to accommodate the wide wheels—with 7in rims at the front and 8in at the back—and there was also the "tea-tray" spoiler on the engine lid. Full luxury equipment was fitted, and if the fact that the gearbox only contained four forward ratios seemed to suggest skimping, the truth was that the normal 911 five-speed box would not take Turbo power, and this was a new and altogether beefier gearbox. However, the Turbo customer was deprived of two options—neither the Sportomatic transmission, nor the Targa body were available. The Targa structure is not quite as strong as the coupé, and Porsche deemed it prudent to make their most powerful car in coupé form only; this has not stopped several enterprising customisers in Germany and abroad from offering converted Turbo Targa models. Racing versions of the Turbo, the types 934 and 935, appeared for the 1976 season after Porsche had taken another year's break from works racing; but these were by then so removed from the 911 road car family that they will be dealt with in a following chapter devoted to Porsche's racing cars.

The 3-liter engine size from the Turbo was introduced on the Carrera model from 1975, as was the K-Jetronic fuel injection, while the 911 and 911 S still retained the 2.7-liter engine. However the 911 S was offered exclusively in the US market for the 1976 and 1977 model years. All 1976 models had the body

Above and above left: This 1975 Targa incorporates a Turbo-type rear spoiler. The Targa is still in production despite the introduction of the cabriolet model.

Right: Porsche's pleasant surprise for the 1980s: the return of the cabriolet body for the first time since 1965. The 911 SC cabriolet is now one of the most sought-after models.

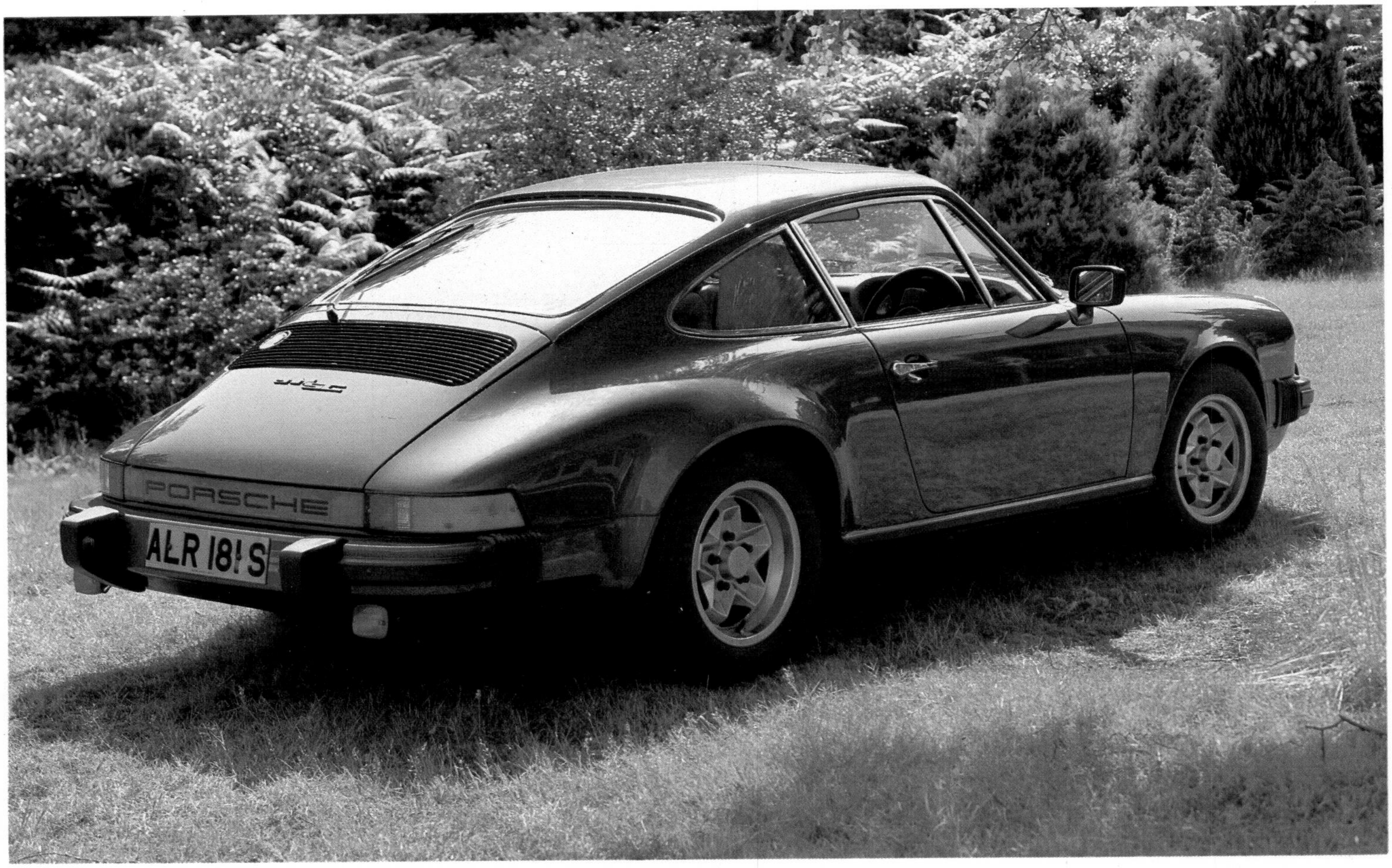
PORSCHE
ALR 181 S

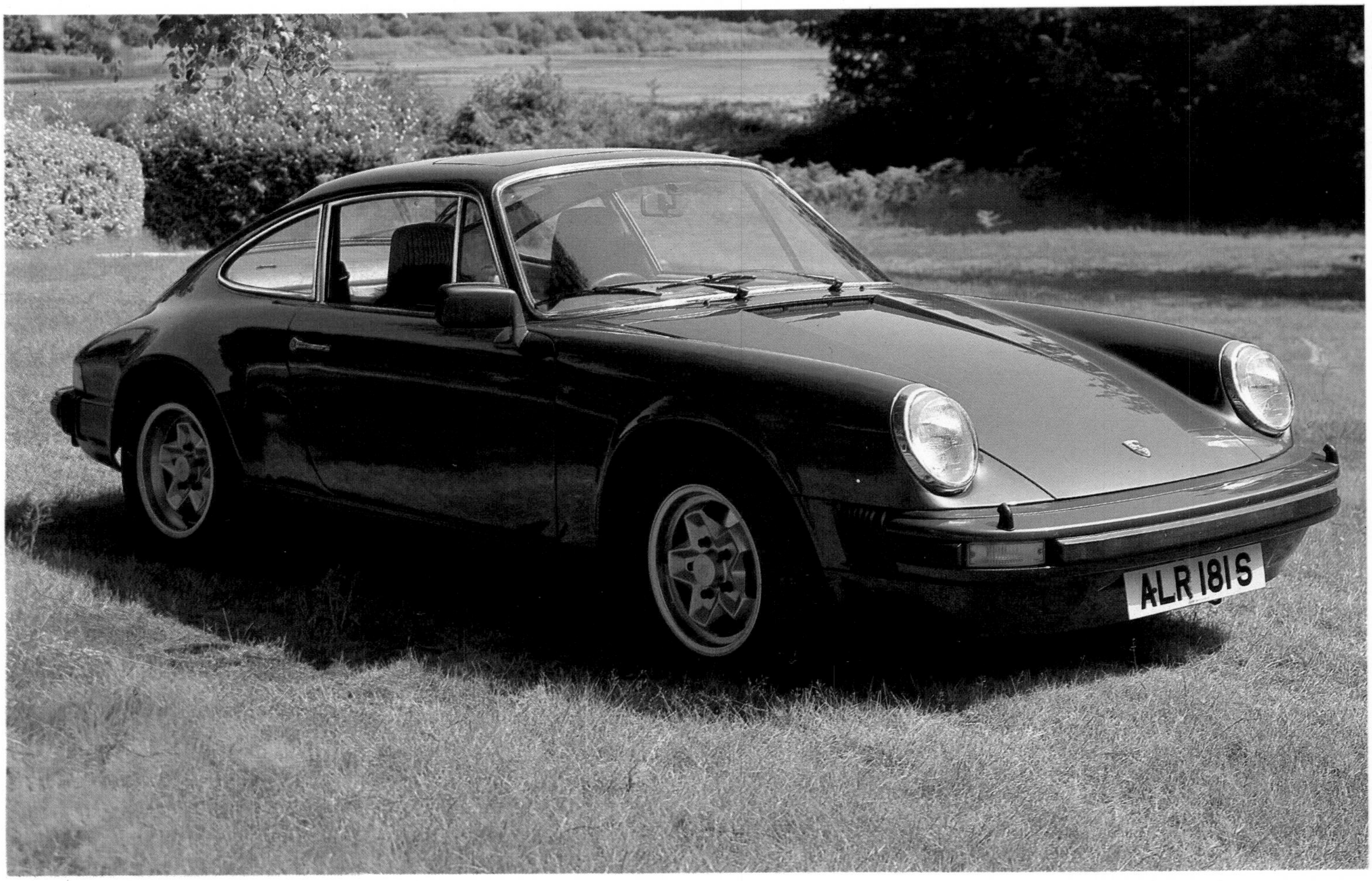
ALR 181 S

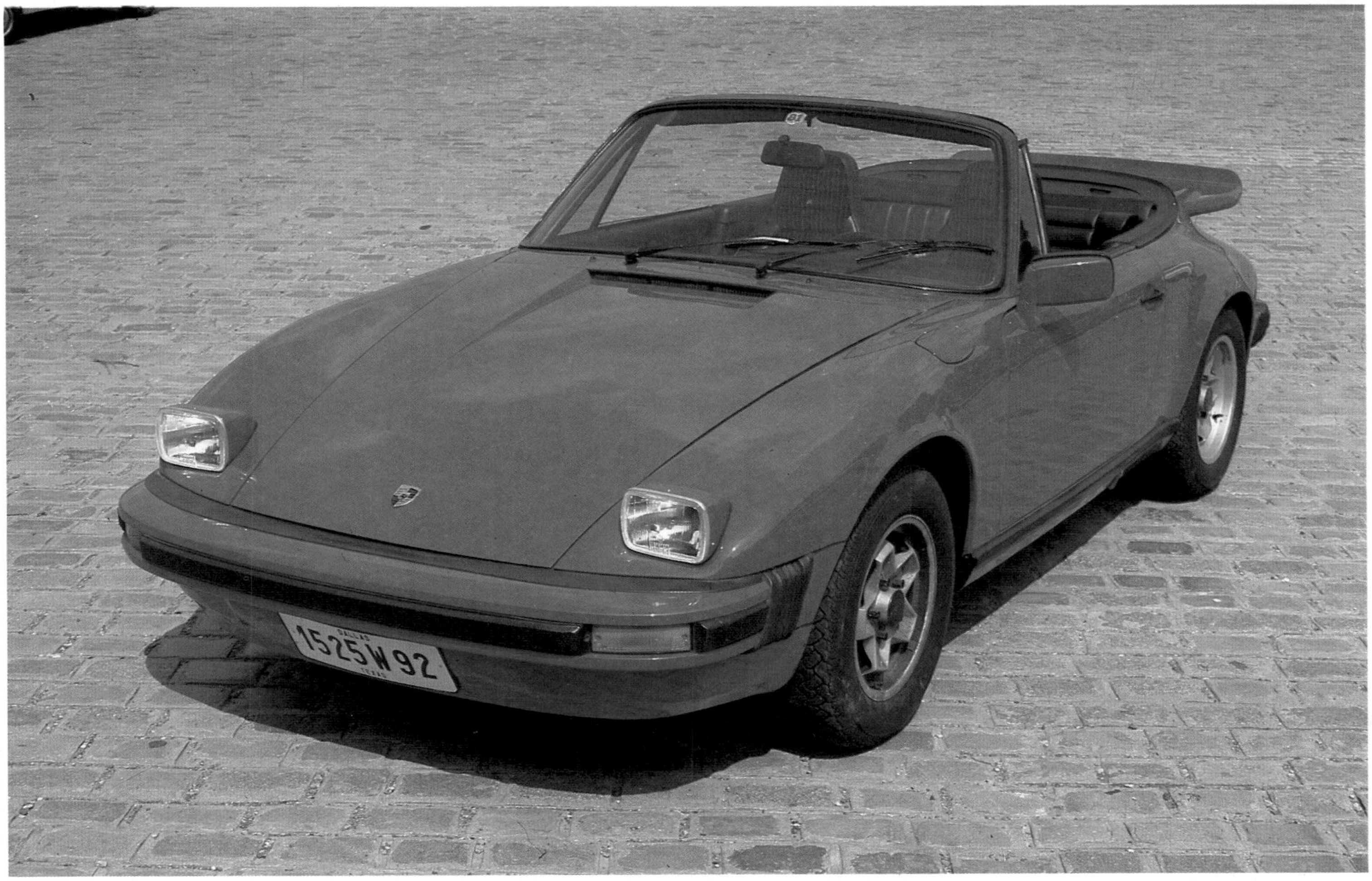
DALLAS
1525W92
TEXAS

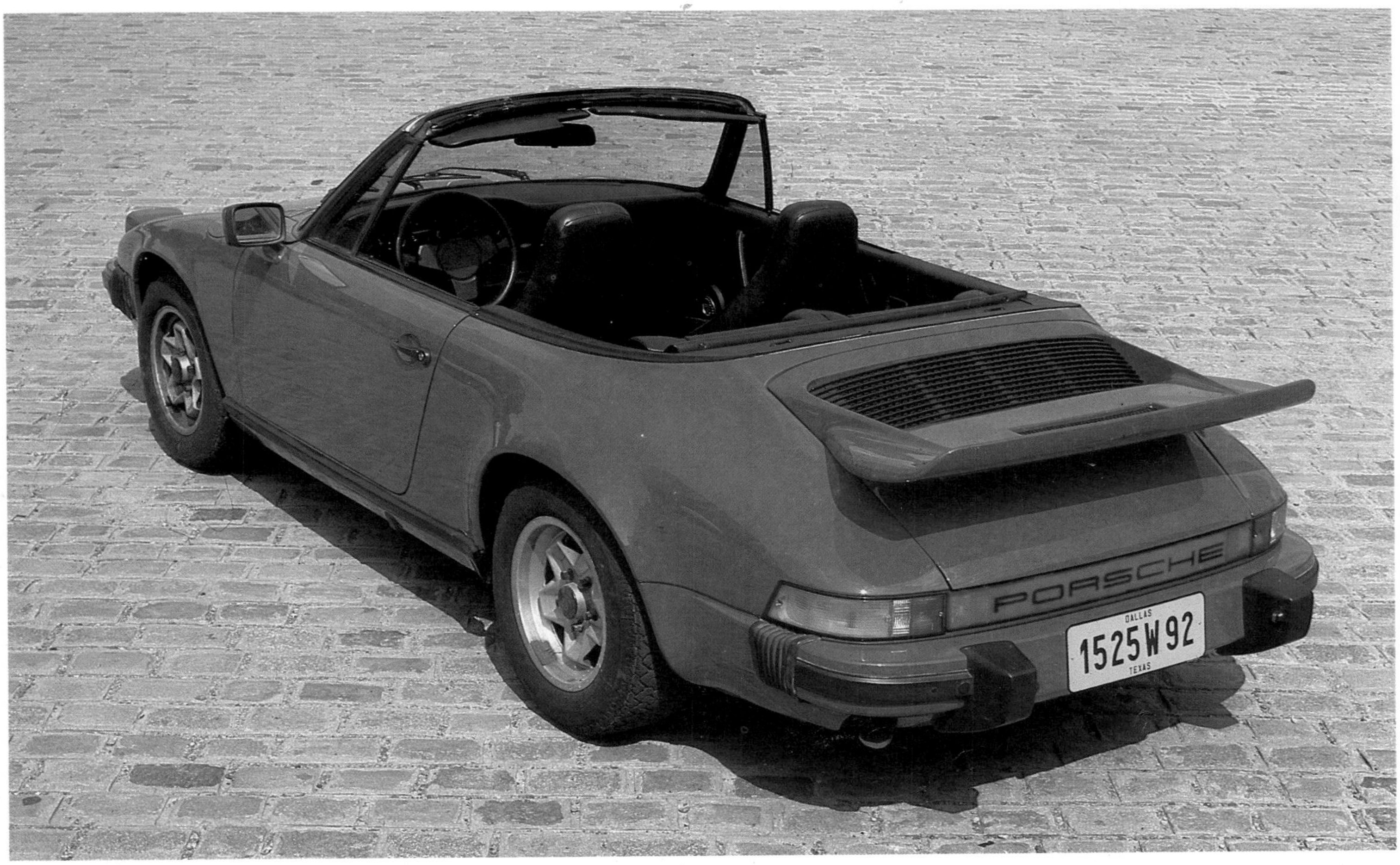
PORSCHE
DALLAS
1525W92
TEXAS

1357 NO

F PR1

PORSCHE

with a power output of exactly 300bhp. A feature of the new engine was an air-to-air intercooler built into a revised rear spoiler. In this form Turbo top speed was over 160mph (258km/h), and the model comfortably kept its position as top Porsche despite the introduction early in 1977 of the 928 model.

With the introduction of the new generation of front-engined Porsches, observers began to predict the demise of the 911 models. It was clear that future product development would center on the 924, the 928 and eventually the 944; the 911 range had already been pared down to the SC coupé and Targa, and the Turbo. But despite all predictions, the 911 refuses to lie down, nor does it show any sign of fading away. The 1980 911 SC models had slightly increased power at 188bhp, while at the end of 1979, the Turbo was withdrawn from the US market as Porsche acknowledged their defeat in the battle to keep the model abreast of ever-tightening US regulations. The 1981 SC models were more powerful still, with 204bhp actually topping the old Carrera. A real surprise was in store for the 1982 Geneva Motor Show: for the first time since 1965, Porsche offered a full cabriolet model. Few people had expected a new body style for the 911 in its 19th year, but the cabriolet got off to a flying start with long waiting lists for the model in Germany and on export markets. The 911 SC cabriolet dispensed with the roll-over bar of the Targa (which remained in production) and had a normal folding top. For the 1983 model year, the Sportomatic transmission was finally discontinued.

So the 911 entered the 20th year of its life. Porsche will be celebrating the anniversary by installing a 230bhp 3.3-liter engine in the 911 SC, and rumors abound of a revised Turbo with two turbochargers for the future, together with an all-wheel drive 400bhp rally version; already a four-wheel drive 911 has been displayed at motor shows. A road-going production four-wheel drive

Pages 124–125: The straightforward factory item is still to many the most attractive 911—and who would say no to a bright red 911 Coupé?

Pages 126–127: "b+b" of Frankfurt are responsible for some extravagant 911 custom cars. Their Turbo Targa was perhaps better than most other similar attempts, using a 928-inspired flat front end.

This page: In virginal white, Germany's classic racing color, the 911 Cabriolet awaits your pleasure, whether for a gentle run with the top down through the countryside on a fine spring day, or for a 150mph (240km/h) burst down a highway.

911 cannot be far behind, and this particular avenue of technology is something that the Porsche engineers can seek inspiration for in their own archives, as the 1950s *Jagdwagen* employed precisely this system.

But the question remains, how long can the 911 survive? Probably for as long as there are enough wealthy enthusiasts who can indulge themselves with that particular kind of motoring which the 911 and the Turbo offer—a rare commodity in the modern world. What is certain is that these cars will be the last of their line; there will be no new rear-engined air-cooled Porsches, once the 911 models disappear. The future belongs to cars like the 928 and the 944; excellent cars, in so many ways better than the 911, yet their competence may seem bland compared to the sheer character of the 911.

The most remarkable feature of the 911 story is not so much the long life of the car as the fact that this 20-year-old design is still one of the world's top supercars. This bears witness to the tireless efforts which the Porsche team has poured into the development of the car; although the basic design and package is unchanged, there are now few if any parts which are the same as in 1963. It may also be mentioned that in mid-1983, the Turbo broke through the DM100,000 price barrier in Germany, and that the "basic" 911 SC coupé now costs DM58,000; to be sure a hefty increase over the original 1964 price of DM21,900 but not so unreasonable when it is remembered that apart from inflation taking its toll (inevitable even in Germany), the 911 buyer is now getting a 3-liter supercar which even in its 145mph (233km/h) SC form is among the fastest sports cars in the world, while in the 1960s, the 911 was a 2-liter GT coupé, fast certainly, but easily outclassed by some of the competition. Now—and for quite some time—it is Porsche which has been setting the standards by which other supercars are judged.

9: TOWARDS THE ULTIMATE

Previous page: A 910 dogfight at Laguna Seca in 1982.

The years from 1966 to 1970 saw the meteoric rise of the house of Porsche in motor racing. Until 1966 Porsche's track record had been impressive enough, but so far the company's racing cars had all been below the two-liter threshold and while the name of Porsche had figured in the result lists often enough, there were more class than outright wins. By the mid-1960s, with the rather irrelevant Grand Prix racing program safely behind them, Porsche could concentrate its efforts and was ready to make a bid for supremacy in the elite field of top sports car racing.

At the time, Ferrari was the undisputed leader. They had six consecutive Le Mans wins to their credit, and were world champions from 1960 to 1963. Of their fellow Italians, Maserati had suffered singularly bad luck and finally withdrew from racing in 1965, after a final luckless appearance at Le Mans. Alfa Romeo had yet to rejoin the fray with the Tipo 33 which was first seen in 1967. There were no serious British contenders after the disappearance of Aston Martin and Jaguar from the race circuits—only a few small-capacity production sports cars, such as MG, Triumph or Austin-Healey which might score a very occasional class win but which impressed more by reliability than by performance. The renaissance of French sports car racing was about to begin, with both Matra and Alpine-Renault launching three-liter cars in 1967. But there was a new and unexpected challenger—Ford whose GT 40 was first seen in 1964, and two years later had been sufficiently developed to do what it had always been intended to do: win the 24-hour race at Le Mans.

It was the appearance of Ford in sports car racing, as much as Porsche's attempts, which wrestled the crown from Ferrari, and for four years Porsche was content to play a waiting game, letting the giants from Detroit and Modena fight it out while Zuffenhausen and Weissach schemed and developed. During those years the Porsche racers were steadily improved and upgraded from two to three liters, and by 1969, when the CSI again reduced the number required for homologation in the sports car category from 50 to 25, Porsche stunned the world by showing off just that number of a completely new car—the 4.5-liter flat-twelve engined 917, which eventually became perhaps the most powerful sports racing car the world has ever seen.

It will be remembered that it was a similar reduction in homologation numbers which had encouraged Porsche to abandon the 904 in 1965 in favor of a new design, the 906 Carrera 6 which was a much more specialized piece of machinery, designed for racing without any concessions toward being a road car (not that the 904 had many of those!). Much of the running gear from the 904 was carried over on the new model but instead of the 904's box section frame, the 906 had a tubular space frame, reverting to traditional Porsche practice. The engine was the same as used in some works 904s—basically a derivative of the two-liter flat-six used in the 911 road car, giving some 210–235bhp depending on the stage of tune. The gearbox was a newly developed fully-synchronized five-speeder, with numerous different sets of ratios from which to choose to suit different events and circuits.

The body of the 906 was a lightweight fiberglass skin stretched around the frame, with a characteristic appearance resulting from the almost semicircular section of the greenhouse which incorporated gull-wing doors, and the long louvered engine cover which was made in one piece from plexiglass and sloped from the roof down to the rear end which was abruptly cut off, Kamm-style. The windshield was shaped like a wedge of lemon and in order to clear the front wheels, the wings rose high above the flat "hood" which hid the oil cooler and spare wheel. In the hands of private owners—as most of the 58 or so 906s were sold—the 906 ran with the six-cylinder engine, but some works cars ran as prototypes with the 2195cc (133.9cu in) type 771 flat-eight. Some of these had the experimental *Langheck* (long-tailed) bodywork.

The first races for the 906 were in the USA where the new car scored 6th place in the Daytona 24-hour, and 4th place in the Sebring 12-hour race. Then in May 1966 came the Targa Florio (incidentally the 50th in the series of the great Sicilian road races). Always a happy hunting ground for Porsche which had won five Targa Florios until then, the 1966 race added further laurels for Porsche as Mairesse and Müller won in a 906. The 1000-kilometer race at the Nürburgring was by contrast a fiasco for the home team which suffered several retirements and could do no better than a 4th place.

The 1966 Le Mans will always be remembered for the 1-2-3 victory for Ford, with the photo-finish of McLaren/Amon and Hulme/Miles underscoring the American company's new-found supremacy; but the three Fords were followed home by four Porsche 906s which on distance were not terribly far behind, despite making do with two liters where the Fords disposed of almost seven. The two-liter class win, and the sports car category win, both went to Porsche as did the Index of Performance. Porsche's efforts throughout the season were consistent enough to be rewarded with the World Championship for makes, in both the prototype and GT categories. In addition, Gerhard Mitter took the hill-climb championship, and Porsche's next racing model was developed on the basis of Mitter's eight-cylinder "Bergspyder" or hill-climb special.

At a glance the 910 was almost indistinguishable from the 906, but it used smaller 13-inch wheels with center-lock hubs, following a one-off hill-climb car which had used Lotus hubs and wheels. The gull-wing doors were replaced by front-hinged doors and these permitted a removeable roof

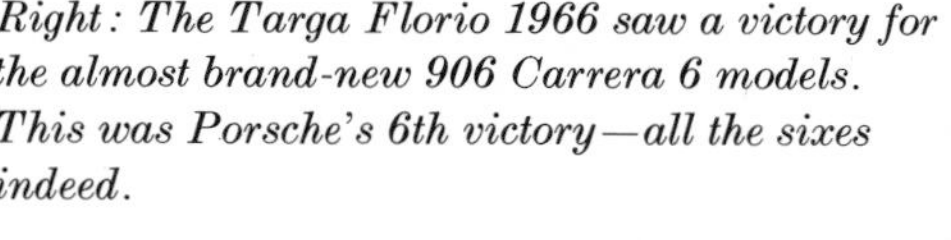

Right: The Targa Florio 1966 saw a victory for the almost brand-new 906 Carrera 6 models. This was Porsche's 6th victory—all the sixes indeed.

DUNLOP
DUNLOP
DRIVE KENNING
Shell
14
LEONARD
MARTINI

panel so the 910 could be run either as a coupé or as a spyder; some later versions intended solely for hill-climbs were completely open. It was raced with various engines, either the two-liter flat-six or the flat-eight in two and 2.2 liter forms. It was intended solely as a works racer, and had a relatively short career, being used in long-distance racing during 1967 and afterwards usually seen only in hill-climbs.

Its career closely followed that of its 906 predecessor. The 910 was first raced at Daytona and Sebring, placing 4th and 3rd respectively. Another 3rd place came Porsche's way in the Monza 1000-kilometer race, and a 910 was 2nd at Spa-Francorchamps. Success again came in the Targa Florio in May 1967 where Hawkins and Stommelen drove an eight-cylinder 910 to victory, followed home by two six-cylinder sister cars; and in the same month, Porsche filled the first four places in the Nürburgring race. Even then the career of the 910 was drawing to its close, as the new model 907 made its first appearance at Le Mans in June and it was a 907 which scored Porsche's highest place, 5th, followed by a 910. The final races for the 910 works cars were at Mugello where they came 1st and 2nd, and the six-hour race at Brands Hatch which resulted in a 3rd place. Henceforth the 910 became a hill-climb car and enabled Gerhard Mitter to retain his championship title for both 1967 and 1968.

As mentioned the 907 made its debut at the 1967 Le Mans race. It was developed on the basis of the 906/910 design but was given a completely new body with a much lower drag co-efficient; both short tail and long tail versions were seen. While engines and transmissions were substantially the same as in the 910, there were two modifications worthy of note: ventilated disk brakes were used, and right-hand drive was fitted to suit races which are run clockwise. For Le Mans, the model's first race, two 907s—both fitted with six-cylinder engines—were entered, together with two 910s and two 906s. A 907 in the hands of Siffert and Herrmann was 5th, followed by a 910 and the 906s, while the two other cars retired. The 907 also won the two-liter class and

908 developments included the 908/02 (left) and the 908/03 (below).

Left: The prototype 16-cylinder version of the 917, intended for Can-Am racing.

the Index of Performance, and was 2nd in the Index of Thermal Efficiency. An eight-cylinder 907 was 4th at Brands Hatch, following the 910 in 3rd place.

The 1968 season opened well for Porsche, with outright wins for the 907s at both Daytona and Sebring; but by now the CSI had introduced a 3-liter limit for prototype sports cars, and Porsche had decided to tackle the opposition head-on by developing a completely new 3-liter engine, type number 908. This was again a flat-eight but the most important change in design was that the two overhead camshafts per bank were now to be chain-driven rather than shaft-driven as on the old type 771 engine. Dimensions were settled at 85 × 66mm (3.3 × 2.6in) for a capacity of 2997cc (182.8cu in) and power output was a reliable 350bhp, with 370bhp being available on occasion. Initially a six-speed gearbox was used but eventually a new five-speed box was designed. The new engine fitted neatly in the existing 907 structure, without any need for drastic modifications, and thus the Porsche 908 was born.

Throughout extensive testing in the early months of 1968 many teething troubles were however encountered, and in their 1st race, the Monza 1000 kilometer, the 908s could do no better than 11th and 19th place—a 907 saved Porsche's honor by finishing 2nd. The 908s were not entered in the Targa Florio but Elford and Maglioli in a 907 scored yet another win for Porsche. The 908's day came in May when Siffert and Elford won the Nürburgring 1000-kilometer race. They were followed by a 907 in 2nd place, and it was evident that the 908 3-liter car was not as yet very much faster than the 2.2-liter 907, besides using a great deal more fuel.

The fact that in 1968, the Le Mans race was delayed until September due to the political unrest in France, gave Porsche some much-needed time to sort out some of the bugs in the 908, and have the new five-speed gearbox ready. Porsche entered four 908s but in the race it soon became apparent that the model was still not sufficiently reliable. After eight hours, three had retired, and the sole survivor driven by Stommelen and Neerpasch who eventually finished 3rd, suffered problems with the belt drive to the cooling blower and also with the alternator. They were in fact beaten by a privately-entered 907 which finished 2nd after the winning Ford GT 40. This in itself was compensation as it was Porsche's best place at Le Mans until then, and the highest placed Porsche since the miraculous 3rd place 10 years before.

At about this time, toward the end of the 1968 racing season, the short-lived 909 Bergspyder appeared in the European hill-climb championship; it was developed on the basis of the 910 Bergspyder and was still fitted with the 2.2-liter type 771 flat-eight engine, but in the interest of better weight distribution it had the gearbox mounted between the engine and the final drive, instead of being overhung at the rear, while the driving position was moved further forward. This particular model was never sufficiently developed to meet with any success, and was only entered for two events anyway, but it was to influence later developments of the 908.

With the opening of the 1969 racing season came the CSI's dual capacity rule for the world championship endurance races. Prototype cars taking part

Following page: This beautiful 1970 917 Kurzheck *in the Gulf colors (owned by Classic Autos) is on display in the Midland Motor Museum at Bridgnorth, England. The year 1970 was indeed the* annus mirabilis *for John Wyer's Gulf-Porsche team which, with the exception of Le Mans, won all the important races of the season.*

Above: The 917 of Elford/Ahrens in the 1970 Le Mans.

were limited to 3 liters, but sports cars could have 5-liter engines, provided 25 were built for homologation. Porsche decided to back both horses—the 908 would run as a prototype but the ace up their sleeve was a new sports car, the type 917. Rumors had been circulating in the world of motor racing about a new super-Porsche but it was still a surprise when Porsche unveiled the 917 at the Geneva Motor Show in March 1969—complete with a price tag of DM140,000. While the new car was clearly based on the 908, and had the same cylinder dimensions of 85 × 66mm (3.3 × 2.6in) which permitted interchangeability of many engine parts, it was nevertheless a major step forward for Porsche—a flat-12 of 4496cc (274cu in), developing a quoted 520bhp. It was the first 12-cylinder engine from Porsche since the prewar Auto-Union and there were perhaps also other similarities between the 917 and its predecessor of 35 years before.

In April 1969 Porsche invited representatives from the CSI to visit Zuffenhausen where they had proudly lined up 25 917s in the factory yard just to prove their point, and the homologation certificate was duly issued. In the following month, a 917 appeared in its first race at Spa but failed to finish, while at the Nürburgring a 917 had to be nursed to finish in 8th place. The other opening races of the 1969 season had produced mixed results for Porsche; in the USA, no 908s finished at Daytona, while at Sebring problems were encountered with chassis breaking during the race, leading to the retirement

Right: This impressive line-up of 25 917s greeted CSI's homologation inspectors when they arrived at Zuffenhausen in 1969.

Right: The unmistakable profile of the 917 Langheck *version.*

Below: The front view of a 917 Kurzheck *at the Laguna Seca.*

of most Porsches although even with a broken chassis, a 908 finished 3rd. But in Europe, the 908s were victorious in virtually all of the races qualifying for the World Championship; they won at Brands Hatch, Monza, Spa and the Nürburgring, as well as in the Targa Florio, and often as not there were 908s in 2nd and 3rd places as well.

Le Mans however still eluded Porsche. Porsche completely dominated the list of entrants which apart from several 911s in the GT category included three 917s in the sports car category, and four 908s and two 910s in the prototype category. This was where the 917—again repeating Auto-Union history—acquired its reputation as a dangerous car. On the first lap, John Woolfe crashed his short-tailed 917 near the White House corner and was killed. Both the other 917s had *Langheck* bodies and were apparently more stable; the Elford/Attwood car led the race for 18 hours before succumbing to clutch failure, leaving a 908 in the hands of Herrmann/Larrousse as Porsche's main contender in the race. They finished 2nd to the Ford GT 40 of Ickx/Oliver, with one of the closest margins ever in Le Mans history. The 917 did win one race in 1969, at the Osterreichring, but clearly there was a lot of work to be done before it was reliable as well as safe; brute force was not enough. However, thanks to the successes of the 908, Porsche was World Champion for 1969.

Before turning to the 1970 racing season and the further development of the 917, let us briefly consider the subsequent career of the 908 model. The original works racers were sold off after the 1969 season, as Porsche decided to concentrate on the 917, but a 908 derivative, the 908.03 model, was prepared for the slower and more winding circuits such as the Nürburgring and the course of the Targa Florio, where the performance of the rather unwieldy 917 could not be fully exploited. The 908.03 was a small spyder-bodied car inspired by the 909; it was incredibly light, at 545kg (1199lb). It was successfully raced by the factory in 1970–71, winning the Nürburgring 1000-kilometer race in both years and the Targa Florio in 1970.

When Porsche withdrew from the World Championship after the 1971 season, the cars were sold to private owners, but the 908s continued their racing careers for several years, becoming Porsche's longest-lived racing model since the original Spyder of the 1950s. Three for instance were entered by the Jöst team in the 1975 Le Mans and one of these finished 4th, the highest-placed Porsche that year. In other races, the old 908s appeared with turbocharged flat-six 2.1-liter engines although these converted cars were not always as reliable as the originals. The 908s proper were not seen in racing after 1976, but the Jöst team still fielded their so-called 908/80s at Le Mans in 1980—where Ickx and Jöst drove the car into 2nd place—and 1981. However, the 908/80 had more in common with Porsche's later 936 model (see chapter 11).

For the 1970 racing season, there were to be no Porsche works entries as such—instead two teams of 917s were entrusted to the British Gulf-sponsored John Wyer team, and to the Austrian Porsche-Konstruktionen which later became the Martini racing team. Both teams enjoyed the direct support of Porsche—Wyer had direct access to the research department at Weissach—and with the combined efforts of Porsche and the two new teams, the 917 soon found its form. The Wyer cars came 1st and 2nd at Daytona at the start of the new season and proved victorious in all important races throughout the year, except at Le Mans where their Austrian rivals scored Porsche's 1st victory in the 24-hour race. The drivers were Herrmann and Attwood; their red-and-white striped car may today be seen in Porsche's museum. The year 1970 again brought Porsche the world championship. Much of the development

LEONARD PARFUMS
5
5

LÉONARD PARFUMS
PARIS

Gulf-Porsche
1
Gulf

Left: To spoil or not to spoil? Porsche's controversial moving rear spoiler was soon banned by the racing authorities.

work on the 917 had gone into the bodywork, to improve the aerodynamics for greater stability, and the modified short-tail (*Kurzheck*) bodies were far more stable without losing much speed over the *Langheck* bodies. But there was also an even bigger engine, of 86 × 70.4mm (3.3 × 2.8in) and 4907cc (299.3cu in), with something like 600bhp on tap, and much wider rear wheels to get the power onto the tarmac.

The year 1971 would be more of the same. The 917 engine capacity was increased fractionally to 4998cc (304.9cu in) by boring out to 86.8mm (3.4in), so 630bhp were now available, and the *Kurzheck* bodies were fitted with tail-fins. With eight victories in 11 races, Porsche had yet another world championship in the bag, and Le Mans in particular proved a most extraordinary occasion: Marko and van Lennep, from the team now sponsored by Martini, won at an average speed of more than 138mph (222km/h) which has yet to be beaten 12 years later. Another unbroken record was Jackie Oliver's fastest race lap at almost 152mph (245km/h), in a Gulf-Wyer 917, and his teammates Attwood and Müller finished 2nd. We may add that 33 of 49 starting cars were Porsches, and that 10 of 13 finishers were of this make; 911s dominated the GT Special class, and a 907 won the prototype category. A rather special 917 made its appearance in the 1971 Le Mans: a 917/20, similar to the Can-Am 917s, but with French-made bodywork, painted pink and decorated like a butchery chart of a pig. "Big Bertha" was a memorable car, even if she did not finish the race.

There was not much Porsche could do to follow up three world championships and two Le Mans wins, and as the CSI after the 1971 season reduced the maximum capacity for sports cars to 3000cc (183cu in), the 917 had to be

Previous page: 917s are now revered museum pieces but they are occasionally aired for demonstration runs, rather than serious racing. These Gulf-liveried cars appeared at Montlhery in 1982 (top left and main picture) and at the Laguna Seca (top right).

Top: 1973 saw the final appearances of the Turbo 917 driven by Mark Donohue in Can-Am racing.

Above: "Big Bertha" or the "Pink Pig" at the 1971 Le Mans.

pensioned off. Porsche withdrew from the championship series and instead entered the Can-Am races in North America. A 917 spyder in the hands of Jo Siffert had been run in Can-Am races in 1969, known as the 917 PA from the initials of the sponsoring American sales organization Porsche+Audi. It was not raced during 1970 but a more powerful 4.9-liter version was ready for 1972; Siffert raced this car with some success before being killed in a BRM Grand Prix car.

In Europe 917 spyders were raced in the Interseries, but the Can-Am races merited more attention and Porsche introduced a turbocharged version of the 917—the 917/10 which at first used the 4.5-liter engine, in turbocharged form this gave some 850bhp. Later capacity was increased to five liters and power output went up to 1000bhp, while the final 917/30 version of 1973 had a 5.4-liter engine with no less than 1100bhp. While one may question these quoted power output figures, there is no doubt that the Can-Am 917s were formidable racing cars. George Follmer and Mark Donohue were the Porsche drivers in the Can-Am series; Follmer was the champion in 1972, and Donohue took the honors the following year. The result was inevitable—for 1974 Can-Am rules were changed to handicap turbocharged cars. It was not quite the end of the line for the 917, as turbochargers were permitted for another season in the European Interseries and Herbert Müller duly won this championship in a 917 Turbo.

Cars such as the 917 have probably had their day; throughout the 1970s endurance racing cars in the Group 6 prototype category were limited to three liters' capacity, or, if turbocharged, to 2.1 liters. The world of motor racing had become fuel economy conscious. The 917 was not suitable under these circumstances, even less so the experimental 16-cylinder version which displaced up to 7.2 liters and yielded close to 900bhp, or a theoretical 2000bhp in turbocharged form. This short-lived 1970 experiment was intended for Can-Am racing but nothing came of it. The likely final race appearance of a 917 was in the 1981 Le Mans where a 917 replica was entered by Kremer racing; it proved disappointingly slow to those who remembered the race 10 years before, and soon retired. Even if we have returned to an endurance race formula—the Group C regulations—which allows unlimited capacity, there are still effectively rules limiting fuel consumption which will curb supercars of the 917 kind. Most 917s are now museum pieces; except possibly the one which was re-built as a road car for Count Rossi of the Martini company. The 917 is now history, but it wrote the most glorious chapter in Porsche's racing history.

10: THE CO-OP CAR

XAA

Three factors influenced the conception of the VW-Porsche 914. First, there was Ferry Porsche's concern that his company was moving upmarket and that the average sports car enthusiast could no longer afford a Porsche. Then there was Heinz Nordhoff, the chairman of Volkswagen, who wished to broaden his company's range and liked the idea of having a sports car at the top of the VW model line-up. And thirdly, there was the idea of building a mid-engined road car.

This last was not a new idea to the Porsche men. Before the war, Dr Porsche had designed the Auto-Union racing cars with mid-engines, and had toyed with the idea of a road-going version; he had also studied a number of other mid-engined sports car projects, some of them based on the original Volkswagen. The first Porsche of 1948 had had its engine in front of the rear wheels, and so had countless Porsche racing sports cars since 1953, with the 904 of the 1960s coming close to being a road-going as well as a racing sports car. Elsewhere in the motor industry, the mid-engined concept was also making progress. Since the first appearance of mid-engined Grand Prix Coopers in

Previous page: The characteristic nose of a VW-Porsche 914, which bore little family resemblance to other Porsches.

1958, motor racing had become completely attuned to mid engines, both in single-seaters and in sports cars; the years from 1961 to 1967 for instance saw the wholesale introduction of mid-engined prototype cars at Le Mans.

The first mid-engined road sports cars appeared during 1966 and 1967, including the spectacular Lamborghini Miura and deTomaso Mangusta, the Ferrari Dino, and on a humbler level, the Matra 530 and the Lotus Europa. Behind the scenes, several other manufacturers were developing similar cars although many never went into production, such as Jaguar, Rover and MG. During the 1960s it was a popular theory that all true sports cars of the future would have their engines behind the driver's seat but in front of the rear wheels; the possibility of almost ideal weight distribution and the low polar moment of inertia by keeping the main masses close to the center of the car were cited as the most important advantages of this type of layout.

Below: The sideview of the 914 was perhaps the best aspect of the car. The Targa top afforded the pleasure of open-air motoring.

So Porsche began to study a mid-engined sports car. This time however, it would be totally different from the racing or near-racing cars of the past; indeed, the new car would be down-market from the established 911, it would

replace the 912 and mark a return to the original Porsche philosophy of making a sports car from mass-production components. With this brief, Ferry Porsche went to Heinz Nordhoff, and found enthusiastic backing for the idea. Throughout the 1960s Nordhoff had expanded the Volkswagen range, with the introduction of the type 3 1500/1600 models and the Karmann-Ghia coupé version; a further new Volkswagen was being readied, the type 411 which was to be the ultimate expression of the original VW design with a rear-mounted air-cooled flat-four engine. The 411 was coming on the market in 1968, and was to be fitted with an all-new engine of 90×66mm (3.5×2.6in), 1679cc (102.4cu in).

A deal was struck between Porsche and Nordhoff. The new sports car would be developed by Porsche, and Karmann at Osnabrück would build the bodywork and undertake final assembly. There would be two versions: a Volkswagen using a fuel-injected version of the 411 engine, and a Porsche which Porsche would assemble with its own engine, but using the same basic Karmann bodyshell. The initial plans assumed that the two cars would be marketed and sold separately by VW and Porsche.

Development of the new car, given Porsche project number 914, went on apace. It was deliberately decided that the 914 should not look like a Porsche, so a proposal from an outside styling consultant was adopted. This was a low, rather square body, with a rear deck under which there was some luggage space in addition to the front luggage compartment. Prominent features were the pop-up headlamps, the well-integrated bumpers and a fixed roll-over bar similar to the 911 Targa with a removable rigid roof panel. Access to the engine was gained by a panel set beneath the roll-over bar, directly behind the rear window.

The chassis design of the 914 owed much to previous Porsche practice, but with the mid-mounted engine it became necessary to lengthen the wheelbase to 2450mm (95.6in), although the overhangs were very short. The front suspension and steering were borrowed from the 911 but as the engine was in the way, the 911 rear suspension with transverse torsion bars could not be accommodated. Instead, a novel rear suspension was developed, which used semi-trailing arms combined with coil spring and shock absorber struts mounted just behind the wheel hubs. Brakes were disk all round, with dual circuits.

The Volkswagen engine was in exactly the same state of tune as found in the 411 which changed from carburetors to fuel injection in 1969, a year after its introduction. This engine developed 80bhp. The engine chosen for the Porsche model was the two-liter carburetor version of the 911 engine with 110bhp, found in the 911 T until 1969 when the 911 range had engines increased to 2.2 liters. Both cars had a five-speed gearbox, and although Sportomatic was listed as an option for either model, very few cars were in fact so equipped.

Before the new sports car could be introduced to the public at the Frankfurt Motor Show in the autumn of 1969, there were quite a few problems to be solved concerning the co-operation between the two companies. These stemmed from the appointment of a new chairman at Volkswagen. Nordhoff suffered a heart attack in the summer of 1967 and was not able to work full time again before his death in the spring of the following year. His successor had been designated already, before his illness—Kurt Lotz who was not a motor industry man but a top manager from Brown Boveri, the Swiss engineering combine. Perhaps the fact that Lotz lacked car experience led to his premature resignation after only three and a half years; he was, whether unjustly or not, accused of having failed to stem the loss of Volkswagen business due to a range of old-fashioned and not wholly popular models.

The appointment of Lotz had an immediate effect on the relationship between Volkswagen and Porsche. Lotz did not see much point in having a VW sports car but was on the other hand reluctant to allow Porsche to sell their own version of the 914. In the end, a compromise was reached whereby the two companies set up a mutual sales company, the VW-Porsche Vertriebsgesellschaft GmbH. This company was established with headquarters at Ludwigsburg outside Stuttgart, in premises built and owned by Porsche. That the new company also took on the marketing of the established Porsche range, was seen by some observers as a first step toward a complete absorption of Porsche by Volkswagen which had but recently taken over the Auto-Union Audi and NSU companies, but this was flatly denied by Ferry Porsche. On the other hand, there is no doubt that Lotz was keen on reinforcing the ties between the two companies; in effect, he wanted Porsche to become the research and development department of the VW group, and commissioned Porsche to design the VW of the future—the ill-fated EA.266. This prompted Porsche to step up the building of their new design and testing department at Weissach.

So when in 1969 the 914 came on the market, it was neither a Volkswagen nor a Porsche. A new hyphenated and uneasy-sounding marque name had been invented—the VW-Porsche, under which the cars were sold except in the

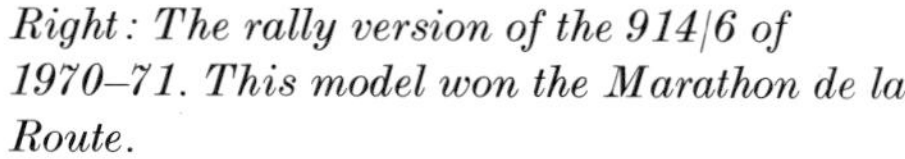

Right: The rally version of the 914/6 of 1970–71. This model won the Marathon de la Route.

Right: The very special eight-cylinder 914 built for Ferdinand Piëch. Wider headlamps and the special front bumper give the game away.

OHR 699M

Previous page: This 1974 914/4 does not display a Porsche badge but the VW is in evidence on the hubcaps.

USA, where they became Porsches, although handled by VW of America Inc. through the newly-established Porsche+Audi Division. The two models were known as the 914/4 and the 914/6 respectively, and prices were fixed at DM12,560 and DM19,000 in the German home market. This in fact put the six-cylinder model uncomfortably close to the cheapest real Porsche, the 911 T which was less than DM1000 more expensive. On the other hand, the four-cylinder car was more expensive than any Volkswagen, appreciably dearer than the Type 3 Karmann-Ghia coupé which had cost DM9145 and which it was supposed to replace.

The naming and pricing of the new cars did not help, and their reception was very mixed. The road-holding and handling were probably all that VW-Porsche claimed for it, and the 914 was found to have almost neutral handling and a very forgiving nature—which could not be said about other Porsches! On the other hand, the 914 was—if sufficiently provoked—liable to spin like a top, especially on wet or icy roads: the penalty one paid for the low polar moment of inertia. While the performance of the 914/6 rivaled the 911 T, the 914/4 was found to be disappointingly slow by Porsche standards—the testers conveniently forgetting to measure it against Volkswagen standards. The styling was disliked by most, and although there was sufficient luggage space and the cockpit was just about wide enough to accommodate three people, there was the usual mid-engined car drawback of no stowing space behind the seats for odds and ends. Equipment was spartan and furnishings austere, and the minor controls were too obviously of Wolfsburg ancestry, including a VW badge on the steering wheel!

The cars were soon popularly referred to as "Volks-Porsches"—sometimes shortened by Germans to "Vo-Po" which also refers to the dreaded East German gendarmerie, the Volks-Polizei! The demand for the 914 did not live up to VW-Porsche's anticipations, especially not for the 914/6 which sold only 3332 before it was quietly discontinued in 1972. The four-cylinder models did rather better, reaching the creditable total of 115,646 cars until the model was phased out at the end of 1975. The introduction of more powerful versions helped; the 914/6 was replaced by a four-cylinder car with a fuel-injected two-liter engine (94×71mm [3.7×2.8in], 1971cc [120.2cu in], 100bhp) which was built by Volkswagen specially for this model. With the new engine, top speed was 120mph (193km/h), a useful increase from the 110mph (177km/h) attained by the original 1.7-liter model and not far short of the 125mph (201km/h) possible in the 914/6. For the 1973 model year, the basic 1.7-liter model was replaced by a 1.8-liter version, using a carburetor version of the uprated 1795cc (109.5cu in), 93×66mm (3.6×2.6in) engine from Volkswagen's improved 412 model, and this gave a top speed of almost 115mph (185km/h). The two new models were more reasonably priced at DM14,700 and DM15,700, and 1973 proved to be the best single year for 914 sales.

In true Porsche tradition however, the 914 did spawn some much more exciting derivatives. First came the 914/6 GT which was actually listed in the 1971 catalog as a Group 4 car, available from the Porsche racing department. In fact very few were built, and all of those probably before the catalog was published. The 914/6 GT was fitted with a much-tuned engine; although capacity was kept at 1991cc (121.5cu in) and Weber carburetors still used, it developed some 210bhp. The model was first raced at the end of May 1970, and a single car was entered by the French Porsche importer Sonauto—where Auguste Veuillet was still in charge—for Le Mans the following month. This was driven into an excellent 6th place by Chasseuil and Ballot-Lena, who also won the GT category of the 24-hour race. Later in the year, a team of three GTs finished 1-2-3 in the arduous Marathon de la Route, and there were

Above: Almost identical to the one on the previous pages, this 914 sports the optional alloy wheels.

other race successes as well. By contrast, Porsche's gamble of entering only the 914/6 models, and not the 911s, in the 1971 Monte Carlo Rally, backfired and the highest place achieved was a 3rd by Björn Waldegaard, shared with an Alpine-Renault. There were also two specially built 914/8s, into which the flat-eight three-liter engines from the 908 had been squeezed, but these were strictly playthings for Ferry Porsche and Ferdinand Piëch! Ferry's car is now in the Porsche museum.

A production version of the 914/6 GT almost happened, and experts opine that some 20 were built in preparation for a launch at the 1971 Paris Motor Show. This was called the 916, and shared the distinctive widened flared wings of the GT; it also had 911 style five-spoke alloy wheels, and integrated body-color bumpers, with an oil cooler mounted in the front bumper. The roof panel was of metal and welded in place. Power was 190bhp, from a fuel-injected 2341cc (142.8cu in) engine as fitted to the 911 S. But two weeks before the launch, the project was dropped as Porsche planners were worried about the commercial viability of such a specialized car in the unpredictable sports car market.

For the final production year of 1975, the two 914s were given reinforced bumpers, but by now the model was dying on its feet. Since Kurt Lotz had resigned from the chair of VW in 1971 and been replaced by Rudolf Leiding, it had become clear that Volkswagen was no longer wedded to the air-cooled rear engine. Leiding saw it as his primary task to develop a completely new Volkswagen of the future, a car so thoroughly up-to-date that it would set the standard in the small car class, as the Beetle had done in its day. Looking around the VW empire, Leiding found little that pleased him. Sales of the Beetle were flagging, the rear-engined type 3 and type 4 models were by VW standards commercial disasters and the technically interesting front-wheel drive K.70, a project inherited from NSU when Volkswagen took over the company, was altogether too big and expensive a car to fall in line with the

The original Porsche importer in Great Britain, AFN Ltd, retains a close link with Porsche Great Britain Ltd and prepared this 924 works race and record car in 1978, taking the British 24-hour record. This car is now on display in the Midland Motor Museum at Bridgnorth, England.

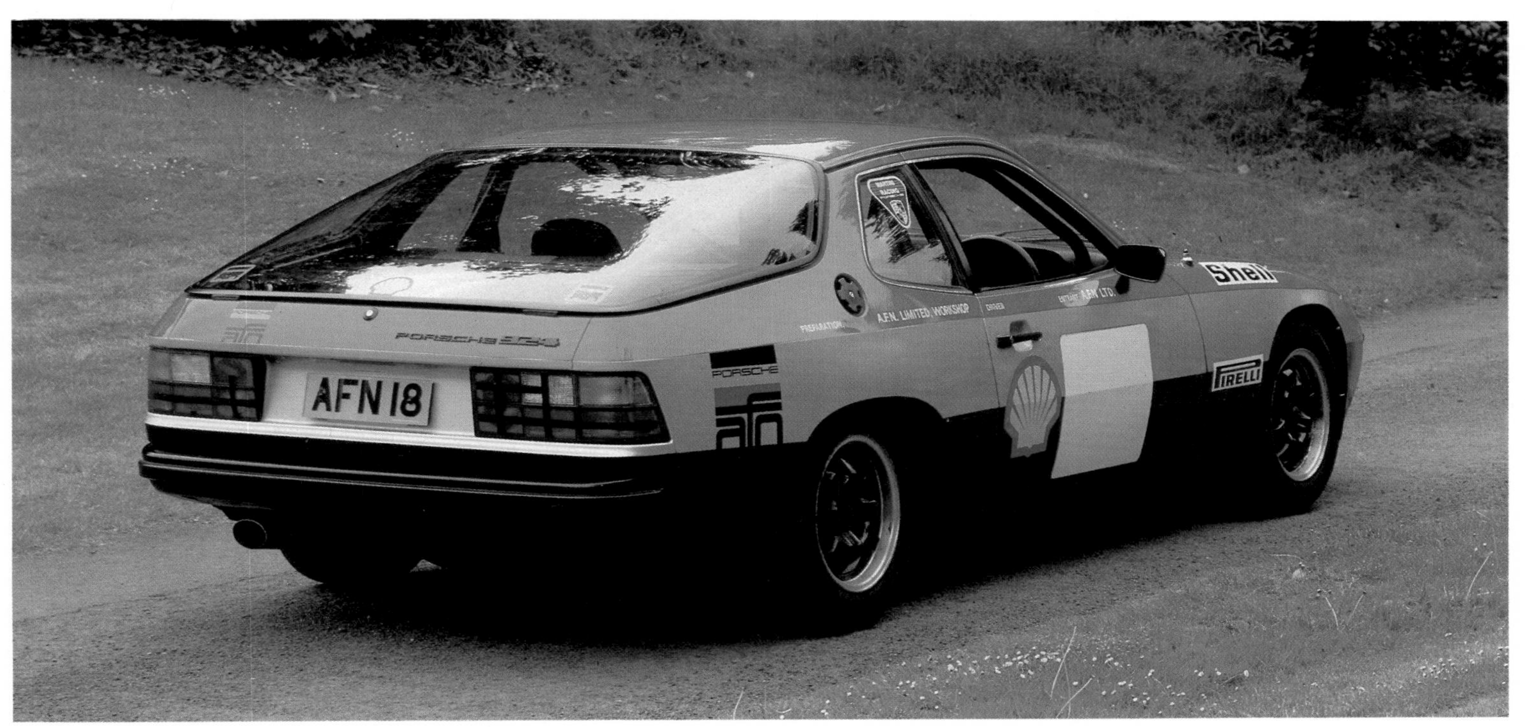

Shell
PIRELLI
AFN 18
PORSCHE
A.F.N. LIMITED WORKSHOP

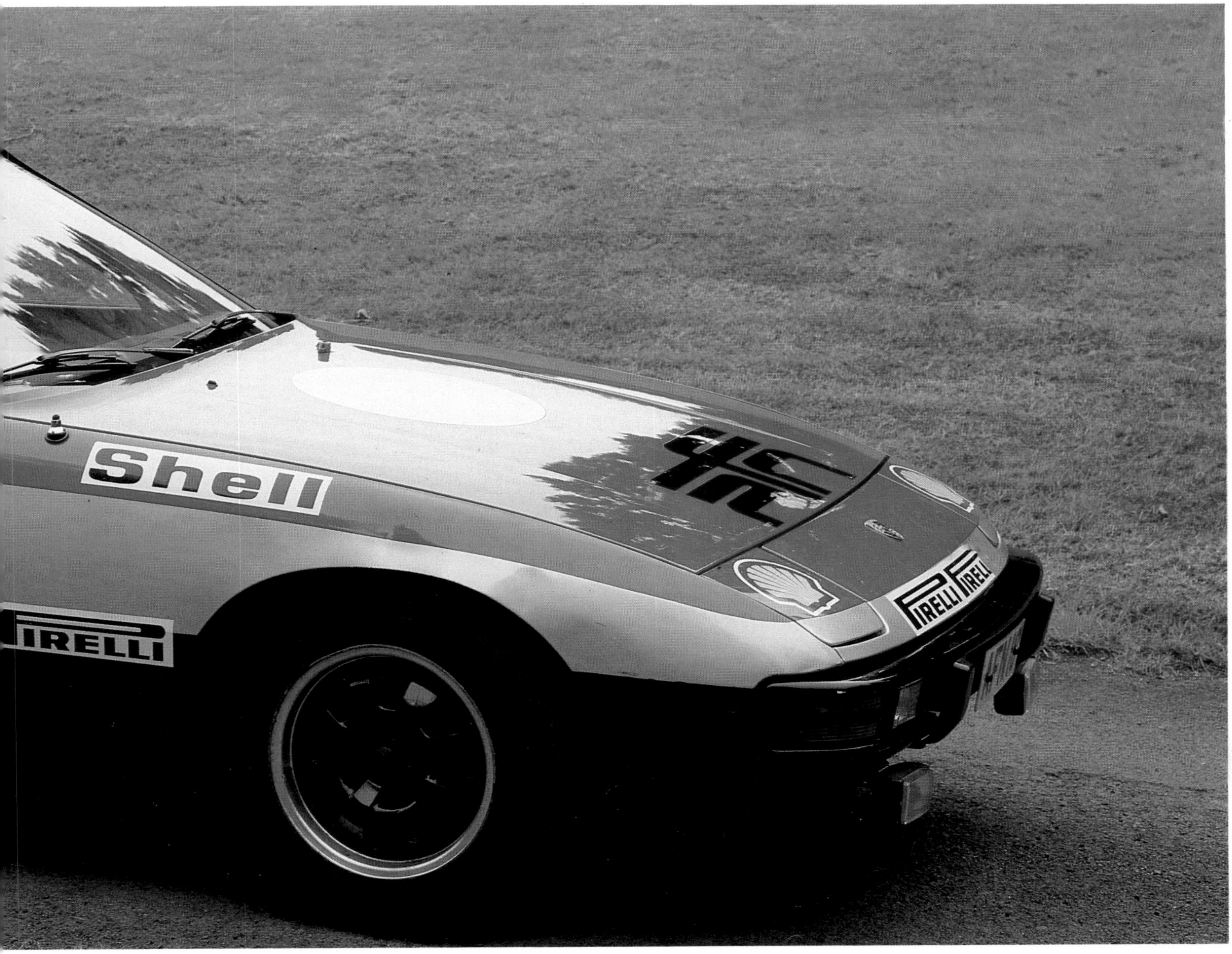
Shell
PIRELLI
PIRELLI PIRELLI

established Volkswagen image, and also competed directly with the 411/412 range.

Leiding was able to look to the other half of the VW group, the Audi company at Ingolstadt which had a tradition of front-wheel drive cars going back to the prewar DKW. Two new models were under development, the medium-sized Audi 80 and the small Audi 50 which were to reach the market place in 1972 and 1974. Leiding seized the opportunity to bring out badge-engineered Volkswagen versions of both these cars, which became the VW Passat of 1973, and the VW Polo of 1975. He also got Wolfsburg's designers and engineers started on their own new small front-wheel drive car, launched in 1974 as the Golf together with a sports coupé version the Scirocco, both with bodywork styled by the Italian master Giugiaro. These cars have indeed achieved everything expected of them as the real replacement for the once-ubiquitous Beetle.

In the middle of all these events at Volkswagen, the Porsche-designed EA.266 became a Cinderella. The car was an engineering marvel, with a water-cooled in-line four-cylinder engine transversely mounted, but lying on its side under the rear seat. The concept was Ferdinand Piëch's and there is little doubt that the car was brilliant in engineering terms. But if it had been put on the market as a Volkswagen, it is very questionable whether it would have done the ailing Wolfsburg giant much good. True, it would have been a unique and possibly revolutionary car, but it might not have achieved the commercial success reaped by the Golf, for the simple reason that by the 1970s the car-buying public of Western Europe had come to expect small cars to be front-wheel drive hatchbacks. The Golf conformed to this pattern; the EA.266 would have been an oddity. So in 1971 Leiding cancelled the EA.266 program which by that time had reached the stage of testing a fair number of prototype cars. This incidentally is still one of the skeletons in the cupboards of VW and Porsche, and even after the passage of more than 10 years the detailed story

Top: An early model of the EA.266, Porsche's proposal for a new Volkswagen.

Above: The EA.425 prototype which with a few modifications became the 924.

Left: The Porsche 924 at the 1975 introduction in the South of France.

of the EA.266 has yet to be told.

The cancellation of the EA.266 project left Porsche's Weissach complex somewhat deprived of work. However what Leiding had torn down with one hand, he was ready to build up with the other. Like Nordhoff before him, Leiding fancied the idea of a sports model at the top of the VW-Audi range, and Porsche was the natural source for a project of this nature. The outcome was another potential VW-Porsche co-op car, codenamed EA.425. It was seen as a replacement for the 914, and like its predecessor—even like the original 356—the EA.425 would use the maximum number of parts out of the VW parts bin, and would be clothed in a sports coupé body. The difference was that by now, the VW bin contained rather different components. The engine for the new car came from the Audi 100—a front-mounted water-cooled single overhead camshaft in-line four of two liters' capacity. The McPherson strut front suspension was typical of the new VW-Audi models, while the trailing arm rear suspension with transverse torsion bars was actually borrowed from the latter-day VW Super Beetle. Although VW-Audi was firmly committed to front-wheel drive for their bread-and-butter cars, it was felt to be more appropriatè for a sports car to have rear-wheel drive. The apparent absence of a suitable gearbox for a rear-wheel drive car was elegantly solved by the Porsche engineers who took the Audi 100 transaxle and put it in the back of the sports car, connecting the engine and the transaxle with a 20mm (.8in) diameter shaft running in a tube which was rigidly connected to both engine and gearbox, with the clutch at the engine end. Another Volkswagen influence resulted in the use of drum brakes on the rear wheels, with disks at the front only; a retrograde step as all Porsches since the 356 C had had disks on all four wheels.

The EA.425 project suffered from several changes of heart by the Volkswagen board. In 1973, the formal Volkswagen and Porsche co-operation in the VW-Porsche sales company came to an end when this was dissolved and Porsche bought out Volkswagen's share. EA.425 then became a Volkswagen project, and Porsche would be deprived of a share of the sales of the car. Then at the end of 1974, it was Leiding's turn to resign from the Volkswagen chair; although he had seen the new generation of VWs through to production, the cost of the development program had been so enormous that the company was deeply in the red, with existing models not selling well enough to generate the funds necessary for the new cars. Leiding's replacement was ex-Ford man Toni Schmücker whose first task was to make economies and slim the VW-Audi group down to manageable proportions. The EA.425 project was an early casualty, the plans to manufacture the car as a Volkswagen (or Audi) in the company's Salzgitter plant were dropped, and another of Schmücker's drastic reforms was to close down one of VW-Audi's eight German factories. This was the former NSU plant at Neckarsulm near Stuttgart which produced Audi 100 saloons and coupés, in addition to small numbers of the costly and unreliable Wankel-engined NSU Ro80.

After a long period in 1974 when the whole EA.425 project was in abeyance, a solution was found. Porsche bought back their design from VW-Audi, reputedly at a much lower cost than VW-Audi had already paid them for the design and development work, and a deal was negotiated whereby Volkswagen would build the car for Porsche in the Neckarsulm factory, with the body being made on site and components sourced from other branches of the VW-Audi empire. Effectively Porsche leased the plant but paid Volkswagen an agreed sum for each car manufactured. The launch of the new car was planned for 1975, and finally EA.425 was given its proper designation: The Porsche 924.

11: PORSCHE INVINCIBLE

46
LONGINES
MECCARILLOS

Previous page: The 935, here at Le Mans in 1980, was the ultimate development of the 911 and the most successful Group 5 racing car of the period.

Porsche's retirement from the World Championship of Makes in sports car endurance racing might fancifully be compared to the abdication of a popular monarch after a long and benevolent reign; seeking a quiet retirement away from the hustle and bustle of official affairs, wishing to let a younger successor take over the reins, escaping from the spotlight of public life. But this is where the fable stops and the real-life story begins. Porsche did not stay out of racing—the 917 indeed continued its devastating career in Can-Am and Interserie racing—and as we have seen, by the 1973 racing season Porsche were back in the Championship, with the 911-based Carrera (see chapter 8) which successfully contested a number of important races.

It could be argued that the emergence of proper racing versions of the 911 was to some extent a stop-gap designed to keep Porsches in racing after the 917 was overtaken by the new regulations limiting prototype sports cars to a capacity of three liters. Porsche very much wanted to keep on racing, mindful of the prestige and publicity gained from victories on the race track, and it made a great deal of sense to shift the emphasis to recognizable 911 derivatives which would give that model an extra boost—while the new 924 and 928 models were emerging on the drawing boards, Porsche at the beginning of the 1970s anticipated that the 911 would be kept in production, possibly even until 1980. How wrong they were. . . .

Right: At the start of the 1976 Le Mans, the ultimate winner, the Ickx/van Lennep Porsche 936, was already well to the fore (No 20).

Right: 1976 gave Porsche the double world championship in both Group 5 and Group 6. The winning Martini-Porsche team consisted of (from left to right) Schurti, Stommelen, Racing Manager Jantke, Mass and Ickx. They are seen in this photograph with the 935 and 936 racing cars.

The Carrera RS and RSR models were, as it turned out, only a first step along this road. Initially, the Carrera ran as a prototype—as for instance in the 1973 24-hour race at Daytona—but the model was soon homologated in Group 4, and proved invincible in the GT championships on both sides of the Atlantic in 1973 and 1974, besides winning the 1973 Targa Florio and Sebring races. Basically, the original Carrera RSR racing version was quite close to the road-going RS model, or indeed to the straightforward 911; but the cars were specially lightened, with thinner-gauge metal for the bodywork and deletion of all superfluous luxury items such as soundproofing. Racing engines were of 92×70.4mm (3.6×2.7in) for a capacity of 2806cc, developing 300bhp at 8000rpm, and the model could be immediately identified by the oil cooler built into the front air dam. The 1974 RSR models had engines bored out to 95mm (5.8in) and a capacity of 2993cc (116.7cu in), resulting in 330bhp.

The year 1974 also saw the appearance of the first turbocharged Carrera RSR. This ran as a prototype, and to keep within the three-liter limit under the CSI's 1.4 equalization formula for forced-induction engines, it was fitted with a 2142cc (130.7cu in) engine of 83×66mm (3.2×2.6in) bore and stroke. This developed up to 500bhp, with a single KKK turbocharger similar to those used on the 917 turbo. It proved to be quite competitive even against the very fast normally-aspirated Matra V-12 prototypes and the outstanding result of the 1974 racing season was van Lennep and Müller's 2nd place at Le Mans. But even Carreras without the turbocharger were still keeping up in racing; notable wins included the Daytona 24-hour in 1975 and 1977, the Sebring 12-hour in 1976, and the GT class at Le Mans in 1978.

Porsche was by now convinced that the future belonged to the turbocharger—certainly in the world of racing but possibly also on the road. The first pre-production version of the 911/930 Turbo road car had appeared at the 1974 Paris Motor Show. In the racing world there was some confusion over the introduction of new regulations for the endurance racing championship; it had been expected that this would be run for Group 5 cars in 1975 but the CSI postponed this until 1976. Porsche decided on another strategic withdrawal and did not field works entries in the World Championship for 1975; this did not prevent them from taking 2nd place, thanks to the efforts of private

MARTINI RACING
Renault
20

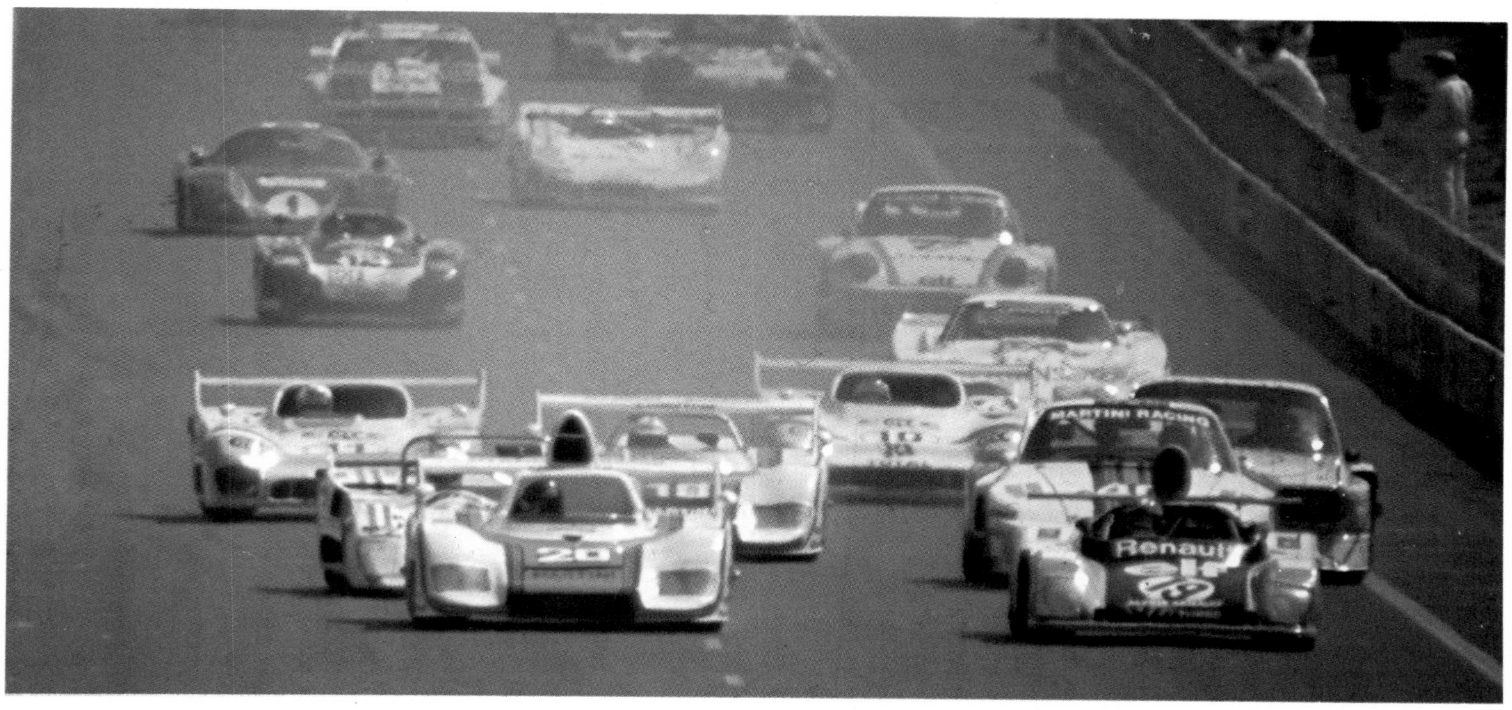

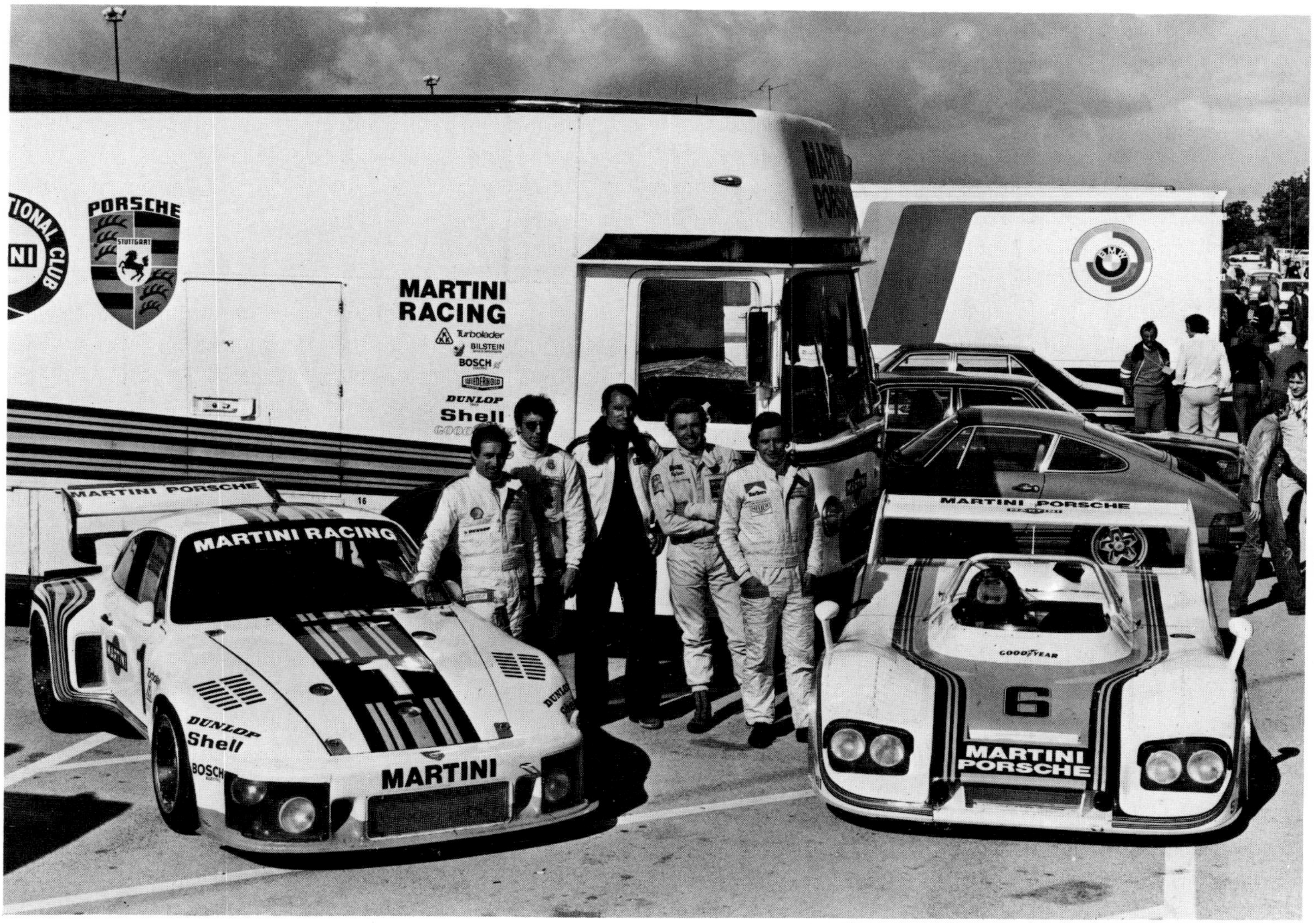
PORSCHE
MARTINI RACING
Turbolader
BILSTEIN
BOSCH
DUNLOP
Shell
MARTINI PORSCHE
MARTINI RACING
DUNLOP
Shell
BOSCH
MARTINI
MARTINI PORSCHE
GOODYEAR
6
MARTINI
PORSCHE

entrants and drivers who scored sufficient points mainly in re-engined turbocharged 908s.

Meanwhile a new generation of racing cars was under development at Weissach. Porsche typically did not put all their eggs in one basket, which turned out just as well as the 1976 long-distance races were opened to both Group 6 prototype cars competing for a World Championship for Sports Cars, and to the Group 5 cars which would contest the World Championship for

Dick Barbour Racing
70
garretson enterprises
BP
BP BP BP
MARCHAL
Dick Barbour RACING

Previous page, left center: The 934 Group 4 car was the "tamest" of the 1970s racing Porsches but nevertheless a formidable weapon in GT racing.

Previous page, right and left below: The win of the 935 in the 1979 Le Mans was the high point in the model's career. Even greater interest was centered on the 2nd-placed car shown here, which was driven by Paul Newman with Barbour and Stommelen.

Right: 935s won 5th place as well as Group 5 and IMSA categories in the 1980 Le Mans.

Following page, top, all three: The Jöst/Ickx 908/936 was the only Porsche entered in Group 6 in the 1980 Le Mans and did well to finish 2nd.

Following page, main picture: A Porsche 935 in the 1980 Le Mans.

BP
MARCHAL

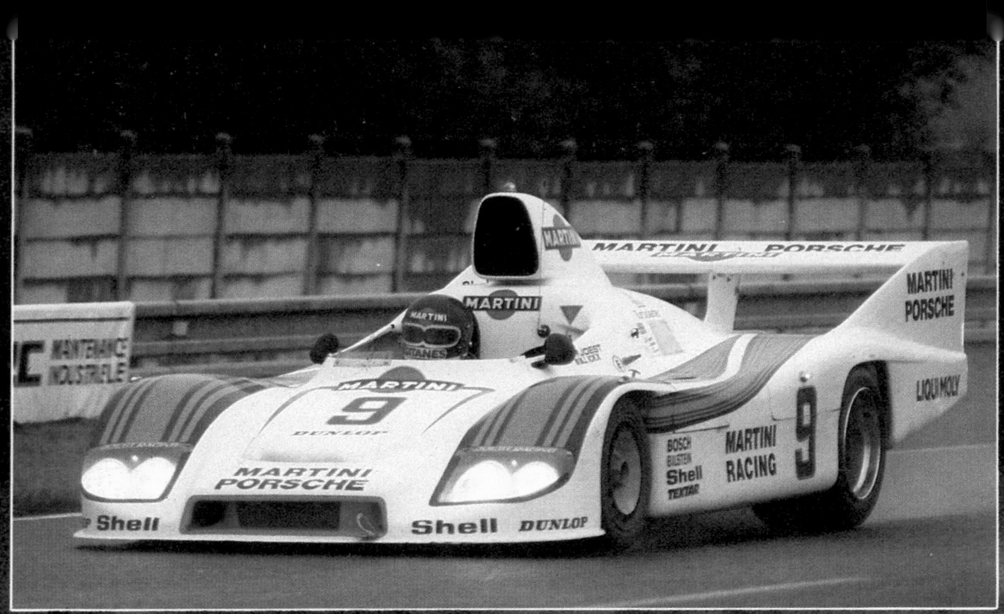

MARTINI
MARTINI PORSCHE
MARTINI
PORSCHE
MARTINI
9
DUNLOP
MARTINI
PORSCHE
Shell
Shell
DUNLOP
MARTINI
RACING
9
LIQUI MOLY
MAINTENANCE
INDUSTRIELLE

MARTINI
MARTINI
9
DUNLOP
MARTINI
PORSCHE

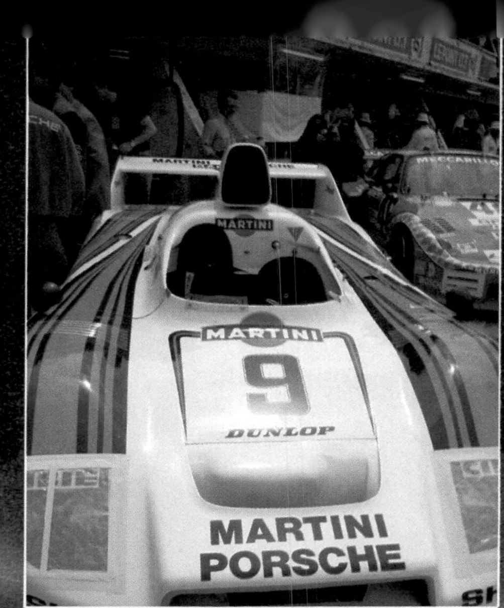

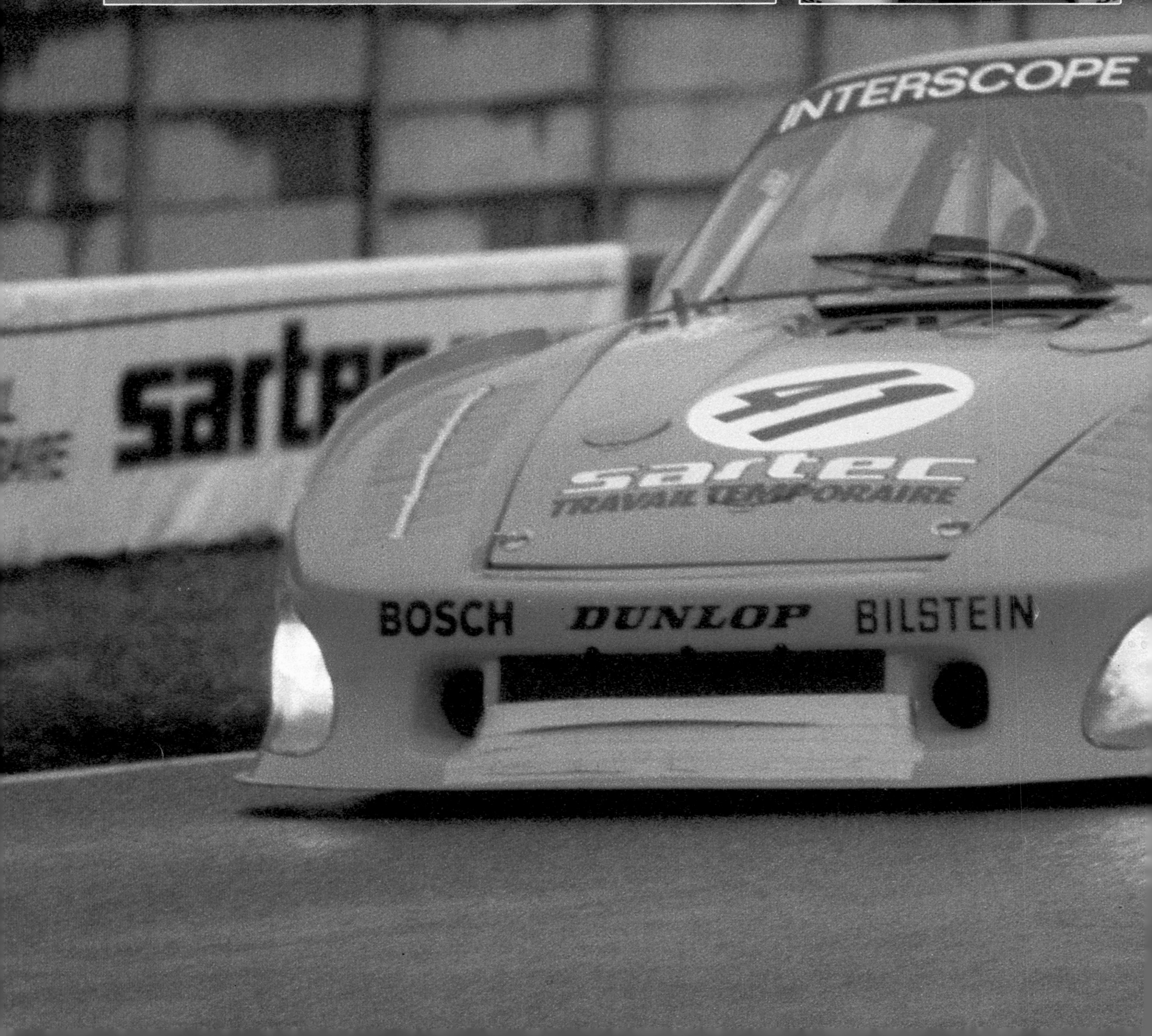
INTERSCOPE
sartec
BOSCH
DUNLOP
BILSTEIN

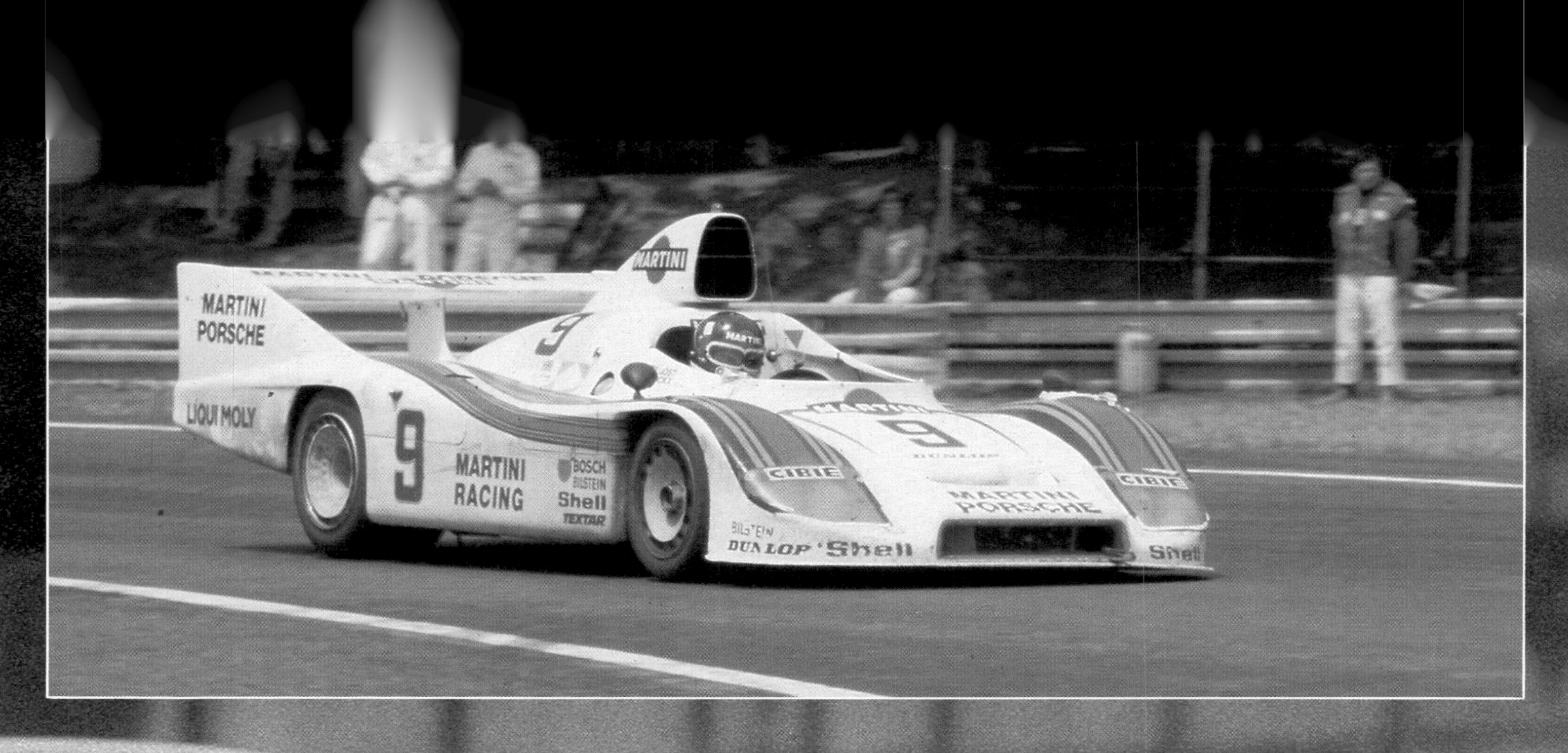

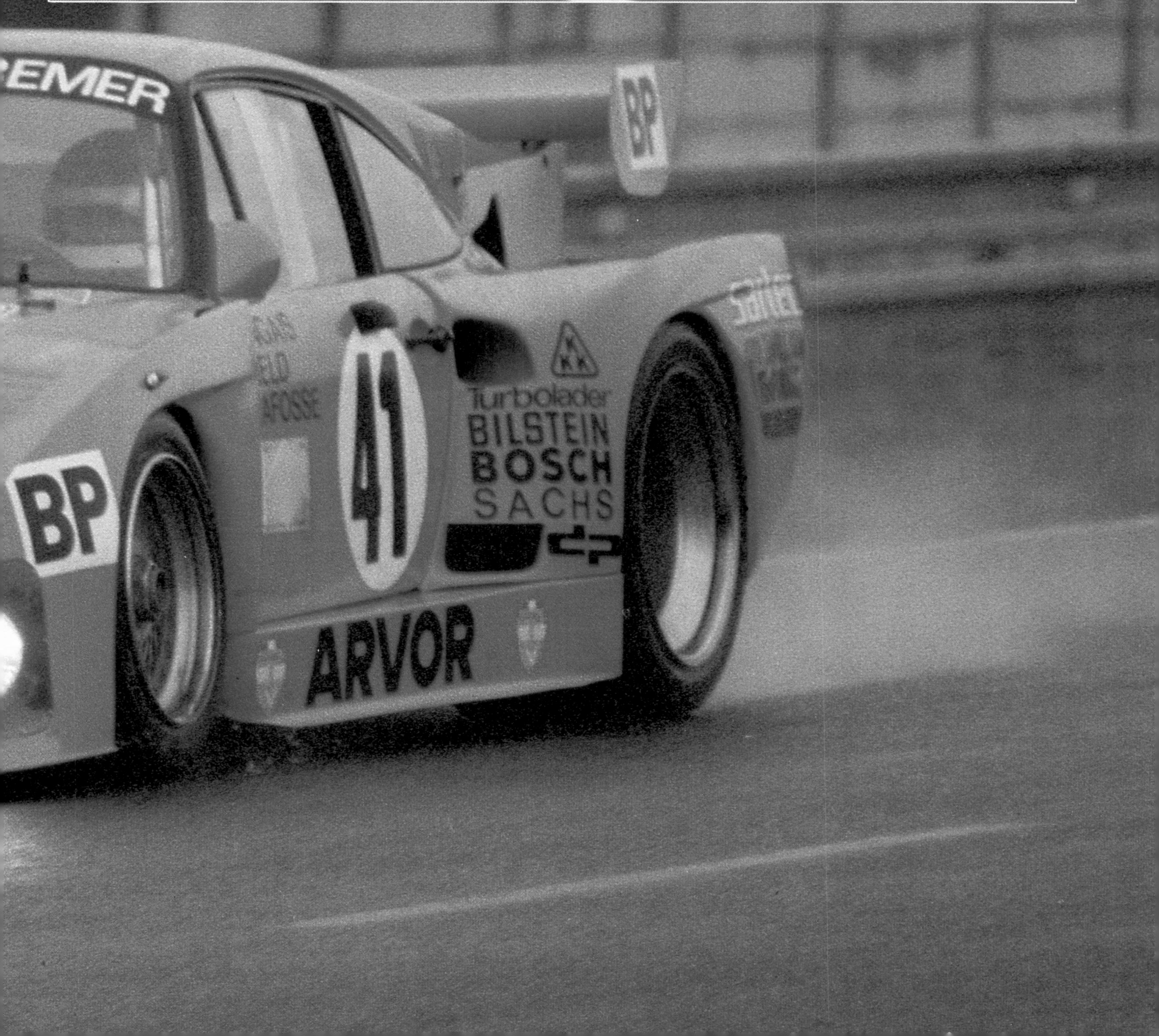
BP
41
Turbolader
BILSTEIN
BOSCH
SACHS
ARVOR
MARTINI
MARTINI
PORSCHE
LIQUI MOLY
9
MARTINI
RACING
BOSCH
BILSTEIN
Shell
TEXTAR
MARTINI
9
CIBIE
MARTINI
PORSCHE
BILSTEIN
DUNLOP 'Shell
Shell

Makes. The new Porsches were distinguished by new type numbers, and there were three of them: the 934, the 935 and the 936. These numbers indicated that they all had some relationship with the 930 Turbo, and were intended for Groups 4, 5 and 6 respectively. Visually, the 934 and 935 confirmed the 911/930 parentage; the 936 was Porsche's return to the open spyder-bodied mid-engined prototype racing car, and was a direct descendant from the 908 and 917.

Engine-wise, all three cars used versions of the turbocharged flat-six. The 934 being closest to standard used the full-sized 2993cc (182.6cu in) engine—the same capacity as the production Turbo—but nevertheless suitably modified to give a healthy 485bhp. The 935 used a slightly smaller 2806cc (171.2cu in) engine; multiplied by 1.4 this equaled just under four liters—not that Group 5 cars were hampered by a capacity limit but the minimum permitted weight increased with capacity under the Group 5 regulations. With a higher turbo boost, this engine gave 590bhp. The 936 engine had to fit within the three-liter Group 6 limit so actual capacity was 2142cc (130.7cu in) as the 1974 Carrera Turbo had been, but the output was still a respectable 520bhp.

In terms of body and chassis, the 934 was again closest to the standard car, as only modest body changes were allowed, especially in respect of aerodynamic aids, and wheel width was limited. The production run required for homologation was 400 in a two-year period which was amply met by the 930 Turbo. The minimum weight specified was 1120kg (2464lb) so a standard bodyshell was used and no special lightening was necessary, beyond the deletion of soundproofing and some trim. Wheels were 16in in diameter with a 12.5in wide rim; the wheels fitted were composite magnesium castings by BBS with a very elegant multi-spoke pattern. Technically, the 934 was a production model—some 30 were in fact built; including tax it was listed at DM108,000 in Germany. It was a fairly mild car, being mainly intended for GT racing, and appeared in the GT classes in endurance races such as Le Mans where 934s won the Group 4 GT class in 1977, 1979, 1981 and 1982, being placed as high as 4th in the 1979 race.

The 935 was a rather different animal. These Group 5 racing cars of the

Right: In 1977 the 936s were only raced once, at Le Mans, where Ickx, sharing the Haywood/Barth car, won again.

Below and below right: The next Le Mans victory for Ickx and the 936 came in 1981. Derek Bell was the co-driver on this occasion and Jules Aftershave the most prominent sponsor.

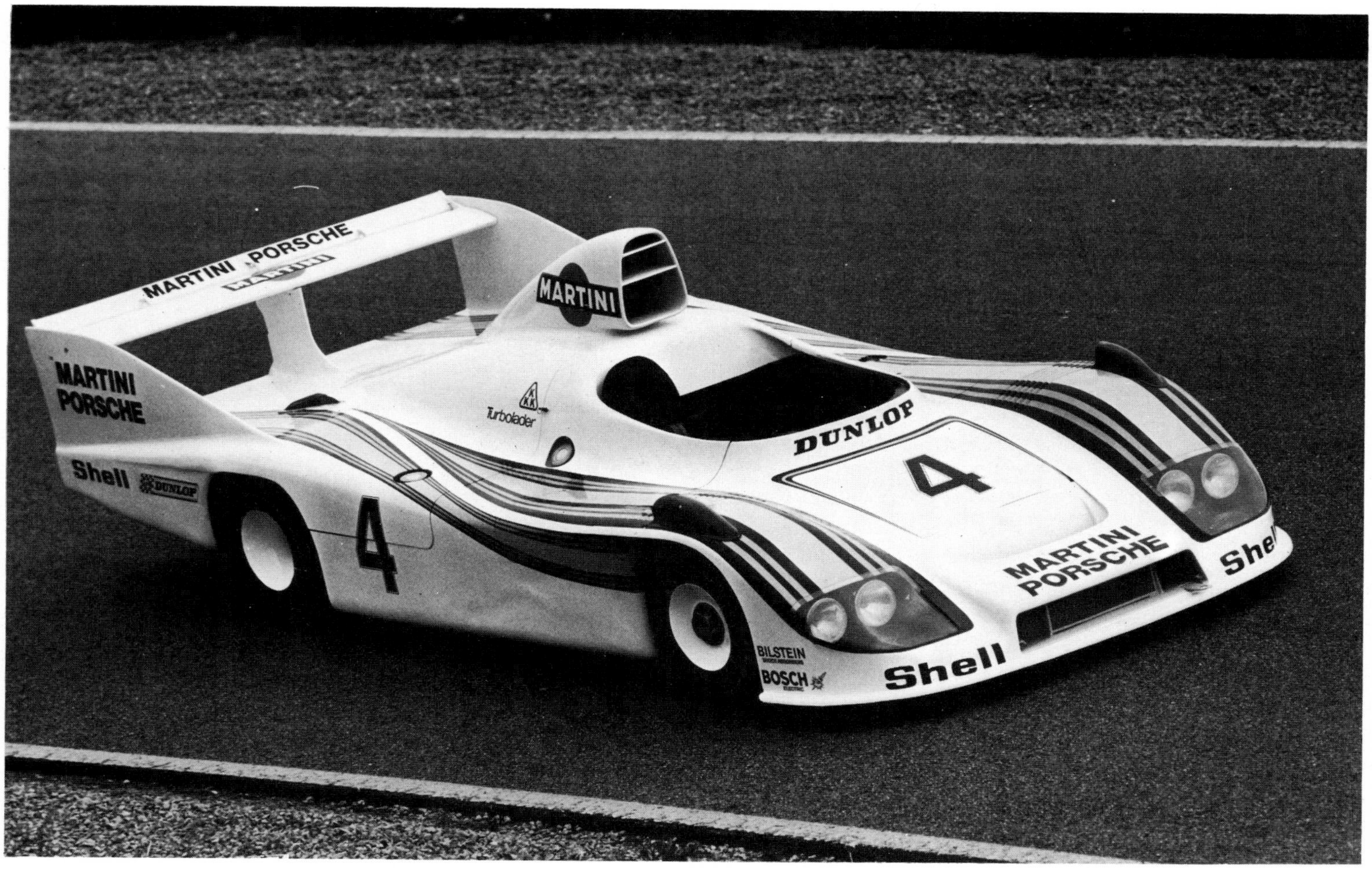
MARTINI PORSCHE
MARTINI
MARTINI
PORSCHE
Shell
DUNLOP
Turbolader
DUNLOP
4
4
MARTINI
PORSCHE
Shell
BILSTEIN
BOSCH
Shell

Jules
PORSCHE
11
Shell
Jules
Jules
Jules
Jules
CIBIE
DUNLOP
BILSTEIN

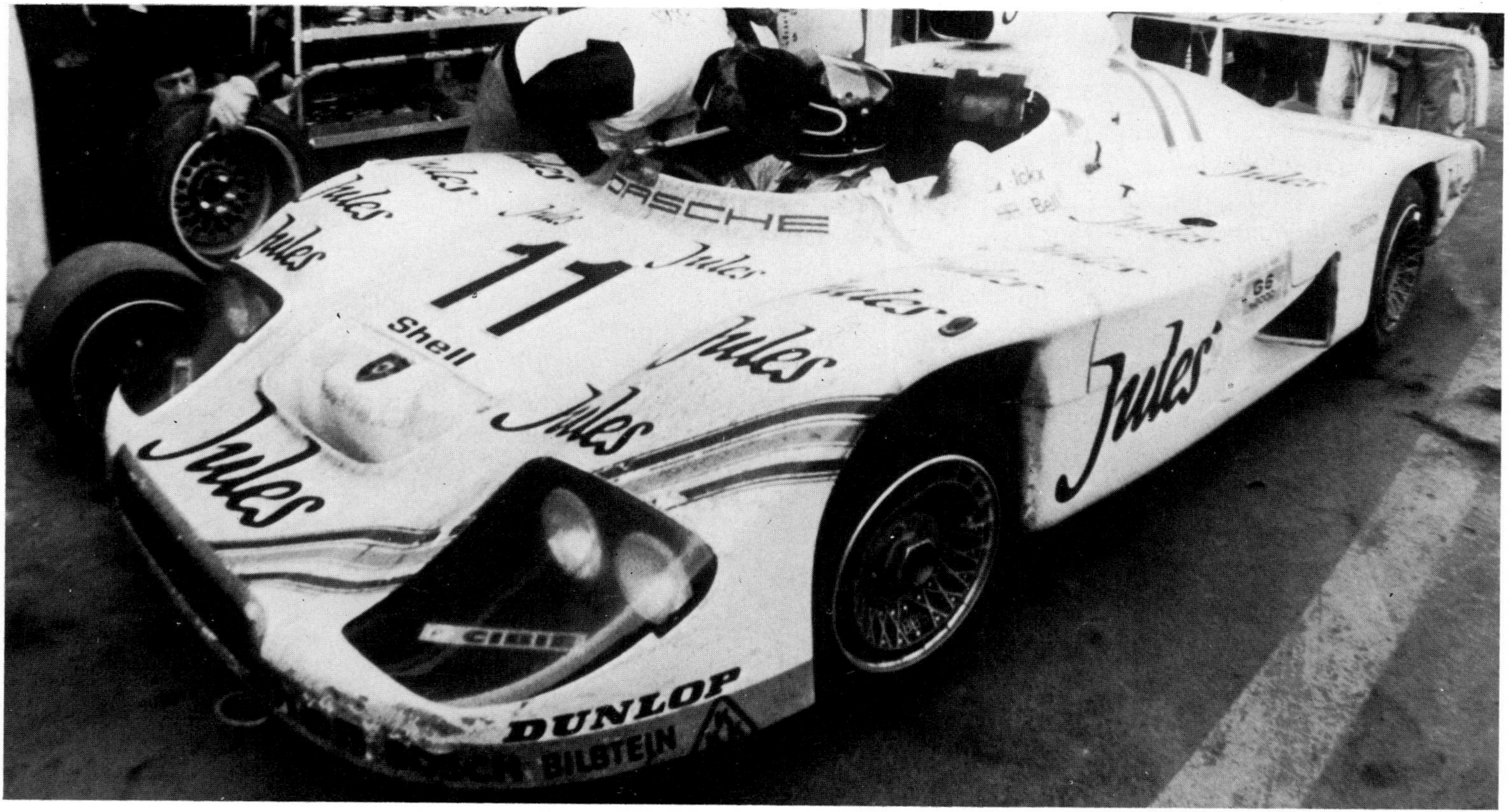

1976–82 period could aptly be described as "silhouette" racers; bearing an outward resemblance to production road sports cars but built to a much more advanced specification. The 935 was quite simply *the* Group 5 car in the late 1970s and among few competitors were various BMWs—from the CSL to the M.1—and the Lancia Monte Carlos. The 935 shared the floorpan and basic body structure with the 930/934 but most of the removeable skin panels were in an incredible lightweight polyurethane foam sandwich construction, with an easily detachable front end which combined wings and front air dam in one unit; at first the outline of the front wings and headlamps resembled the 911 but soon the characteristic sloping "flatnose" appeared. Front and rear wheels were 16 by 11in, and 19 by 15in respectively, and obviously required substantial wheelarch extensions to preserve some kind of modesty. At the rear was a gargantuan spoiler which gradually became more and more integrated with the main bodyshape, as development of the 935 continued and tailfins grew up to meet the spoiler.

Right and right below: 935s came in any number of variations, both privately entered and works cars. The Martini team car (below) was seen at Silverstone in 1978.

The 935/78 for 1978 had the bodywork modified still further, with a much longer tail which in fact was a bolt-on section, hiding the normal engine lid underneath to satisfy regulations. A new range of engines was developed—these still retained the standard crankcase and air-cooled cylinders, again as per regulation requirements, but had new water-cooled cylinder heads with twin overhead camshafts per head and four valves per cylinder. A range of engine sizes from 1.4 to 3.2 liters was foreseen; a 1.4 liter 935 "Baby" had already contested the Group 5 two-liter category in 1977, and it has been suggested that Porsche's engineers were seriously considering a turbocharged version of a 1.5-liter type 935 engine as a possible contender in Formula 1, where the capacity limit is three liters and the equalization factor for forced induction engines is 2 rather than 1.4. The new engine range included the 2649cc (161.6cu in) version foreseen for Indianapolis; although Porsche's attack at this most famous American car race in 1980 was thwarted by a change in regulations, this engine was put to good use later on.

In the same way that the 934 proved invincible in Group 4 GT racing, the 935 dominated Group 5 racing. In its first season, there were wins at Mugello, Vallelunga, Watkins Glen and Dijon—sufficient to regain the World Championship for Makes for Porsche. The year 1977 was a repeat performance; the 935s won seven out of nine races (the remaining two fell to a 934 and a Carrera RSR) and was World Champion again. In 1978 the only difference was that 935s won *all* the qualifying races for the Championship. 1979 saw the Championship for Makes contested by both Group 5 and Group 6 cars; this did not make much difference to Porsche, they took the Championship for the 4th year running and the 935 had its finest hour when Ludwig and the Whittington brothers came first in a Kremer-entered 935 at Le Mans, after the retirement of the works Porsche 936s. In this particular race the 935 won its category every year from 1976 to 1982.

Returning now to 1976, let us consider the 3rd ace up Porsche's sleeve, the 936. The separate Sports Car Championship for Group 6 cars—an anomaly that lasted for two seasons—would be contested by this car. As described, the engine was a small-capacity derivative of the 934/935 flat-six but the remainder of the car was more influenced by the 917 from which much of the running gear was borrowed. Everything was fitted to a new aluminum tubular chassis and cloaked in a plastic two-seater spyder body, its shape reminiscent of the 908 spyder. Apart from the first version of the 936 seen in early 1976, notable features of the car were a high full-width aerofoil and the engine air intake towering over the cockpit. Development time was very short and the car quickly proved reliable; less than eight months passed from the project being

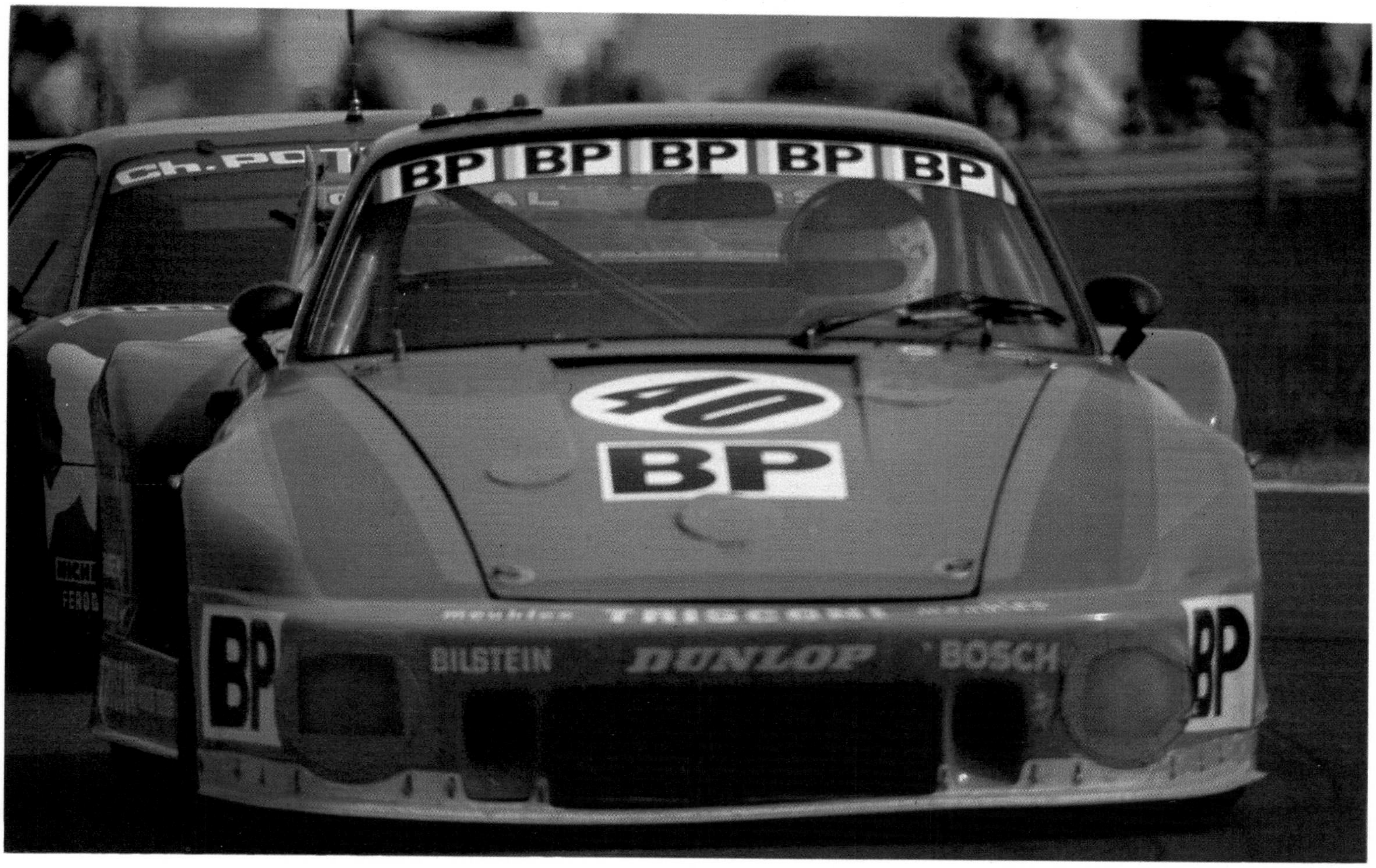
BP BP BP BP BP
40
BP
BP
BILSTEIN
DUNLOP
BOSCH
BP

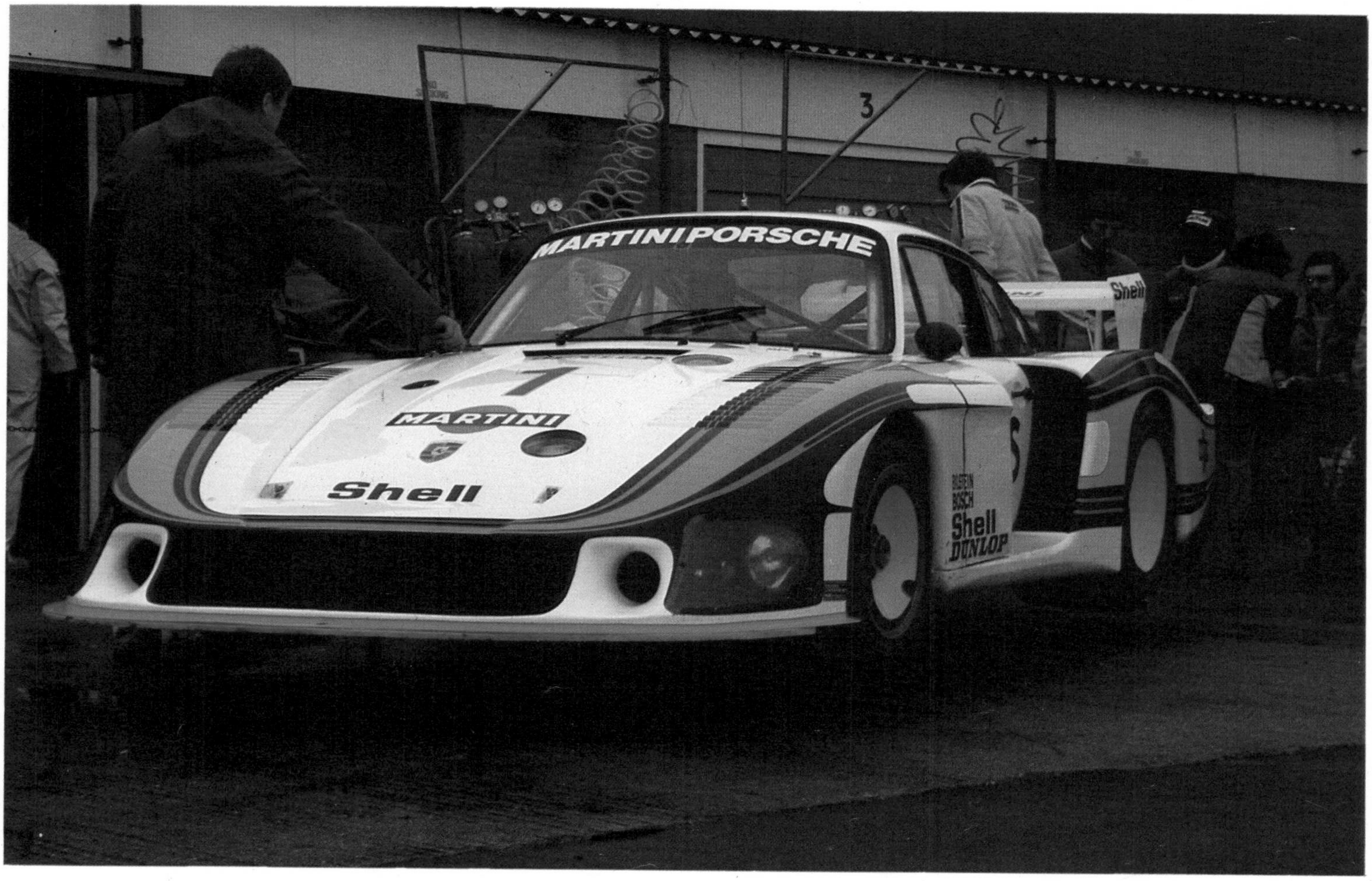
MARTINI PORSCHE
7
MARTINI
Shell
Shell
Shell
DUNLOP

given the go-ahead until the first race at the Nürburgring in April 1976.

This was won by privateer Jöst in his old faithful 908 but after that all the remaining races that season counting toward the Sports Car Championship became a triumphant procession for the Porsche 936. There were six races; in five of these, only one 936 was entered, winning each time. The exception was Le Mans where Porsche entered both of their 936s—while the car driven by Jöst/Barth retired with gearbox failure (the model's Achilles heel), Ickx and van Lennep scored Porsche's 3rd Le Mans win. The other 936 works drivers in 1976 were Mass and Stommelen. The year 1977 was by contrast an easy season for the 936s; Porsche decided to concentrate on the Championship for Makes, leaving Alfa-Romeo to walk-over the Sports Car Championship. The 936s became Le Mans specials, and Le Mans was not a championship race that year. Both cars were entered, driven by Ickx/Pescarolo and Haywood/Barth. It seemed that this would be a luckless outing when Pescarolo blew the engine of one 936 early in the race, with the other car well down the field after fuel pump trouble; but Ickx joined the other team of drivers—now a possibility under Le Mans regulations—and steadily pulled the car back up the scoreboard, helped by the retirement of the entire Alpine-Renault team. Then with the car in the lead and less than a hour to go a piston broke, but Barth was able to nurse a very sick 936 round for the last two laps for one of the most dramatic Le Mans victories in modern times.

In some ways 1978 was a peculiar year; there was no championship for the Group 6 cars as such, and Le Mans had still not regained championship status but to Porsche this was the most important race and the only one that the 936s contested—in response to a direct challenge from Alpine-Renault. An extra 936 was built and the cars were now fitted with the four-valve engine which had appeared in the 935 for this season. But this was not to be Porsche's year; in the race, the 936s were dogged by mechanical problems, chiefly with transmissions, and although Porsche's mechanics became experts in quick gearbox rebuilds during pit stops, the team was still beaten by the Alpine-Renault and had to be content with 2nd and 3rd places. Nor was 1979 a good year for the 936; again, Le Mans was the only race entered, the two 936s now changing from the traditional Martini-Porsche colors to those of the Essex Motorsport Team. Ickx was disqualified for accepting outside assistance, and the other car retired, leaving the 935s to defend Porsche's honors—which as we know they did most effectively.

Porsche took a back seat in racing in 1980 and 1981 and let Lancia run away with the Championship for Makes in both years. The year 1980 saw a works

Right: The pre-race line-up at Le Mans 1976.

Right, below: The winner of the 1977 Le Mans: the 936 of Ickx/Haywood/Barth.

Left: 1979 was a luckless year for the 936s. Two cars were entered by Porsche and Essex Motorsport but Ickx was disqualified and the other car retired.

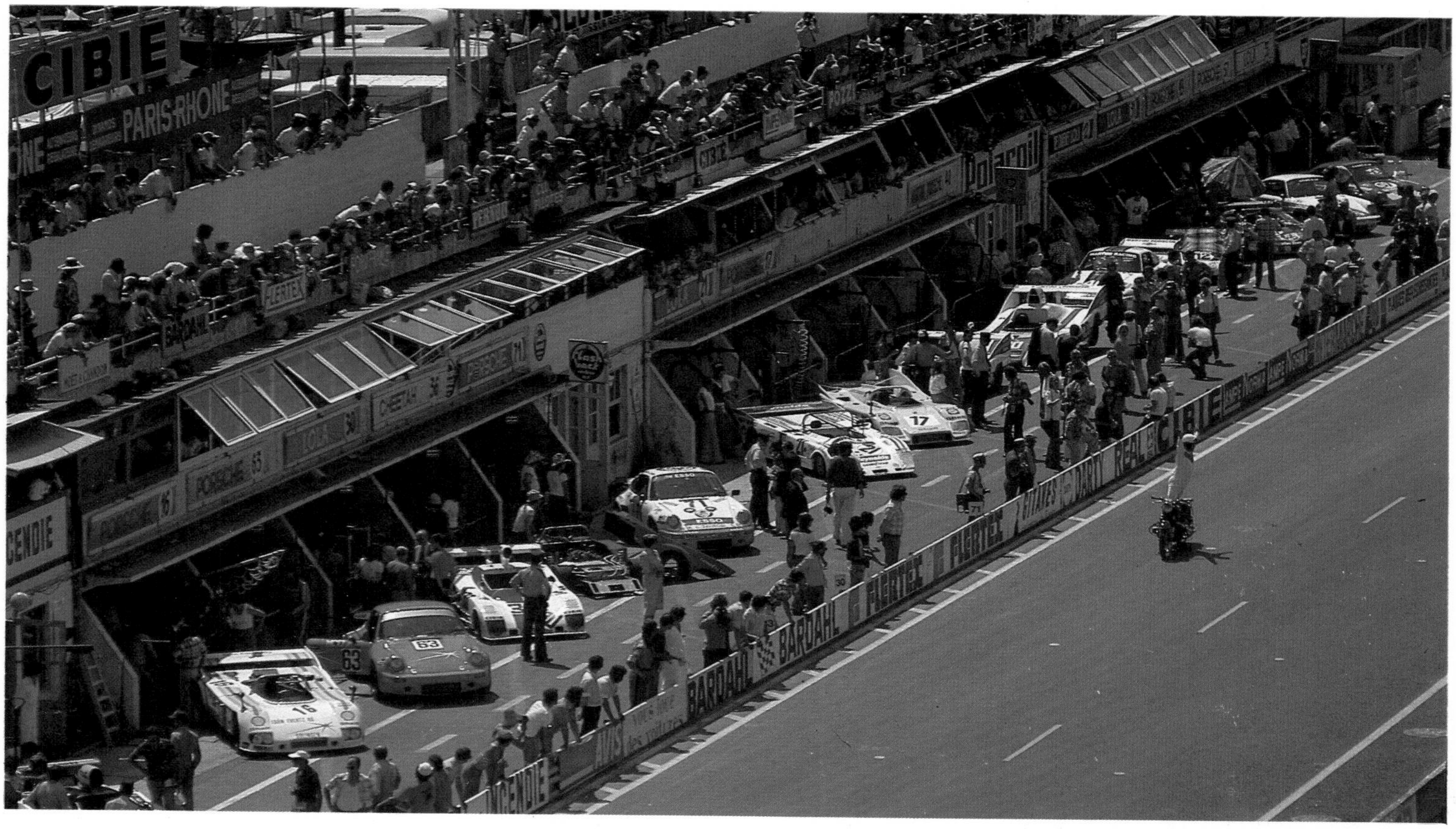
CIBIE
PARIS-RHONE
BARDAHL
FIERTEX
CHEETAH
PORSCHE
DARTY
63
17

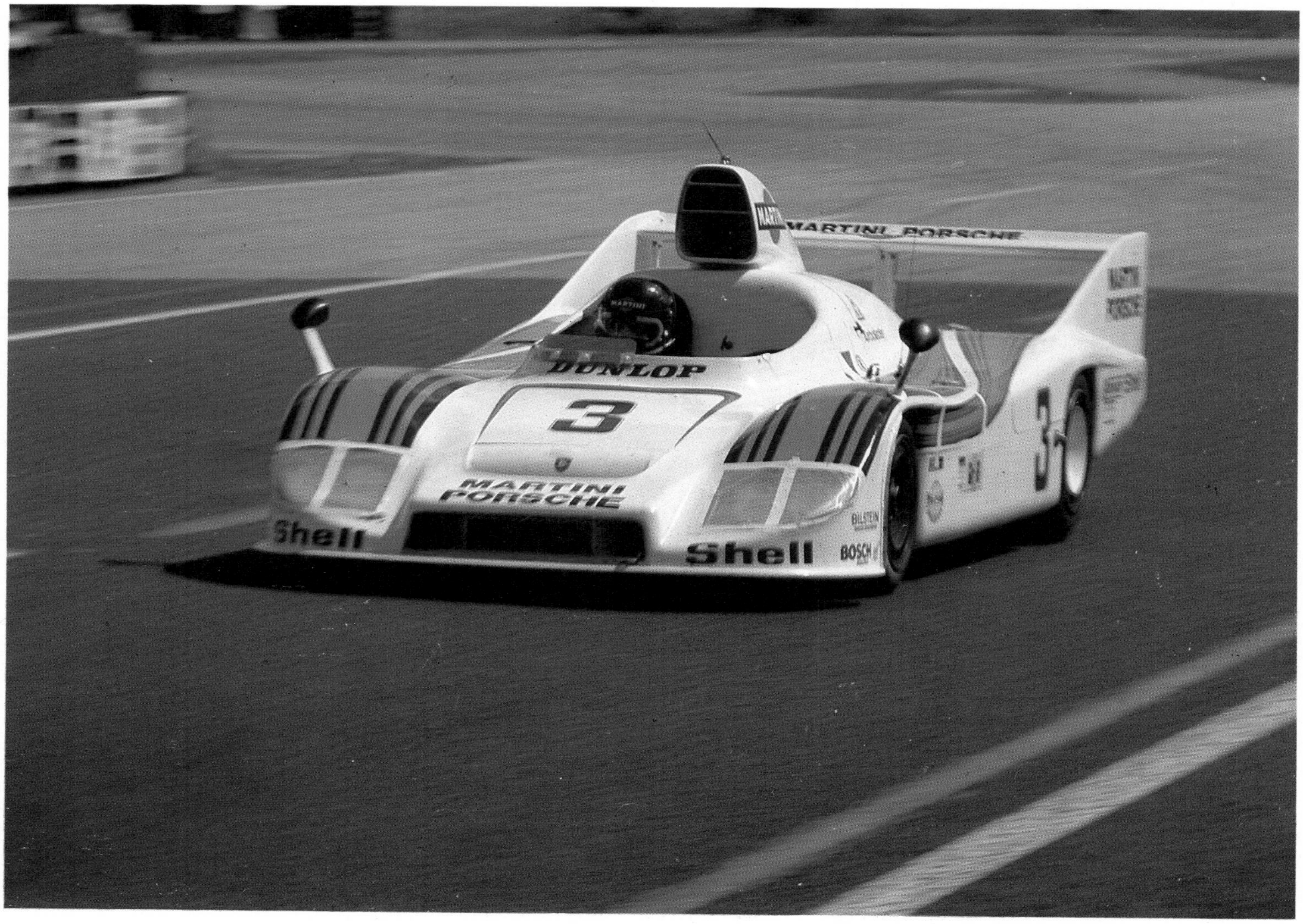
MARTINI PORSCHE
MARTINI PORSCHE
DUNLOP
3
MARTINI PORSCHE
Shell
Shell
BOSCH
BILSTEIN

Left: The aging but faithful 908/03 with Turbo engine in the 1000-kilometer race at the Nürburgring 1975.

Left: Stillborn contender: the Porsche intended for the 1980 Indianapolis 500-mile race.

Left: New departure: the turbocharged 1.5-liter engine for the TAG-McLaren Formula 1 car in 1983.

Above: The Porsche procession at Le Mans 1982: Numbers 1, 2 and 3 finished 1st, 2nd, and 3rd.

Below: What the 956 is all about: a ghost view from the German magazine Auto Zeitung.

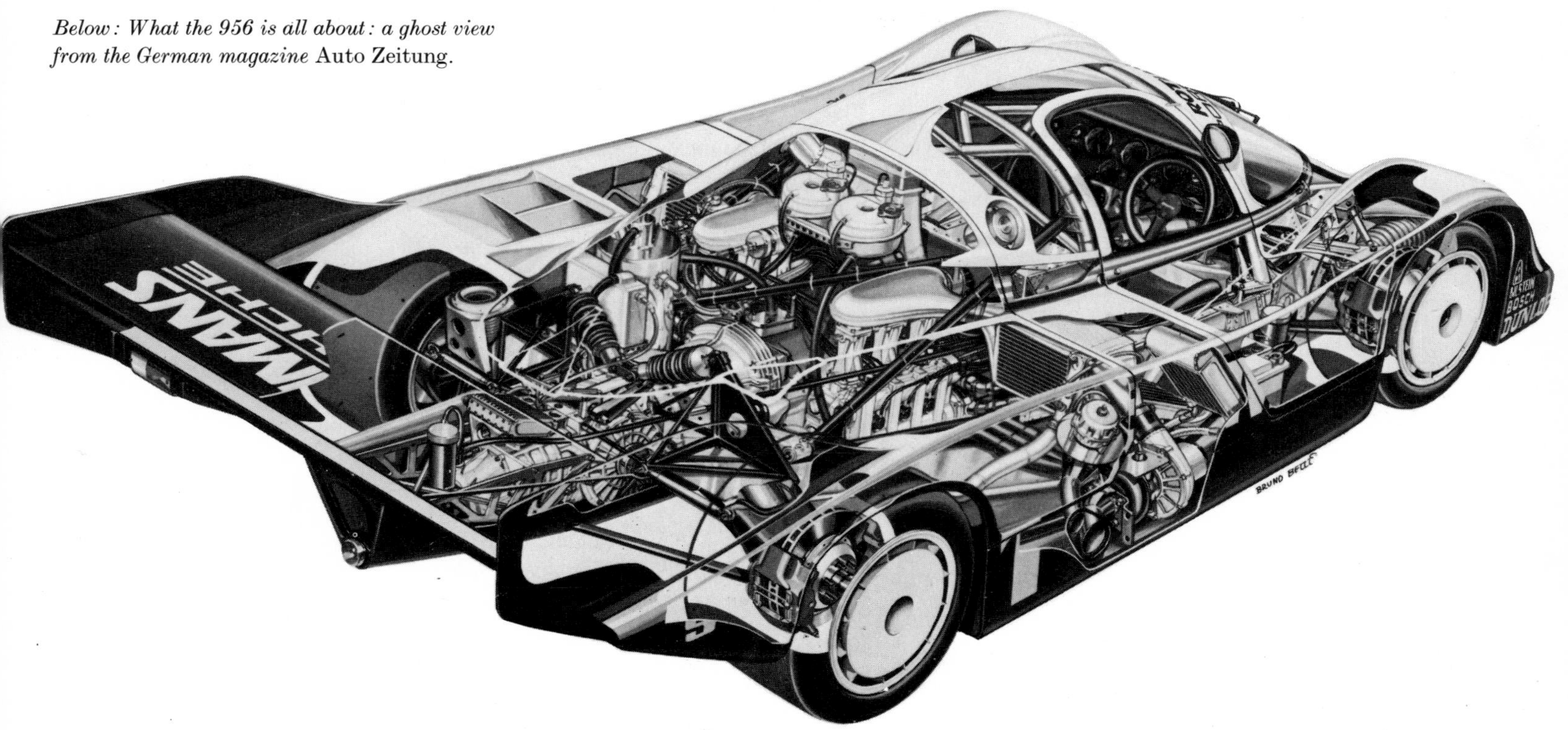

Above: The 956 made its sensational debut at Le Mans in 1982. Number 3 was the Haywood/Holbert/Barth car which finished 3rd.

Right, all pictures: Studies of the winner, the Ickx/Bell 956 in the pits and during the race.

ROTHMANS
PORSCHE
Shell
3
ROTHMANS
PORSCHE
BOSCH
BILSTEIN
TELETRON
UNLOP

PORSCHE

ROTHMANS
PORSCHE
Shell
ROTHMANS
1

team of 924s appear in the GT prototype category at Le Mans, while Ickx and Jöst shared a Martini-entered Porsche 908/936 cross-breed which was specially built for this race and which came 2nd after a French Rondeau. In 1981 the 936s made their final appearance after a year's absence; again Le Mans was the target, like Jaguar in the 1950s Porsche were quite happy to disregard the Championship as a whole in favor of the single race which to them was most important and prestigious. The 936/81 featured the 2.6-liter Indianapolis type engine and also four-speed gearboxes which were rather more robust than the five-speed boxes which had given so much trouble in 1978 and 1979. One car was driven by Mass/Schuppan/Haywood, the other by Jacky Ickx, Derek Bell—the winning team from 1975—and Jürgen Barth. While Haywood put in the fastest race lap, it was the "old firm" of Ickx/Bell/Barth who won the

Top: The Ickx/Bell 956 speeds past the grandstand, Le Mans 1982.

Below: Porsche's Number 2 was the Mass/Schuppan 956.

race, with the other car finishing 13th. For the 936 it was the 3rd and final Le Mans win—Jacky Ickx had driven on all three occasions, and for him it was a personal triumph as he became the first driver to win Le Mans five times.

With 1982 a new set of regulations loomed up for the World Championship. The CSI decided to drop the old groups 1 to 6 and instead introduced a simplified system based on Groups A, B and C. The Championship for Makes would be contested by Group C cars which could be of unlimited capacity but with rules acting as a curb on fuel consumption, there would still effectively be a limit to engine size. The year 1982 was a transitional year in which some Group 6 cars were still being raced, including a Porsche 936 modified to meet the Group C regulations, but Porsche—now with sponsorship from the Rothman tobacco company—had a new weapon ready to do battle with the new Fords,

Rondeaus, WM-Peugeots and Nimrods in Group C, together with the Lancias which ran in the still-permitted under two-liter category in Group 6. The new Porsche was the 956 which very soon proved a worthy heir to the 908, 917 and 936 models of the past.

As the 904 model had been 20 years before, the 956 was a break with Porsche tradition in that it abandoned the tubular chassis and instead used Porsche's first aluminum monocoque construction. This was covered by a light fiberglass coupé body (the 1983 works cars had still-lighter kevlar bodywork), obviously derived from the 936 Spyder body but suitably modified to meet Group C regulations. The engine was the same as in the later 936s—the 2649cc (161.6cu in) flat-six with watercooled cylinder heads containing two overhead camshafts each, and with four valves per cylinder. With two KKK turbochargers and Bosch fuel injection, maximum power was around 615bhp and the top speed as measured at Le Mans in 1982 was just over 220mph (354km/h). To make full use of the limited ground effect permitted in Group C, it was a fairly large car with a wheelbase of 2.65 meters (8.6ft), and overall length and width almost at the maximum dimensions of 4.8 by 2 meters (15.6 by 6.5ft); but weighing only around 830kg (1826lb), some 30kg (66lb) over the minimum permitted weight.

The first race for the 956 was at Silverstone in May 1982 where Jacky Ickx and Derek Bell finished in a worthy 2nd place; a short circuit such as Silverstone did not suit the 956 which could not be extended properly and was deliberately held back, cruising to conserve fuel. It was still the highest placed Group C car as the winner was a Group 6 Lancia. The next race for the 956s was Le Mans, where three cars came to the start with race numbers 1, 2 and 3—driven by Ickx/Bell, Jochen Mass/Vern Schuppan and Haywood/Holbert/Barth—and after a magnificent race, memorable for the number of retirements of Group C cars other than Porsches, these three cars finished 1-2-3 in exactly the same order. Ickx/Bell in the winning car put up an average speed of almost 127mph (204km/h) for a total distance well over 3000 miles (4830km)—still short of the 1971 records but one of the fastest races in recent years. There were possibly one or two of the other Group C cars which were marginally faster in a straight line than the 956, but none possessed the remarkable reliability of the Porsche. This was the 7th Le Mans win for the marque, the

Above and below left: The 956s returned to Le Mans in 1983 with devastating results. The Rothmans works cars came 1st and 2nd; the winners were Haywood/Holbert/Schuppan (above) with Ickx/Bell running a very close 2nd (below).

6th for Ickx and the 3rd for Derek Bell. Only one other race counted toward the Championship for Makes, at Spa in September, and here Ickx was victorious in the 956 again, this time with co-driver Jochen Mass. This was sufficient to clinch the Championship for the 956, and after further wins in a Porsche 935 in races which only counted toward the drivers' championship, Jacky Ickx was the champion driver as well.

Porsche had made its mark in the first Group C season, and as the 1983 racing season opened one commentator was moved to remark that the worst thing about the endurance races was that they tended to become processions of Porsches—a complaint which might equally well have been made at the beginning of the 1970s. At least there would be some competition for the Porsche works team, in the shape of those 15 956s which were sold to private entrants and drivers—at a cost of DM630,000 each. The other important works team to contest Group C was Lancia with a new car, but in a surprise announcement Ford withdrew from Group C racing after one unsuccessful season. At the first race in 1983, at Monza in April, the winner was in fact a private 956, entered by Jöst racing, with Ickx and Mass in the best-placed works car 2nd; the next five places were also taken by 956s. Silverstone followed in May, and here Derek Bell and new works driver Stefan Bellof redressed the balance for the works team, but with Mass running out of road there were only five 956s heading the result list. At the end of May the 1000km (621 miles) race was held for the last time on the old North Circuit of the Nürburgring, and this time it was the turn of Ickx and Mass to head the procession of four 956s in the first four places.

18 June 1983 saw no less than 11 Porsche 956s start for the 24-hour race at Le Mans—three works cars, with Ickx and Bell in pole position after a 155mph (250km/h) practice lap by Ickx, together with eight privately entered cars. In addition there was a Porsche 936, six Porsche 930s, a single 928 S and two Porsche engined Kremers among the 51 starting cars. Some 24 hours later, nine 956s were still in the running—Mass/Bellof's works car and one privateer had retired—and not unsurprisingly, eight 956s filled the first eight places with the final car coming 10th. The winners were Schuppan, Haywood and Holbert from the works team, at an average of almost 131mph (over 210km/h); the finish was not without drama as their engine overheated and threatened to

seize up, and the Ickx/Bell works car ran a very close second. Porsche also won the Group B category with a 930 placing 13th among 26 finishers. With this rather incredible result it was clear even only halfway through the season that Porsche had won the World Endurance Championship again, so overwhelming was the number of points accumulated after four of the seven races.

Apart from the continuing success story of Porsche in sports car endurance racing, the company has now also got a toe-hold back in Formula 1 Grand

Below: The 1983 Le Mans winner.

Prix racing. Porsche announced in March 1983 that they were developing a turbocharged 1499cc (91.4cu in) watercooled V-6 engine on behalf of TAG, for use in the Marlboro-McLaren. At the time of writing this 600bhp engine was undergoing tests in a McLaren Formula 1 car at Porsche's Weissach test track, and it remains to be seen when it will appear in a Grand Prix race and with what results. But the very idea of a Porsche-engined Formula 1 car will undoubtedly create still more interest for Porsche's future racing plans. . . .

12: A NEW BEGINNING

Previous page: 1977 and a new shape noses into Porsche's future: the 928.

The start of the 1970s marked a watershed in Porsche history. We have seen how the Porsche and Piëch families stepped back from the day-to-day running of the company; Ferry's place as chairman was taken by Dr Ernst Fuhrmann while Helmuth Bott took charge of all engineering development and Helmut Flegl became director of research. Butzi Porsche was replaced in the styling studio by the ebullient ex-GM stylist, Latvian-born American citizen Anatole Lapine. The main projects then occupying the Porsche team were the EA.266 for Volkswagen, and a range of sports cars based on it. When EA.266 was cancelled, it had a disastrous effect on Porsche's long-term plans. The intention had been to phase out the 911 by the middle of the decade and return to something closer to the original 356 with the introduction of the EA.266-based cars. What was to happen instead?

For the time being, the designers were being kept busy on a continuation program for the 911, and there was the 911/930 Turbo to be considered. Then in a move which harked back to the end of the 1950s when Porsche decided to introduce a new car up-market from the 356, the company investigated the idea of introducing another completely new concept for Porsche, a large front-engined sports car with a water-cooled V-8 engine. The initial proposal for this car was approved by Ernst Fuhrmann in the autumn of 1971, in fact a few months before Leiding commissioned Porsche to design the EA.425 which would eventually become the Porsche 924. The other new project, from the start Porsche's own, was given project number 928 and engineer Wolfgang Eyb was appointed project leader. Although project 928 was conceived fractionally earlier than 425/924, the two cars were under development at the same time, so it was only natural that they should share several design features; but the fact that the 924 was designed to use stock VW-Audi components permitted that car to go into production first, at the end of 1975; while the debut of the 928 did not take place for another 18 months, at the 1977 Geneva Motor Show.

We have already considered the engineering of the Porsche 924. The package foreseen for the 928 was broadly similar, with a front-mounted water-cooled engine and the gearbox at the rear. In terms of size and price the 928 would be a rival to the Mercedes-Benz coupés, and if Porsche looked at the Mercedes V-8 engine before designing their own who could blame them? There were certainly some similarities in the two engines, both used a single overhead camshaft per cylinder bank but the more modern Porsche engine employs a toothed belt driving both camshafts where the Mercedes engine has chain-driven camshafts. Both had a 4.5 liter capacity but Porsche chose slightly more oversquare dimensions than their colleagues and rivals on the other side of Stuttgart—the Porsche 928 engine had dimensions of 95×78.9mm (3.7×3.1in) for a capacity of 4474cc (272.9cu in). The valve operation by hydraulic tappets was an unusual feature for a European engine, but Bosch electronic fuel injection was a natural choice for Porsche. The new engine in production form developed 240bhp.

Unlike the 924, chassis design of the 928 was not hampered by the need to use VW components. The transaxle incorporated either a five-speed manual box, or a completely automatic transmission supplied by Daimler-Benz (an automatic option was also available on the 924, and these cars became the first fully automatic Porsches). The 928 suspension employed coil springs all round, at the front with upper and lower wishbones, while rear suspension was looked after by the sophisticated Weissach axle, with a lower wishbone and an upper link, designed to countereffect any rear wheel steering tendencies in cornering and control rear wheel toe-in under braking. Steering was by rack and pinion as on the 911 and the 924, and there were ventilated disk brakes on all wheels.

Right: The ghosted view of the 928 highlights both styling and mechanical features . . .

Right, below: . . . while this "chassis" clearly shows the distribution of the main mechanical elements.

Below: Proud parents (from left to right): Dr Ernst Fuhrmann, Helmut Bott, Wolfgang Eyb and Wolfgang Möbius with the 1977 Car of the Year.

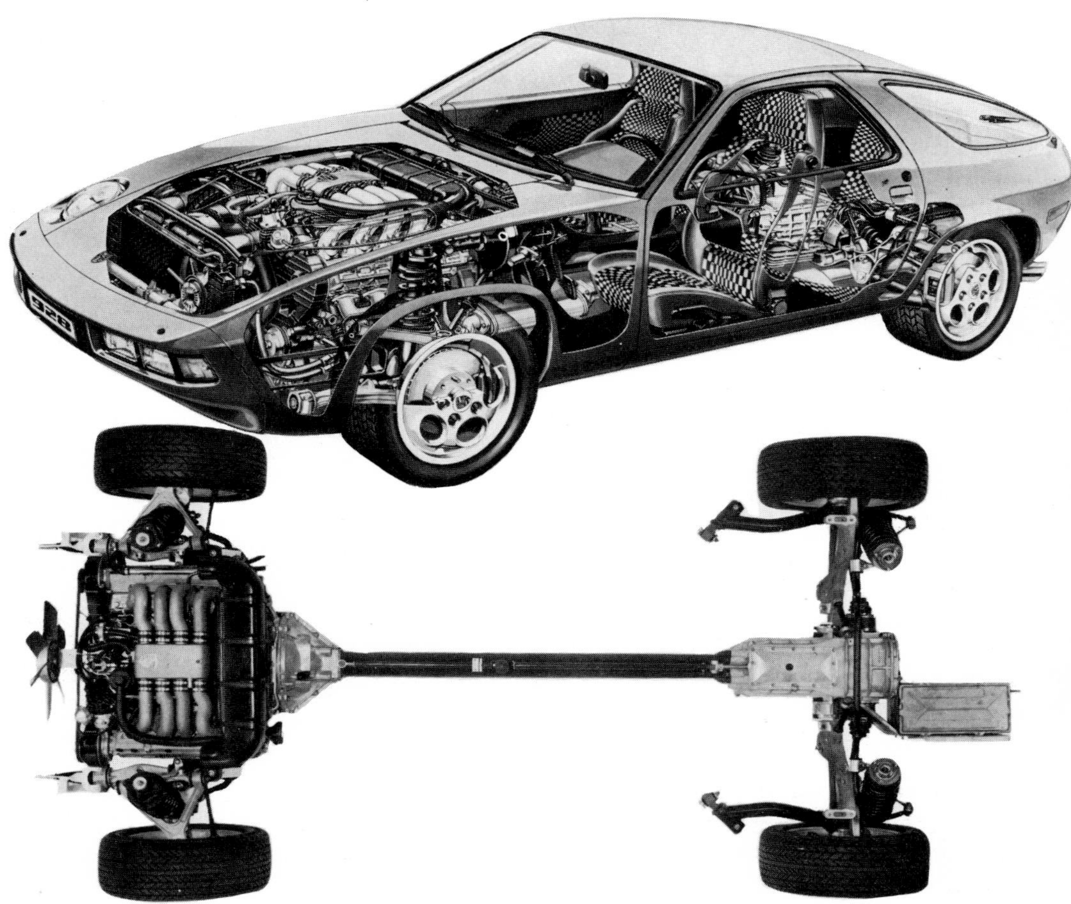

An important difference between the 924 and the 928 packaging was that whereas the 924 had its Audi-based gearbox behind the rear axle line, the 928 gearbox was in front of the axle and final drive. This meant that despite a slightly longer wheelbase (2500mm [97.5in] as against 2400mm [93.6in] on the 924) the 928 was only a two-plus-two rather than a full four-seater, as the gearbox hump intruded in the rear seat area. But this was what Porsche wanted; there were no plans to make the 928 anything other than a sports car.

The 924 and 928 bodies were developed in parallel by Lapine's styling team. The 924 has been credited to Dutch stylist Harm Lagaay, while Wolfgang Möbius was responsible for the 928. Both had unitary construction bodies, and

The dramatic shape of the 924 Carrera was developed from the 914 but was a major improvement in the eyes of most people.

both were fastback two door two-plus-two coupés; both also had affinities with previous Porsche styling. But if the 924 was the more conventional of the two cars, it must be remembered that it was designed to fit in with the VW-Audi range; the 928 was a much more revolutionary design statement, yet clearly in the Porsche tradition. In principle, the difference between the two cars may be summed up by saying that where the 924 is "lines," the 928 is "form." Where the 924 had hidden pop-up headlamps and integrated bumpers in body color, the 928 headlamps were designed to fold back into the car so their lenses were flush with the hood in the retracted position, and instead of conventional bumpers, the 928 had complete front and rear end sections in soft

impact-resistant plastic painted the color of the bodywork, so to the casual observer a 928 does not have bumpers. Neither car had a radiator grille—which would have been unwanted on the nose of a Porsche—but both had discreet air intakes built into the front spoiler below the front number plate. The most dramatic feature of the 924 was its large wrap-around window which opened to give access to the luggage space; so did the rear window of the 928 but this was a more simply shaped piece of glass. The overall effect was still striking, with a wide B/C pillar just aft of the door and a rear quarterlight almost butting up to the rear window itself.

For much of its body hardware and equipment, the 924 relied on Volkswagen bits and pieces, but the 928 was free from these constraints. For instance, the 924 door handles were the standard VW-Audi item, but the 928 had door handles mounted flush with the bodywork. The 924 interior betrayed the Volkswagen connection too, with minor controls, some instruments and hardware being of obvious VW origins; even the check pattern upholstery was rather like that seen on the VW Scirocco. The 928 interior was more obviously a Porsche design, if completely different from the 911 interior. All instruments except the clock were mounted in a large binnacle in front of the driver who could adjust the height of the binnacle together with the steering column. The fascia panel itself was cleverly integrated with the central console and the door trim, and set a new standard for interior design. The unusual but eye-catching op-art upholstery pattern evoked the quip that it was copied from Lapine's old sports jacket. . . . It was later replaced by a discreet pinstripe; obviously the chief stylist had bought himself a business suit.

Above and right: Details of the Carrera: the dashboard and interior are similar to the 924; but under the hood the scene is very different, dominated by the intercoder for the turbocharger. The main headlamps pop out but are supplemented by driving camps in the front spoiler. The rear spoiler is attached directly to the opening rear window.

At the 1975 launch of the 924, there were some disparaging comments on the Volkswagen ancestry of the car. The critics did not consider it a "real" Porsche although it was conceded to be a much superior successor to the little-lamented 914. The absence of a 5th speed in the gearbox was criticized, and not wholly favorable comparisons were made with the hottest Volkswagen, the new 110bhp Scirocco GTI/GLI. The Scirocco accelerated quicker, and its 115mph (185km/h) top speed was not far short of the 924's 125mph (201km/h); apart from that, the Scirocco had much more useable space in both the rear seat and the trunk, and cost approximately 25 percent less than the Porsche. It could be considered a 924 competitor, and others included the Triumph TR 7 and the Matra Bagheera—both cheaper, if slower, than the 924, the TR 7 with very controversial styling suggesting it was a mid-engined car which it was not; the Matra was, and had the problems by now associated with this layout. Another mid-engined competitor was the Lancia Beta Monte Carlo. Some two and a half years after the launch of the 924, the Japanese Mazda company paid Porsche the compliment of introducing a near-copy of the 924, the Savanna RX-7, which however differed in the important respect of having Mazda's Wankel-based rotary engine. The RX-7 was cheaper than the 924, and just as quick.

As had been the case with the early 911s, the first 924s suffered from several minor problems, and it took some time for build quality to reach an even standard. One Porsche executive who ran an early 924 during the winter of 1975–6 detected a strange knocking sound from the rear of the car; but despite exhaustive experiments, none of the chassis engineers could pin this down to any rear suspension component. Finally the problem was solved by a long-time employee of the experimental bodyshop; it turned out that water had leaked through the rear window seal and had accumulated in the built-in toolboxes, where it froze overnight in cold weather. As the car was driven away in the morning, a lump of ice would detach itself and start to rattle around in the tool compartment. . . .

The 924 road testers found the engine rather rough and drew their reader's attention to the fact that this was basically the same engine as found in the new Volkswagen LT van. Certainly the noise and vibration levels were initially rather high, and some cars suffered from drive shaft vibration. At least all critics were generous in their praise for the road behavior of the 924, while the styling pleased but was found unexceptional, almost bland, compared to other Porsches. The way most of the road test reports could be summed up was as a plea to Porsche to continue development of the car. The 924 was basically a fine car but needed a little more attention to bring it up to true Porsche standards.

Right, all pictures: The 928 shape rewards close and detailed study. The rear end is particularly harmoniously resolved, the integral bumpers and rear lamp clusters blending neatly with the shape of the bodywork. The original alloy wheels were of a unique design, much copied by other stylists, but since replaced by Porsche on the 928 S model. This particular car is in the British Nigel Dawes collection and is also featured on the following page.

Porsche was not slow to respond to such criticisms. First and foremost, a five-speed gearbox was made optional for the 1978 model year and standardized two years later, with the three-speed automatic remaining on the option list. The equipment was also gradually improved, taking the 924 up-market away from the plain-Jane VW image, and refinement has been much improved over the years of production. The 924 still has the original VW-Audi engine, of almost square dimensions (86.5×84.4mm [3.4×3.3in], 1984cc [121cu in]) developing 125bhp; but it is worth noting that this engine is now made exclusively for the 924, as the Audi 100 has acquired a five-cylinder engine instead and the Volkswagen LT is now fitted with VW's straight-six engine. At one time the engine design and tooling were going to be sold to American Motors which used this engine in their Gremlin and Spirit compact cars; AMC actually took over the engine production in Germany and sold engines back to VW-Audi and Porsche. But this arrangement has ended and with Renault having taken a stake in AMC, they have stopped using the Audi engine. It is likely that the 924 will receive a new engine in the future, probably a 130bhp two-liter version of Porsche's own four, first seen in the 944 in 1981. At the time of writing, the basic 924 has already been discontinued in the US market in favor of the 944.

However, there was also an answer to those who expected more performance from the 924. The 924 Turbo was launched at the end of 1978, and featured a turbocharger which boosted engine output to 170bhp, later increased to 177bhp. The Turbo had such identification features as extra air intake slots above the fender, and a NASA duct in the hood admitting air to the turbocharger; it was fitted with special multi-spoke cast alloy wheels and was normally finished in two-tone paintwork. The five-speed gearbox was fitted from the start, and there was no automatic option. Top speed was improved to almost 145mph (233km/h), far more acceptable to the Porsche clientele; in fact the 924 Turbo was slightly faster than either the 911 SC or the 928, and to cope with the increased performance, Porsche installed disk brakes on the rear wheels instead of the drums still found on the basic 924. Then at the Frankfurt Motor Show of 1979, Porsche exhibited the first 924 Carrera as a foretaste of things to come. This was fitted with much-extended wheel arches and front and rear spoilers, with a 210bhp engine and a 150mph (242km/h) top speed. With the need to build 400 cars for homologation purposes, this became a production model as the Carrera GT in 1980, and three cars were entered at Le Mans that year—the first front-engined water-cooled Porsches to take part in this prestigious race. Highest placing was 6th but they lost the GT prototype category to a French Rondeau which finished 3rd. For 1981, a second-generation 924 Carrera appeared, the GTS model with 245bhp and a top speed nudging 155mph. Furthermore, this could be developed into a full-blown racing or rally car, the Carrera GTR with dry-sump lubrication, mechanical fuel injection and anything up to 375bhp and 180mph (289km/h).

While the 924 Carreras continued to show the Porsche flag on the race

35T

with the 100mph (161km/h) mark coming up in less than 15 seconds. The 928 S was getting close to the 911 Turbo in performance, while it was some 10 percent cheaper and a far more civilized car — what some people would undoubtedly call "softer," but doing what was required of it by appealing to a completely different sector of the market than the 911 Turbo. In 1982 the "cooking" 928 was discontinued, leaving only a slightly revised 928 S model available.

Turbo is the keyword to much of Porsche's future. The 944 Turbo is the flagship Porsche 2.5-liter model. Developing 220 bhp (DIN), it carries forward dramatically the Porsche policy of crowning a road- and race-proven series with an all-powerful turbocharged version. With a maximum speed of 152mph, the 944 Turbo represents the very latest advance in production car turbo techology. However, there may still be those who are not content even with what Porsche offers, but such customers can always go to one of Germany's custom car builders who will do things to Porsche that Porsche officially disapproves of. One such specialist is Nordstadt, the VW dealers of Hannover, who managed to squeeze a complete set of 928 mechanicals under the admittedly lengthened and widened skin of a VW Golf. A wolf in sheep's clothing indeed. The Buchmann Brothers of Frankfurt, trading as "b + b," gave us a 911 Turbo Targa which had also had a 928-type nose job, and then proceeded to take the roof off a 928. Their first 1979 effort was a Targa with a roll-over bar but in 1982 they had progressed to a full cabriolet 928. One wonders whether Porsche will ever do likewise but at least these extravagant exercises generate extra publicity for the marque.

Below: Porsche's own model line-up at Geneva with the 928 S in the foreground.

The 924 Carrera GT.

S-DY 4659

Below: A cutaway artwork showing at a glance the 1987 Porsche 911 Carrera.

Above: The Porsche 911 Speedster, which was launched on 8 September 1987.

Independent suspension with wish-bones. MacPherson struts and torsion bars, 22mm anti-roll bar. Hydraulic, dual circuit braking system with internally ventilated disk brakes all round. Light alloy cast 6J × 15 road wheels with 185/70 VR 15 tires.

2 + 2 seating accommodation with individually folding rear backrests to increase luggage capacity. Ergonomically optimised seating available in fabric, leather or leatherette combinations. Driver's and passenger's seat electrically adjustable.

Right: 1987 Model Year Porsche 911 Carrera Coupé.

All-galvanised steel construction. Aerodynamic body shape results in low drag co-efficient of Cd = 0.39 and a frontal area of 1.77 m^2. Maximum speed is 152 mph. Acceleration from 0–62.5 mph in 6.1 seconds.

Air-cooled light alloy 6-cylinder four stroke "boxer" engine with two horizontally opposed banks of 3 cylinders. Digital fuel injection and ignition system. 3.2 liter capacity. Output 170 kW (231 bhp DIN) at 5.900 rpm, torque 284 Nm at 4.800 rpm.

The optional large rear spoiler enhances the car's performance by improving straight-line running and reducing wind resistance, increasing stability and reducing lift at high speed.

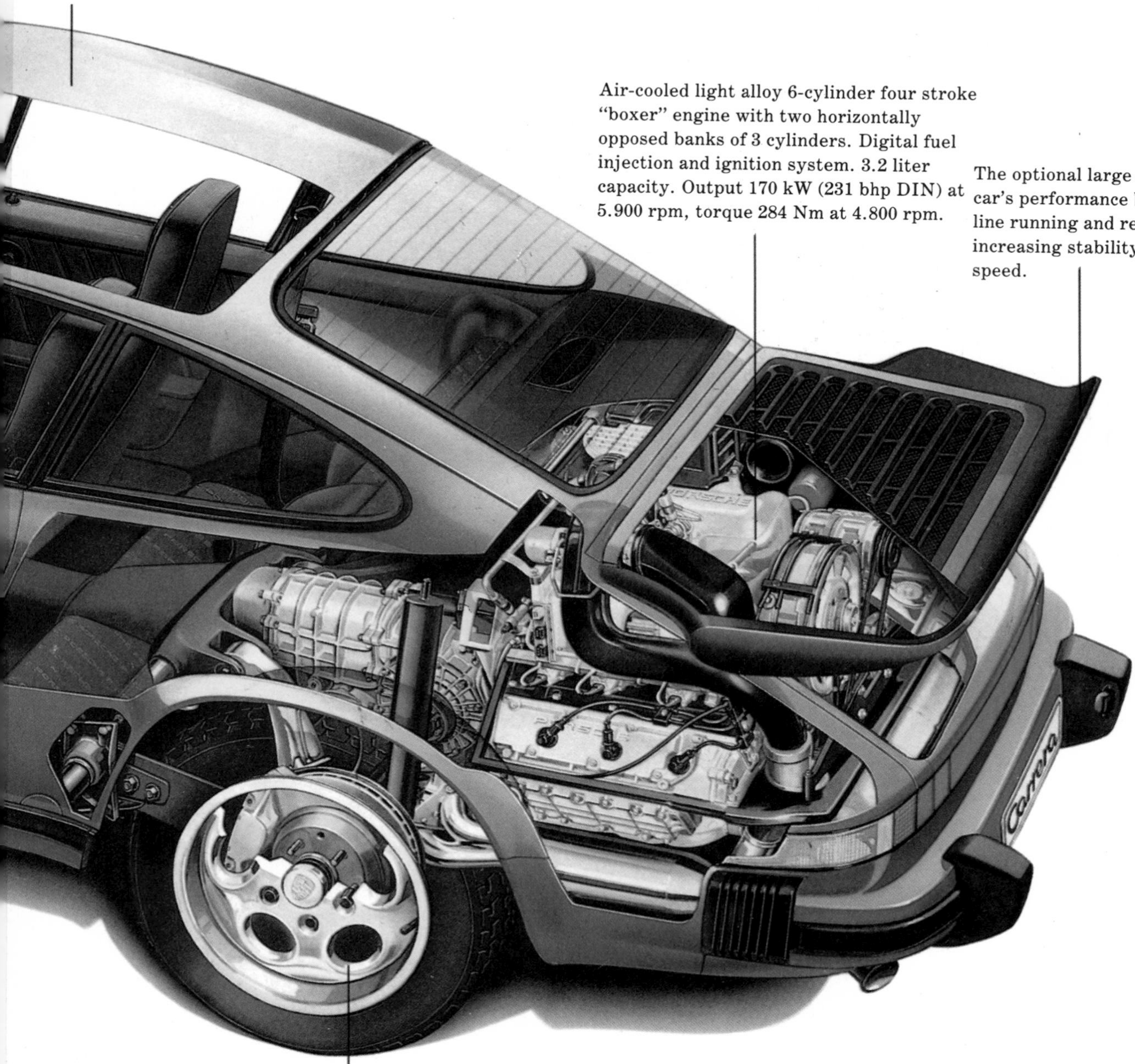

Rear, independent semi-trailing arms with transverse torsion bars per wheel. 21 mm anti-roll bar. Light alloy cast 7 J × 15 road wheels with 215/60 VR 15 tires.

Above: New for 1987, the 250 bhp Porsche 944 Turbo with Sport Equipment and, in the foreground, the then unavailable Porsche 944 Cabriolet.

Below: The cutaway shows features of the 1987 Porsche 928 S series 4.

8–cylinder, light alloy water cooled engine with new 32-valve cylinder head. Digital fuel ignition system. 5.0 liter capacity. 320 bhp (DIN) at 6,000 rpm. Torque 430 Nm at 3,000 rpm.

Totally revised polyurethane front nose section with integral spoiler, recessed driving, fog and indicator lamps. Automatic air inlets adjust in accordance with vehicle speed and engine cooling required. Disk brake ventilation ducts.

Hydraulic dual circuit braking system unit. Anti-lock braking system. Servo-assisted, internally ventilated, 4-piston capiler disk brakes all-round. Front wheel suspension via double, light alloy wishbones, coil springs and internal shock absorbers. Anti-roll bar. Forged alloy 7J × 16 road wheels with 225/50 VR 16, ultra-low profile tires.

All-galvanised steel and aluminum body construction. Revised aerodynamic body shape results in a low drag coefficient. Maximum speed: 167 mph. Acceleration from 0–62.5 mph in 5.9 seconds.

All-new polyurethane spoiler on tailgate and new rear section to optimise air-flow and reduce tail lift at high speeds.

Unique "Weissach" self-correcting rear axle assembly incorporates single light alloy wishbones, anti-roll bar, coil springs and shock absorbers. 8J × 16 wheels with 245/45 VR 16 ultra-low profile tires.

Rear mounted, 4-speed automatic or optional 5-speed manual gearbox. Engine power transmitted via the rigid torque tube of the Transaxle driveline system.

2 + 2 seating accommodation with individual folding rear backrests to increase luggage capacity. Ergonomically optimised seating design incorporates full electric adjustment of front seats for legroom, height, squab and backrest angle, via seat-mounted controls. Seats available in leather combinations or with various cloth inlay options.

Right: 1987 Model Year Porsche 944 S.

Above: The 1988 Porsche 944 Turbo.

Below: A cutaway drawing of the Porsche 2.5-liter model

Right: 1988 Model Year Porsche 924 S.

All-galvanised steel construction. Aerodynamic body shape results in a low drag co-efficient Cd = 0.33. Frontal area = 1.76m^2. Maximum speed 137 mph. Acceleration from 0–62.5 mph in 8.2 seconds. Rear spoiler on tailgate to reduce lift at high speed. Glass tailgate enhances all-round rear visibility.

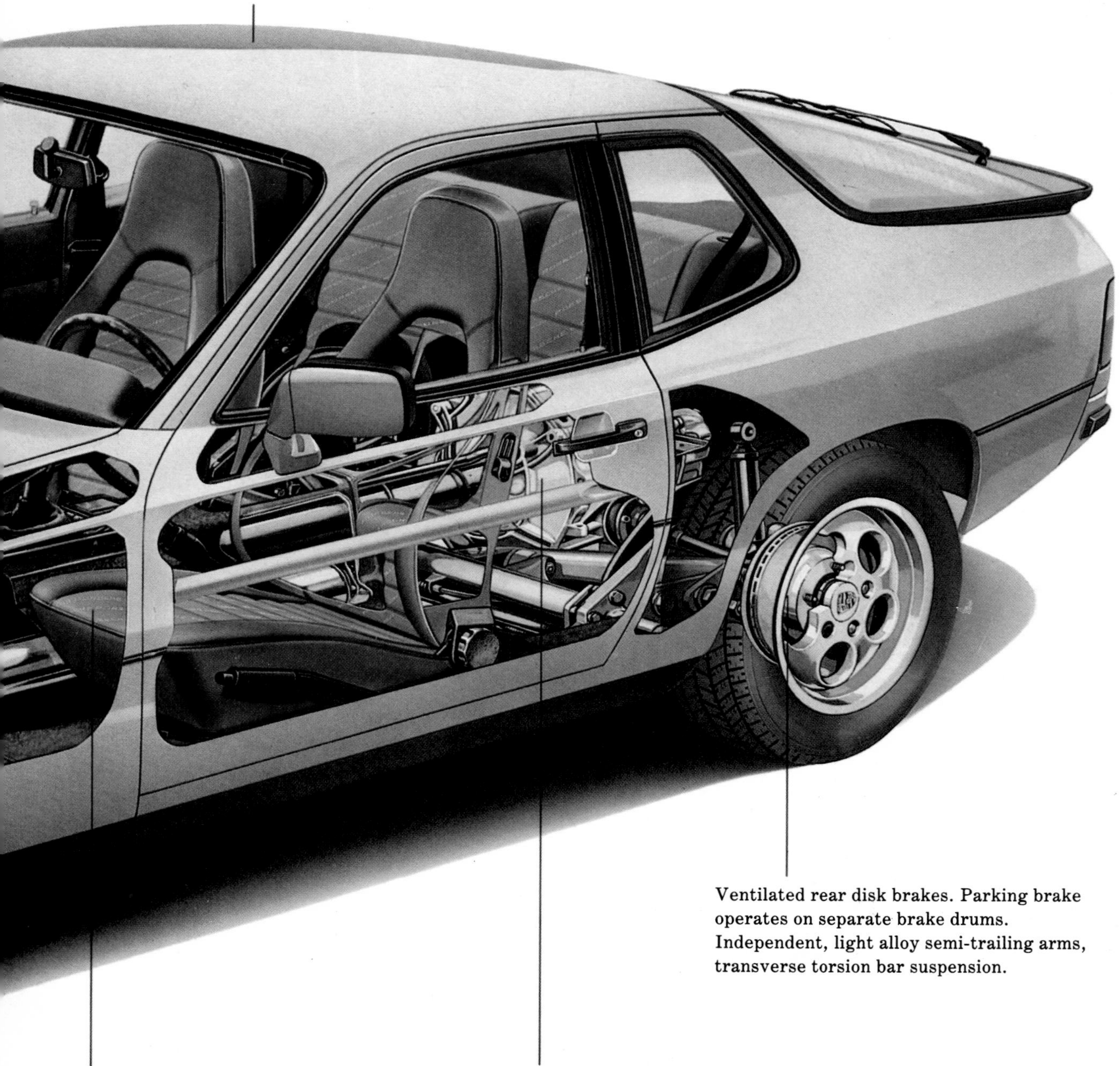

Ventilated rear disk brakes. Parking brake operates on separate brake drums. Independent, light alloy semi-trailing arms, transverse torsion bar suspension.

Rear mounted 5-speed manual or 3-speed automatic gearbox connected to the engine via a Transaxle driveline system. Rear wheels independently sprung, light alloy trailing arms, torsion bar suspension and light alloy torsion tube.

2 + 2 seating accommodation with folding backrest to increase luggage capacity. Ergonomically optimised seating design available in fabric, leather and leatherette combinations.

Ultimate performance within this acclaimed Porsche 911 Series is the prerogative of the unrivalled Porsche 911 Turbo models. The first high performance car ever to be turbocharged, the "Turbo" maintains its position as the world's most coveted supercar. Huge reserves of power, complemented by remarkable limits of roadholding, make it a machine of unparalleled performance. Yet its practicality is vouched for by exceptional reliability, exemplary fuel efficiency and ease of driving.

Fitted with a derivative of the flat six cylinder 911 Carrera engine, this larger 3,299cc turbocharged power unit develops a staggering 300 bhp (DIN) at 5,500 rpm, producing "sling shot" acceleration: 0–62.5 mph in 5.4 seconds and a maximum speed comfortably in excess of 160 mph.

In June 1984, a standard production Porsche 911 Turbo won the title "The Fastest Accelerating Production Car in the World", the first official event of its kind organised by the RAC Motor Sports Association. The final winning time, from a standing start to the one kilometre mark, was 23.985 seconds, with a final speed of 135 mph. To date, this achievement has not been bettered.

As the ultimate in the 911 Series, the Porsche 911 Turbo models have distinctive spoilers to enhance the aerodynamic styling exemplified by the individual 911 Carrera models. The deeper front, rubber-edged, spoiler on the 911 Turbo minimises underbody air turbulence, while the distinctive rear spoiler ensures maximum air cooling to the all-powerful turbo engine, optimises rear stability and increases tire adhesion to accommodate the greater performance.

Left: Today's ultimate: the 911 Turbo.

13: THE SENSIBLE SUPERCAR

Previous page: The long-life car prototype was shown in Frankfurt in 1973. It became the subject of much discussion and has undoubtedly influenced subsequent Porsche designs.

Zuffenhausen is a northern suburb of Stuttgart, on the edge of the city where the Autobahn begins and near fields and forests. If you wish to visit Porsche, you avoid the new ringroad and go up the old Schwieberdingerstrasse, following the tramlines until suddenly you come upon the Porsche factories which straddle the main road. The old No 1 factory, the original 1938 red-brick building which looks more like a school than an office block, is on the corner of Spitalwaldstrasse hiding behind a screen of large trees; this now houses the entire administration, together with the workshops of the service and customer racing departments. On the other side of the main road is what looks like a modern office block but in fact houses the assembly halls for the 911 and 928 models. This is the No 2 factory which was originally the Reutter body plant; you find the entrance by taking two turns off the main road, and you are at 42 Porschestrasse, outside the main gates.

Entering the factory, there is the delivery department on the right, in a building which also houses Porsche's museum; on the left are the halls which house the trim and engine shops, the bodyshop with the paintshop behind, and behind that again is the rear of the assembly building. Close by are the smaller subsidiary No 3 and 4 factories which have been taken over by Porsche more recently. Imagine that you are one of the many customers who come to pick up their cars at the factory (a service that Porsche still offers—but try to do the same in Detroit or at Dagenham) and when you have reported to the delivery center, you will be given a guided tour through the works.

Zuffenhausen is not one of those factories where iron ore enters at one end and is processed into cars which emerge at the other end. Porsche have subcontractors who supply the body pressing, the castings and many of the other parts which come together to make a Porsche—in fact while some 5500 people are on Porsche's payroll, it is reckoned that almost 10,000 work for subcontractors. Body pressings arrive at Zuffenhausen to be welded into the complete 911 and 928 shells which are then rust-proofed and painted. Porsche still offers any color you want—as well as black—and it claims that it has been able to match the color for a car from a lipstick sent in by a customer. Of course the customer pays extra for this sort of capriciousness, but not an unreasonable amount.

The painted bodyshells enter the assembly building on the second floor. Here final body assembly takes place—window glass, bumpers, exterior trim and electrical equipment are all added. Separate assembly lines for the 911 and 928 models share the floor space; assembly line however is a dirty word at Porsche, as the bodies are moved almost leisurely around on individual trolleys, from work station to work station. At regular intervals there are special quality control stations, and there are special areas for complicated operations such as installing a sunroof or other extras. The atmosphere is relaxed, yet purposeful; one imagines it must have been rather like this at Abingdon in MG's heyday.

Once the bodyshell has been finished—which takes the best part of a working day—the car proceeds down to the first floor which is laid out in a similar manner, half the space for the 911s, half for the 928. Here the body is suspended from an overhead conveyor, and the mechanical and chassis components are mated up from below. The engines have come from the neighboring engine shop, where the machined castings are assembled into complete engines; from this shop come all Porsche's own engines including the 944 engines which are despatched to Neckarsulm. A special bench, manned by four workers, is devoted to the assembly of the Turbo engines. In the same building is the trimshop which produces interior trim and rear seats; the front seats are supplied by Recaro. Finished trim also goes to the assembly building and is installed after all mechanical elements are in place.

Finally, the wheels are bolted on, gasoline and oil put in (and in the 928, water) and the car is started up for the first time. It is then handed over to the test department which is housed on the ground floor of the assembly building. Each car is tested on a rolling road in a test cell, as well as on public roads. Only after everything has proved to be in satisfactory order is the car's "birth certificate" signed and it is handed over to the delivery department, to be picked up by the owner or to be despatched to any of the hundreds of different destinations in Germany or abroad. The whole process, from the time when body panels or raw castings are first received in the factory to the moment

Right: The impressive proving grounds at Weissach. The design center itself is at the lower right in this picture.

Right: The main factory at Zuffenhausen today. The 911/928 Assembly Hall is along the main road on the left; behind are the buildings of the original Reutter body factory.

Left: 928 assembly at Zuffenhausen: this car has almost reached the final stage of this long process.

when the car is finally ready, takes on average 10 days of which two and a half days are spent in the test department.

Of course, this applies only if the car is a standard model or at least only fitted with such options as normally appear in the price list. If you want something a little different, Porsche will oblige, and the car is then pulled out of the normal assembly process and turned over to the service department workshops in the Spitalwaldstrasse works. Here almost everything is possible and the sky is the limit on the money you can spend. Recently a Middle-Eastern customer asked Porsche to build him a road-going version of the 935; he was advised that he ought to have a steel body rather than the polyurethane shell of the racing version but that was no problem at all, neither for Porsche's panel-beaters who were quite happy to make a one-off body, nor for the customer who was quite happy to pay. By comparison the solid gold gearlever knobs which other customers have had fitted seem almost mundane.

However let us assume that the car you have come to take delivery of is not quite as special as this. After you have seen the factory, you can spend the rest of the time waiting by browsing round Porsche's museum. This is not a large collection as it numbers only some 30 cars, together with models, engines, race trophies and other memorabilia. Among the cars are race and rally winners, representative examples of most Porsche models of the past but also cars designed by Professor Porsche for other manufacturers, such as the Austro-Daimler, Wanderer, Cisitalia and of course a Volkswagen. Large panels on the wall outline Porsche's history in text and pictures, from the birth of Professor Porsche in 1875 until modern times. A bust of the Professor gazes benevolently at the visitor immediately inside the entrance. When you drive your brand-new Porsche away after the visit, you will retain the impression of a company which works with dedication and enthusiasm, which remains faithful to its heritage and the spirit that governed its past but which at the same time faces the future with confidence and optimism.

It is less likely that the visitor will visit Porsche's other sites. Ludwigsburg is a small town a few miles from Stuttgart, reached in a matter of minutes if you take the Autobahn from Zuffenhausen. You may drive past and notice the modern complex to one side of the road, bearing the Porsche legend in large letters on the roof. This is where most of the sales and service department is housed, with the training school for Porsche mechanics, the technical literature section, the marketing department and the enormous warehouse of the parts department. Some 350 people are employed here. Finally, there is Weissach. Weissach is an enigma; a company the size of Porsche has no right to maintain a research and development center with more than 1500 employees. Weissach is a small village to the west of Stuttgart, halfway to Pforzheim, and there is hardly any evidence of Porsche's presence in the village itself, other than an unpromising-looking side street named Porschestrasse. But turn up this and continue for a couple of miles out of the village, and you will arrive

Below: A view of the Porsche Museum, with the 16-cylinder engine in the foreground. On the left are examples of Professor Porsche's early designs for Austro-Daimler and Wanderer.

at Porsche's real nerve center.

Here, *Zutritt* is very strictly *Verboten:* casual visitors are not welcomed, and you are not likely to be given a guided tour unless you are a VIP from the world of motor racing or enjoy a similarly elevated status. Deliberately, most of the center is hidden away behind the woods so from the road only the main design building is visible; Porsche has no wish to encourage the Hans Lehmanns of this world or other industrial espionage photographers. Very little can be seen of the test track although it occupies almost 100 acres. There are good reasons for this secrecy; at Weissach. Porsche guards not only the secrets of its own future in the engineering and styling departments, but also those of numerous other car manfacturers who have sought its assistance on development projects. Porsche's consultancy business is the reason for the size and scope of Weissach: more work is carried out for customers than for Porsche itself, at hourly rates which start at DM180 and increase to DM400 depending on the nature of the work undertaken. Nor does Porsche confine its activities to the automative field; a major recent project was designing the cockpit interior of the Airbus, and many other areas of industrial design are also familiar to the men at Weissach. Finally, the racing department is housed at Weissach, and the hills occasionally come alive with the sound of a racing car lapping the test track at 115mph (185km/h) or more.

You will by now realize that in many ways, Porsche is a unique company in the motor industry of today. Consider the statistics: Porsche has an output of some 30–40,000 cars per year. If you think of Porsche as a volume car producer, this makes them the smallest independent company in Europe, with a production about half that of SAAB; if on the other hand you feel that Porsche is a specialist car maker, they are well on top of that league. Adding up what might loosely be described as small specialist car makers. Porsche contributes around 50 percent of these manufacturers' combined output, Jaguar-Daimler is second with 30 percent and everybody else (from Ferrari to Rolls-Royce) share the remaining 20 percent. Porsche is the only small independent company which can take on the world's leading car makers on their own terms, and make a success of it. The 924 for instance matched production of the Triumph TR7 over a similar time span; in terms of numbers, this sort of business was not viable to BL, but it made Porsche big. In 1983, daily production figures were running at over 200 cars, of which the Neckarsulum plant contributed 90 944s and 40 924s, while Zuffenhausen's output was composed of 20-odd 928s (of which some 70 percent had automatic gearboxes), 25 911 cabriolets, 20 coupés, five Targas and five 911 Turbos.

The currently fashionable talk about survival in the motor industry, with the wise men claiming that the only hope for car makers is to achieve "economy of scale" by making 200,000 of a given model per year, probably leaves the Porsche directors singularly unimpressed. They are after all in the fortunate position of being able to change more or less what they like for their cars, and there is no lack of customers for a range which starts at DM65,000 for a basic 924 (almost $37,500 in the USA and almost £21,500 in Britain) and ends at over three times that for a 911 Turbo. As this is being written, there are long waiting lists in Germany for the most recent models. The first oil crisis in 1973–5 made a dent in Porsche production, but the second oil crisis and the recession left the company comparatively unaffected. One might have expected differently in the fickle sports car market, and Porsche is after all the world's biggest exclusive sports car manufacturer; and they are heavily dependant on the US market, which takes 50 percent of Porsche production, with about 25 percent being sold in Germany and 25 percent in the rest of the world — percentages which have stayed remarkably similar for the more than

Left, above and below: This 911 Targa bodyshell "in white" demonstrates Porsche's use of zinc-coated steel which has made the six-year corrosion warranty possible.

Above: Project 960 is based on the 928 but has several interesting features, which will find application on future Porsches. Among them is the "4–8" engine which runs on half the cylinders under part load, and has special body members which crumple under impact, absorbing the energy in a head-on collision.

30 years Porsche have been making cars. The American recession and the fall in the value of the Dollar helped to kill off British sports cars, but Porsche not only survived the late 1970s but are now increasing production for the 1980s.

Motor industry observers who think in terms of giant companies like GM, Fiat or BL, and have watched the antics performed by these corporations in recent years, would find it ridiculous that a company the size of Porsche survives and thrives with their complicated model range, based on three totally different families of cars: the 924/944, the 911 and Turbo, and the 928. A Ford-trained rationalization expert would long since have pruned it to just one car, with say five engine options, four trim packages and the odd limited edition to clear stocks of last year's model. But Porsche does not like putting all its eggs in one basket. Its range is effectively split in two groups: the mass-production 924 and 944 models which are put together at Neckarsulm, and the Zuffenhausen-built supercars such as the 911, the Turbo and the 928. One could add a third group—the hand-built racing cars such as the Le Mans-winning 956 which is lovingly assembled in penny numbers in the racing department at Weissach. In the market place, Porsche gives a better coverage of its chosen sector than any other car maker in the world; the average price increment from model to model is less than DM10,000, and there is almost always another Porsche model to change up to, when the customer desires something better, faster or more exclusive to keep up with the Schmidts or Joneses. (This does not quite apply to those who already own a 911 Turbo, but

Above: American but German-born, Peter Schutz has been Managing Director of Porsche since 1980.

we can probably expect Porsche to do something about that in due course!)

Undoubtedly, a Porsche is not a "sensible" car in quite the same way that a 2 CV, a Golf or a Metro might be called "sensible." But in the supercar class they stand apart. Porsche spends more on research and development, and invests more in production facilities than any other supercar maker. It avoids traditional hand-building techniques and has instead embraced mass-production techniques which, together with a rigorous quality control system, enable it to reach standards of build quality and finish which are probably second only to Rolls-Royce. A Porsche model will remain in production for at least 15 or 20 years, and each individual car will have a greater life expectancy than any comparable car from other manufacturers. It is of particular interest to Porsche to make its cars long-lived. In 1973 the company showed its *Langzeit-Auto* (long-life car) as a discussion proposal, a hatchback two-door saloon based on 911 mechanicals. The goal was to make a car with a life expectancy of 20 years which at the same time would be economical to make and thus help to preserve dwindling raw materials and energy resources. Since then the company has introduced the famous bodyshell made from zinc-coated steel, with a six-year warranty against corrosion.

In terms of economy, any given Porsche is likely to use less fuel than any car of comparable performance, and future Porsches are likely to improve their efficiency still further, with more aerodynamical bodywork, sophisticated electronic engine management systems, and engines which will run on half the number of cylinders under part loads—this has already been demonstrated on the 928. It is no coincidence that Porsche should adopt the turbocharger so enthusiastically as this helps to strike the ideal balance between high performance and modest fuel consumption. In much the same way as every other motor manufacturer, Porsche is concerned about safety and has been since seat belts were first offered on the 356 model back in the 1950s. But where many American, post-Nader efforts have been aimed at improving mainly passive or secondary safety, Porsche has also made notable steps forward in the matter of active or primary safety—we have discussed the Weissach rear axle design on the 928 which is an example of Porsche's approach to safety in car design.

What then of the Porsches of the future? Some hints have already been given as to how we can expect current models to develop. In 1984 one of the more sensational German car magazines, eager to give its readers a "scoop," published details of what it called the Porsche 918 and which was claimed to be based on the VW Scirocco. Not much credibility should be given to this type of report, mainly because it is difficult to see where such a car would fit in the marketplace; already, the gap in price and performance between a Scirocco and the 924 is narrower than between any of Porsche's own models. Most Porsches of the late 1980s and 1990s are bound to bear a close resemblance to those we see today but under the skin they will be even better than current models; faster – very likely, but more importantly, they will be safer, more economical and have a better life expectancy. While the 911 and Turbo models are still being developed, there are undoubtedly those within the company who look forward to the day when this venerable pair can be pensioned off. By contrast, the other models in the range are by Porsche standards hardly approaching middle age, indeed the 944 is a mere stripling and both the 924 and the 928 are in their prime. Certainly there will be a new Porsche in the future, but it would be pure guesswork to say when and what specification. Only one thing is certain: it will be a trendsetter in the same way that all other Porsches before it have been, and it will thus be a worthy heir to the unique traditions of the company.

APPENDIX

Specifications of road-going Porsche production models

Specifications are mainly for home-market or European market models and are quoted as Porsche would quote them – i.e. metric. The author wishes to declare his preference for good old-fashioned Bhp rather than new-fangled Kw.

Porsche 356—production period: 1950–55
Engine: Horizontally opposed, light alloy construction. *No. of cylinders:* 4. *Cooling:* Air cooling, fan assisted. *Valves:* Push-rod overhead valves. *Carburation:* 2 Solex. *Electrical system:* 6 volt. *Transmission:* Rear engine built in unit with gearbox and final drive. *Clutch:* Single dry plate. *Gearbox:* 4 forward speeds—1950–52 without synchromesh, 1952–55 fully synchronized. *Chassis and body:* Pressed steel platform chassis welded together with pressed steel bodywork. *Body styles:* Coupé, cabriolet; 1954–55 Speedster. *Front suspension:* Upper and lower trailing arms acting on transverse torsion bars. Anti-roll bar from 1954. *Rear suspension:* Swing axles, with trailing arms acting on transverse torsion bars. *Brakes:* Footbrake hydraulic on all four wheels. Handbrake mechanical on rear wheels only. Drum brakes all round. *Steering:* Worm and peg. *Wheels:* Open centre steel disk type, 3.25 × 16, five-stud fixing. *Tires:* 5.00 × 16 or 5.25 × 16.
ENGINE DETAILS—**1100:** *Bore:* 73.5mm. *Stroke:* 64mm. *Capacity:* 1086cc. *Compression ratio:* 7:1. *Bhp/rpm:* 40/4000. *Production period:* 1950–54. **1300:** *Bore:* 80mm. *Stroke:* 64mm. *Capacity:* 1286cc. *Compression ratio:* 6.5:1. *Bhp/rpm:* 44/4200. *Production period:* 1951–54. **1300 Super:** *Bore:* 74.5mm. *Stroke:* 74mm. *Capacity:* 1290cc. *Compression ratio* 8.2:1. *Bhp/rpm:* 60/5500. *Production period:* 1953–55. **1300 A:** *Bore:* 74.5mm. *Stroke:* 74mm. *Capacity:* 1290cc. *Compression ratio:* 6.5:1. *Bhp/rpm:* 44/4200. *Production period:* 1954–55. **1500:** *Bore:* 80mm. *Stroke:* 74mm. *Capacity:* 1488cc. *Compression ratio:* 7:1. *Bhp/rpm:* 60/4800. *Production period:* 1951–52. **1500:** *Bore:* 80mm. *Stroke:* 74mm. *Capacity:* 1488cc. *Compression ratio:* 6.5:1. *Bhp/rpm:* 55/4400. *Production period:* 1952–55. **1500 S:** *Bore:* 80mm. *Stroke:* 74mm. *Capacity:* 1488cc. *Compression ratio:* 8.2:1. *Bhp/rpm:* 70/5000. *Production period:* 1952–55.
DIMENSIONS—*Wheelbase:* 2100mm (all models). *Track, front:* 1290mm to 1952, 1306mm from 1952–55. *Track, rear:* 1250mm to 1952, 1272mm from 1952–55. *Overall length:* 3870mm to 1952, 3950mm from 1952–55. *Overall width:* 1660mm. *Overall height:* 1300mm (varies with body style). *Weight:* 770 to 840kg, depending on model.
Note: These specifications relate to Zuffenhausen-built cars. The Gmünd-built cars differed in many important respects—some had 1131cc Volkswagen engines and Volkswagen-type mechanical brakes; all had aluminum bodywork (cf. Chapter 4).

Porsche 356 A—production period: 1955–1959
Specification in most respects as for 356 with the following exceptions:
Engine—valves: 1300, 1600: Push-rod ohv. Carrera 1500 GS, 1600 GS: 2 overhead camshafts each side. *Carburation:* 2 Solex; 2 twin-choke Zenith on 1600 models 1957–59; Carrera: 2 twin-choke Solex. *Electrical system:* 6 volt, except some Carrera 1600 GS models which had 12 volt. *Gearbox:* Synchromesh on all forward speeds. *Body styles:* Coupé, cabriolet; Speedster 1955–58; Convertible D 1958–59; Hardtop coupé 1957–59. *Front suspension:* Anti-roll bar on all models. *Steering:* Worm and peg to 1957. 1957–59: ZF worm gear with damper. *Wheels:* 4.5 × 15. *Tires:* 5.60 × 15 or 5.90 × 15; Carrera: 5.90 × 15.
ENGINE DETAILS—**1300:** *Bore:* 74.5mm. *Stroke:* 74mm. *Capacity:* 1290cc. *Compression ratio:* 6.5:1. *Bhp/rpm:* 44/4200. *Production period:* 1955–57. **1300 Super:** *Bore:* 74.5mm. *Stroke:* 74mm. *Capacity:* 1290cc. *Compression ratio:* 8.2:1. *Bhp/rpm:* 60/5500. *Production period:* 1955–57. **1600:** *Bore:* 82.5mm. *Stroke:* 74mm. *Capacity:* 1582cc. *Compression ratio:* 7.5:1. *Bhp/rpm:* 60/4500. *Production period:* 1955–59. **1600 Super:** *Bore:* 82.5mm. *Stroke:* 74mm. *Capacity:* 1582cc. *Compression ratio:* 8.5:1. *Bhp/rpm:* 75/5000. *Production period:* 1955–59. **Carrera 1500 GS:** *Bore:* 85mm. *Stroke:* 66mm. *Capacity:* 1498cc. *Compression ratio:* 9:1. *Bhp/rpm:* 100/6200. *Production period:* 1955–58. **Carrera 1500 GS GT:** *Bore:* 85mm. *Stroke:* 66mm. *Capacity:* 1498cc. *Compression ratio:* 9:1. *Bhp/rpm:* 110/6400. *Production period:* 1957–58. **Carrera 1600 GS:** *Bore:* 87.5mm. *Stroke:* 66mm. *Capacity:* 1588cc. *Compression ratio:* 9.5:1. *Bhp/rpm:* 105/6500. *Production period:* 1958–59. **Carrera 1600 GS GT:** *Bore:* 87.5mm. *Stroke:* 66mm. *Capacity:* 1588cc. *Compression ratio:* 9.8:1. *Bhp/rpm:* 115/6500. *Production period:* 1959.
DIMENSIONS—As for late-model 356 with following exceptions—*Overall width:* 1670mm. *Overall height:* 1220 to 1310mm depending on body style. *Weight:* 815 to 950kg, depending on model.

Porsche 356 B—production period: 1959–1963
Specification in most respects as for 356 and 356 A with the following exceptions:
Carburation: 1600: 2 twin-choke Zenith; Carrera: 2 twin-choke Solex. *Electrical system:* 1600: 6 volt; Carrera: 12 volt. *Body styles:* Coupé, cabriolet, hardtop coupé; roadster 1959–61. *Rear suspension:* Super 90 and Carrera models had additional transverse leaf spring mounted under gearbox. *Brakes:* Carrera 2 (1962–63) had Porsche disk brakes on all wheels. *Tires:* Carrera 2 (1962–63) had 165 × 15 radial ply tires.
ENGINE DETAILS—**1600:** *Bore:* 82.5mm. *Stroke:* 74mm. *Capacity:* 1582cc. *Compression ratio:* 7.5:1. *Bhp/rpm:* 60/4500. *Production period:* 1959–63. **1600 Super 75:** *Bore:* 82.5mm. *Stroke:* 74mm. *Capacity:* 1582cc. *Compression ratio:* 8.5:1. *Bhp/rpm:* 75/5000. *Production period:* 1959–63. **1600 Super 90:** *Bore:* 82.5mm. *Stroke:* 74mm. *Capacity:* 1582cc. *Compression ratio:* 9:1. *Bhp/rpm:* 90/5500. *Production period:* 1960–63. **Carrera 1600 GS GT:** *Bore:* 87.5mm. *Stroke:* 66mm. *Capacity:* 1588cc. *Compression ratio:* 9.8:1. *Bhp/rpm:* 115/6500. *Production period:* 1960–61. **Carrera 2 2000 GS:** *Bore:* 92mm. *Stroke:* 74mm. *Capacity:* 1966cc. *Compression ratio:* 9.5:1. *Bhp/rpm:* 130/6200. *Production period:* 1961–63.
DIMENSIONS—As for 356 A with the following exceptions—*Overall length:* 4010mm. *Overall height:* 1310 to 1330mm depending on body style. *Weight:* 875 to 970kg; Carrera 900 to 1040kg, depending on model.
Note: 1960 356 B Abarth-Carrera (1600 GS GTL) had all-aluminum coupé bodywork.

Porsche 356 C—production period: 1963–1965
Specification in most respects as for 356, 356 A and 356 B with the following exceptions:
Carburation: 1600 C: 2 twin-choke Solex; 1600 SC: 2 twin-choke Zenith; Carrera: 2 twin-choke Solex. *Body styles:* Coupé and cabriolet were the only body styles available. *Brakes:* ATE-Dunlop disk brakes on all wheels. Handbrake in drums on rear wheels. *Wheels:* New type with smaller open centres. *Tires:* 1600 C: 5.60 × 15; 1600 SC and Carrera: 165 × 15 radials.
ENGINE DETAILS—**1600 C:** *Bore:* 82.5mm. *Stroke:* 74mm. *Capacity:* 1582cc. *Compression ratio:* 8.5:1. *Bhp/rpm:* 75/5200. *Production period:* 1963–65. **1600 SC:** *Bore:* 82.5mm. *Stroke:* 74mm. *Capacity:* 1582cc. *Compression ratio:* 9.5:1. *Bhp/rpm:* 95/5800. *Production period:* 1963–65. **Carrera 2 2000 GS:** *Bore:* 92mm. *Stroke:* 74mm. *Capacity:* 1966cc. *Compression ratio:* 9.5:1. *Bhp/rpm:* 130/6200. *Production period:* 1963–64.
DIMENSIONS—As for 356 B with the following exceptions—*Overall height:* 1315mm. *Weight:* 935 to 955kg; Carrera 1020 to 1040kg, depending on model.

Porsche 911 2.0 and 2.2 liter models—production period: 1964–1971
Engine: Horizontally opposed, light alloy construction. *No. of cylinders:* 6. *Cooling:* Air cooling, fan assisted. *Valves:* Single overhead camshaft each side. *Fuel system:* 2 triple-choke Solex carburetors to 1966. 2 triple-choke Weber carburetors on 911 L and T models 1966–69; on 911 S to 1968. 2 triple-choke Zenith or Solex carburetors on 911 T model 1969–71. Mechanical Bosch fuel injection on 911 E and S models 1968–71. *Electrical system:* 12 volt. *Transmission:* Rear engine built in unit with gearbox and final drive. *Clutch:* Single dry plate. *Gearbox:* 4 or 5 forward speeds, fully synchronized. 4 speed semi-automatic Sportomatic gearbox was optional from 1967. *Chassis and body:* All-steel unitary construction body; coupé 1964–71, Targa from 1966. *Front suspension:* Lower wishbones acting on torsion bars, vertical shock absorber struts. Anti-roll bar standard on S model, optional on others. 1968–71: Self-levelling hydro-pneumatic struts on 911 E, optional on T and S models. *Rear suspension:* Semi-trailing arms and transverse torsion bars. Anti-roll bar on S model. *Brakes:* Disk brakes. Dual circuit hydraulics from 1967. *Steering:* ZF rack and pinion. *Wheels:* Steel disk; forged alloy on E and S models 1967–71. 4.5 × 15: 911, 911 S 1964–67. 5.5 × 15: T and L models 1967–71; 911 S to 1968. 6 × 15: 911 E and S models 1968–71. 5.5 × 14: 911 E Sportomatic 1968–69. *Tires:* 165 HR × 15 on 4.5 and 5.5 inch rims. 185/70 VR × 15 on 6 inch rims. 185 HR × 14 on 14 inch wheels.
ENGINE DETAILS—**911, 911 L:** *Bore:* 80mm. *Stroke:* 66mm. *Capacity:* 1991cc. *Compression ratio:* 9:1. *Bhp/rpm:* 130/6100. *Production period:* 1964–68. **911 T:** *Bore:* 80mm. *Stroke:* 66mm. *Capacity:* 1991cc. *Compression ratio:* 8.6:1. *Bhp/rpm:* 110/5800. *Production period:* 1967–69. **911 S:** *Bore:* 80mm. *Stroke:* 66mm. *Capacity:* 1991cc. *Compression ratio:* 9.8:1. *Bhp/rpm:* 160/6600. *Production period:* 1966–68. **911 E:** *Bore:* 80mm. *Stroke:* 66mm. *Capacity:* 1991cc. *Compression ratio:* 9:1. *Bhp/rpm:* 140/6500. *Production period:* 1968–69. **911 S:** *Bore:* 80mm. *Stroke:* 66mm. *Capacity:* 1991cc. *Compression ratio:* 9.9:1. *Bhp/rpm:* 170/6800. *Production period:* 1968–69. **911 T:** *Bore:* 84mm. *Stroke:* 66mm. *Capacity:* 2195cc. *Compression ratio:* 8.6:1. *Bhp/rpm:* 125/5800. *Production period:* 1969–71. **911 E:** *Bore:* 84mm. *Stroke:* 66mm. *Capacity:* 2195cc. *Compression ratio:* 9.1:1. *Bhp/rpm:* 155/6200. *Production period:* 1969–71. **911 S:** *Bore:* 84mm. *Stroke:* 66mm. *Capacity:* 2195cc. *Compression ratio:* 9.8:1. *Bhp/rpm:* 180/6500. *Production period:* 1969–71.
DIMENSIONS—*Wheelbase:* 2211mm to 1968, 2268mm 1968–71. *Track, front:* 1337 to 1374mm, depending on model. *Track, rear:* 1317 to 1335mm, depending on model. *Overall length:* 4163mm.

Overall width: 1610mm. *Overall height:* 1320mm. *Weight:* 1085 to 1125kg, depending on model.

Porsche 911 2.4 and 2.7 liter models—production period: 1971–1977

Specifications in most respects as for 2.0 and 2.2 liter models with the following exceptions:
Fuel system: 911 T 1971–73: 2 triple-choke Zenith or Solex carburetors. 911 E and S 2.4 liter 1971–73, and Carrera 1972–75: Mechanical Bosch fuel injection. 911 S 1973–75, 911 1973–77: Electronic Bosch K-Jetronic fuel injection. *Gearbox:* Sportomatic was not offered on Carrera model 1972–75. From 1975, the 4 speed Sportomatic was replaced by a 3 speed version. *Front suspension:* Anti-roll bar on Carrera from 1972; standard on all models from 1973. *Rear suspension:* Anti-roll bar on Carrera from 1972; optional on other models from 1973. *Wheels:* Steel disk on 911 T, E and 911 to 1975. Forged alloy on 911 S and Carrera. Cast alloy on 911 1975–77 (optional from 1974). 5.5 × 15: 911 T; 911 to 1975. 6 × 15: 911 E, S; 911 1975–77. Carrera: 6 × 15 front, 7 × 15 rear. *Tires:* 165 HR × 15 on 5.5 inch rims. 185/70 VR × 15 on 6 inch rims. Carrera rear tires: 215/60 VR × 15.
ENGINE DETAILS—**911 T:** *Bore:* 84mm. *Stroke:* 70.4mm. *Capacity:* 2341cc. *Compression ratio:* 7.5:1. *Bhp/rpm:* 130/5600. *Production period:* 1971–73. **911 E:** *Bore:* 84mm. *Stroke:* 70.4mm. *Capacity:* 2341cc. *Compression ratio:* 8:1. *Bhp/rpm:* 165/6200. *Production period:* 1971–73. **911 S:** *Bore:* 84mm. *Stroke:* 70.4mm. *Capacity:* 2341cc. *Compression ratio:* 8.5:1. *Bhp/rpm:* 190/6500. *Production period:* 1971–73. **Carrera:** *Bore:* 90mm. *Stroke:* 70.4mm. *Capacity:* 2687cc. *Compression ratio:* 8.5:1. *Bhp/rpm:* 210/6300. *Production period:* 1972–75. **911:** *Bore:* 90mm. *Stroke:* 70.4mm. *Capacity:* 2687cc. *Compression ratio:* 8:1. *Bhp/rpm:* 150/5700. *Production period:* 1973–75. **911 S:** *Bore:* 90mm. *Stroke:* 70.4mm. *Capacity:* 2687cc. *Compression ratio:* 8.5:1. *Bhp/rpm:* 175/5800. *Production period:* 1973–75. **911:** *Bore:* 90mm. *Stroke:* 70.4mm. *Capacity:* 2687cc. *Compression ratio:* 8.5:1. *Bhp/rpm:* 165/5800. *Production period:* 1975–77.
DIMENSIONS—*Wheelbase:* 2271mm. *Track, front:* 1360 to 1372mm, depending on model. *Track, rear:* 1342 to 1380mm, depending on model. *Overall length:* 4147mm to 1973; 4291mm 1973–77. *Overall width:* 1610mm; Carrera: 1652mm. *Overall height:* 1320mm. *Weight:* 1110 to 1135kg, depending on model.

Porsche 911 3.0 and 3.3 liter models, including Turbo—production period: 1975–

Specifications in most respects as for earlier 911 models with the following exceptions:
Fuel system: All models: Electronic Bosch K-Jetronic fuel injection. Turbo: KKK turbocharger; intercooler from 1977. *Gearbox:* 5 speed: Standard on 911 SC and Carrera models. 4 speed: Optional on Carrera to 1977; standard on Turbo. 3 speed Sportomatic optional on Carrera to 1977, on 911 SC to 1982; never available on Turbo. *Chassis and body:* Cabriolet available on 911 SC from 1982. Turbo only available with coupé body. *Brakes:* Servo assistance standard on Carrera and Turbo models from 1976, on 911 SC model from 1977. *Wheels and tires:* Carrera: Forged alloy wheels—dimensions: front 6 × 15, with 185/70 VR × 15 tires; rear 7 × 15, with 215/60 VR × 15 tires. 911 SC: Standard: Dimensions as Carrera, but cast alloy wheels. Optional forged alloy wheels—dimensions: front 6 × 16, with 205/55 VR × 16 tires; rear 7 × 16, with 225/50 VR × 16 tires. Turbo: Forged alloy—dimensions 1975–77: front 7 × 15, with 205/50 VR × 15 tires; rear 8 × 15, with 225/50 VR × 15 tires. From 1977 wheel diameter increased to 16 inch: front 7 × 16, with 205/55 VR × 16 tires; rear 8 × 16, with 225/50 VR × 16 tires.
ENGINE DETAILS—**Carrera:** *Bore:* 95mm. *Stroke:* 70.4mm. *Capacity:* 2993cc. *Compression ratio:* 8.5:1. *Bhp/rpm:* 200/6000. *Production period:* 1975–77. **911 SC:** *Bore:* 95mm. *Stroke:* 70.4mm. *Capacity:* 2993cc. *Compression ratio:* 8.5:1. *Bhp/rpm:* 180/5500. *Production period:* 1977–79. **911 SC:** *Bore:* 95mm. *Stroke:* 70.4mm. *Capacity:* 2993cc. *Compression ratio:* 8.6:1. *Bhp/rpm:* 188/5500. *Production period:* 1979–80. **911 SC:** *Bore:* 95mm. *Stroke:* 70.4mm. *Capacity:* 2993cc. *Compression ratio:* 9.8:1. *Bhp/rpm:* 204/5900. *Production period:* 1980–. **Turbo:** *Bore:* 95mm. *Stroke:* 70.4mm. *Capacity:* 2993cc. *Compression ratio:* 6.5:1. *Bhp/rpm:* 260/5500. *Production period:* 1975–77. **Turbo:** *Bore:* 97mm. *Stroke:* 74.4mm. *Capacity:* 3299cc. *Compression ratio:* 7:1. *Bhp/rpm:* 300/5500. *Production period:* 1977–.
DIMENSIONS—*Wheelbase:* 2271mm. *Track, front:* 1372mm; Turbo 1432mm. *Track, rear:* 1380mm; Turbo 1502mm. *Overall length:* 4291mm. *Overall width:* 1652mm; Turbo 1775mm. *Overall height:* 1320mm; Turbo 1304mm. *Weight:* 1120 to 1160kg for normally aspirated models; Turbo 1300kg.

Porsche 912—production periods: 1965–1969, and 1975–1977

Specifications in most respects as for 911 models with the following exceptions:
Engine—No. of cylinders: 4. *Valves:* Push-rod overhead valves. *Fuel system:* 1965–69: 2 twin-choke Solex carburetors; 1975–77: Electronic Bosch K-Jetronic fuel injection. *Gearbox:* 4 forward speeds standard 1965–69; 5 speeds optional 1965–68, standard 1975–77. Sportomatic never offered. *Chassis and body:* Targa body only available 1966–69. *Wheels:* Steel disk fitted as standard; alloy wheels optional 1967–69. 4.5 × 15 to 1967, 5.5 × 15 on later models. Alloy wheels: 5.5 × 14 or 6 × 15. *Tires:* 6.95 H × 15 (cross ply) until 1968, with 165 HR × 15 radials optional; these were standard on later models, with 185 HR × 15 optional 1975–77—1967–69 cars with alloy wheels had 185 HR × 14 or 185/70 VR × 15.
ENGINE DETAILS—**912:** *Bore:* 82.5mm. *Stroke:* 74mm. *Capacity:* 1582cc. *Compression ratio:* 9.3:1. *Bhp/rpm:* 90/5800. *Production period:* 1965–69. **912 E:** *Bore:* 94mm. *Stroke:* 71mm. *Capacity:* 1971cc. *Compression ratio:* 7.6:1. *Bhp/rpm:* 87/4900. *Production period:* 1975–77.
DIMENSIONS—*Wheelbase:* 2211mm to 1968; 2268mm 1968–69; 2271mm 1975–77. *Track, front:* 1337 to 1367mm, depending on model. *Track, rear:* 1317 to 1343mm, depending on model. *Overall length:* 4163mm to 1969; 4291mm 1975–77. *Overall width:* 1610mm. *Overall height:* 1320mm. *Weight:* 995kg 1965–69; 1160kg 1975–77.
Note: The 1975–77 model, the 912 E, was sold only in the North American market.

VW-Porsche 914—production period: 1969–1975

Engine: Horizontally opposed, light alloy construction. *No. of cylinders:* 4 or 6. *Cooling:* Air cooling, fan assisted. *Valves:* 4 cyl: Push-rod ohv. 6 cyl: Single ohc each side. *Fuel system:* 4 cyl 1.7 and 2.0 liter: Electronical Bosch fuel injection. 4 cyl 1.8 liter: 2 Solex carburetors. 6 cyl: 2 triple-choke Weber carbs. *Electrical system:* 12 volt. *Transmission:* Mid-engine built in unit with gearbox and final drive. *Clutch:* Single dry plate. *Gearbox:* 5 forward speeds, fully synchronized. 4 speed semi-automatic Sportomatic gearbox was optional 1969–72. *Chassis and body:* All-steel unitary construction, coupé with removable roof panel. *Front suspension:* Lower wishbones acting on torsion bars, vertical shock absorber struts. *Rear suspension:* Semi-trailing arms and coil springs. (Anti-roll bars optional front and rear.) *Brakes:* Disk brakes with dual circuit hydraulics. *Steering:* ZF rack and pinion. *Wheels:* Steel disk: light alloy optional. 5.5 × 15 standard on all models, 914/4 1.7 liter 4.5 × 15 optional, 914/6 5.5 × 14 optional. *Tires:* 165 × 15 on all models, 914/4 1.7 liter 155 × 15 on 4.5 inch rims, 914/6 185 HR × 14 on 14 inch wheels.
ENGINE DETAILS—**914/4 1.7 liter:** *Bore:* 90mm. *Stroke:* 66mm. *Capacity:* 1679cc. *Compression ratio:* 8.2:1. *Bhp/rpm:* 80/4900. *Production period:* 1969–73. **914/4 1.8 liter:** *Bore:* 93mm. *Stroke:* 66mm. *Capacity:* 1795cc. *Compression ratio:* 8.6:1. *Bhp/rpm:* 85/5000. *Production period:* 1973–75. **914/4 2.0 liter:** *Bore:* 94mm. *Stroke:* 71mm. *Capacity:* 1971cc. *Compression ratio:* 8.0:1. *Bhp/rpm:* 100/5000. *Production period:* 1972–75. **914/6:** *Bore:* 80mm. *Stroke:* 66mm. *Capacity:* 1991cc. *Compression ratio:* 8.6:1. *Bhp/rpm:* 110/5800. *Production period:* 1969–72.
DIMENSIONS—*Wheelbase:* 2450mm. *Track, front:* 1337 to 1361mm, depending on model. *Track, rear:* 1374 to 1383mm, depending on model. *Overall length:* 3985mm. *Overall width:* 1650mm. *Overall height:* 1230mm; 914/6 1240mm. *Weight:* 940 to 995kg, depending on model.

Porsche 924 and 944 models—production period: from 1975

Engine: In-line, light alloy cylinder head; 924: Cast-iron block; 944: Alloy block. *No. of cylinders:* 4. *Cooling:* Water cooling. *Valves:* Single overhead camshaft. *Fuel system:* 924 models: Electronic Bosch K-Jetronic fuel injection; Turbo and Carrera had KKK Turbocharger, on Carrera with intercooler. 944: L-Jetronic injection. *Electrical system:* 12 volt. *Transmission:* Front engine, rear wheel drive. Gearbox in unit with final drive. *Clutch:* Single dry plate. *Gearbox:* 4 speed: Standard on 924 1975–79. 5 speed: Optional on 924 from 1977, standard from 1979; always standard on Turbo, Carrera and 944 models. 3 speed automatic: Optional on 924 1976–83, optional on 944 from 1981. Not available on Turbo or Carrera. *Chassis and body:* All-steel unitary construction body. *Front suspension:* McPherson struts, coil springs. *Rear suspension:* Semi-trailing arms and transverse torsion bars. (Anti-roll bars front and rear optional on 924, standard on Turbo, Carrera and 944 models.) *Brakes:* 924: Disk front, drums rear. All other models: Disks front and rear. Dual circuit hydraulics, servo assistance. *Steering:* Rack and pinion; servo assistance optional on 944. *Wheels and tires:* 924: Standard 1975–79, 5.5 × 14 steel disks with 165 HR × 14 tires. Optional 1975–79, standard from 1979: 6 × 14 cast alloy with 185/70 HR × 14 tires. 924 Turbo: Standard: 6 × 15 cast alloy with 185/70 HR × 15 tires; optional: 6 × 16 forged alloy with 205/55 VR × 16 tires. 924 Carrera: Standard: 7 × 15 forged alloy with 215/60 VR × 15 tires. Optional, and standard on Carrera GTS: Forged alloy wheels, front 7 × 16 with 205/55 VR × 16 tires, rear 8 × 16 with 225/50 VR × 16 tires. 944: Standard: 7 × 15 cast alloy, with 185/70 VR × 15 tires; optional: 7 × 16 forged alloy, with 205/55 VR × 16 tires.
ENGINE DETAILS—**924:** *Bore:* 86.5mm. *Stroke:* 84.4mm. *Capacity:* 1984cc. *Compression ratio:* 9.3:1. *Bhp/rpm:* 125/5800. *Production period:* 1975–. **924 Turbo:** *Bore:* 86.5mm. *Stroke:* 84.4mm. *Capacity:* 1984cc. *Compression ratio:* 7.5:1. *Bhp/rpm:* 170/5500. *Production period:* 1978–80.

924 Turbo: *Bore:* 86.5mm. *Stroke:* 84.4mm. *Capacity:* 1984cc. *Compression ratio:* 8.5:1. *Bhp/rpm:* 177/5500. *Production period:* 1980–82*. **924 Carrera:** *Bore:* 86.5mm. *Stroke:* 84.4mm. *Capacity:* 1984cc. *Compression ratio:* 8.5:1. *Bhp/rpm:* 210/6000. *Production period:* 1980–81. **924 Carrera GTS:** *Bore:* 86.5mm. *Stroke:* 84.4mm. *Capacity:* 1984cc. *Compression ratio:* 8:1. *Bhp/rpm:* 245/6250. *Production period:* 1980–82. **944:** *Bore:* 100mm. *Stroke:* 78.9mm. *Capacity:* 2479cc. *Compression ratio:* 10.6:1. *Bhp/rpm:* 163/5800. *Production period:* 1981–. (*Production of the 924 Turbo continues in 1983, but only for the Italian market.)
DIMENSIONS—*Wheelbase:* 2400mm. *Track, front:* 1418 to 1475mm, depending on model. *Track, rear:* 1372 to 1475mm, depending on model. *Overall length:* 4213 to 4320mm, depending on model. *Overall width:* 1685 to 1735mm, depending on model. *Overall height:* 1275mm. *Weight:* 1080 to 1190kg, depending on model.

Porsche 928—production period: from 1977
Engine: 90° light alloy V-8. *No. of cylinders:* 8. *Cooling:* Water cooling. *Valves:* One overhead camshaft per bank. *Fuel system:* Bosch K-Jetronic fuel injection. *Electrical system:* 12 volt. *Transmission:* Front engine, rear wheel drive. Gearbox in unit with final drive. *Clutch:* Single dry plate. *Gearbox:* 5 forward speeds, fully synchronized. 3 speed automatic optional. *Chassis and body:* All-steel unitary construction body. *Front suspension:* Upper and lower wishbones with coil springs. *Rear suspension:* "Weissach axle" independent suspension with coil springs. Anti-roll bars front and rear. *Brakes:* Disk brakes front and rear. Dual circuit hydraulics, servo assistance. *Steering:* Rack and pinion, servo assistance. *Wheels and tires:* 928, 928 S: Cast alloy standard (forged alloy optional), 7 × 16 with 225/50 VR × 16 tires. Alternative on 928 1979–82: Cast alloy 7 × 15 wheels with 215/60 VR × 15 tires.
ENGINE DETAILS—**928:** *Bore:* 95mm. *Stroke:* 78.9mm. *Capacity:* 4474cc. *Compression ratio:* 10:1*. *Bhp/rpm:* 240/5250. *Production period:* 1977–82. **928 S:** *Bore:* 97mm. *Stroke:* 78.9mm. *Capacity:* 4664cc. *Compression ratio:* 10:1. *Bhp/rpm:* 300/5900. *Production period:* 1979–. (*928 models from 1977–79 had 8.5:1.)
DIMENSIONS—*Wheelbase:* 2500mm. *Track, front:* 1545mm. *Track, rear:* 1515mm. *Overall length:* 4445mm. *Overall width:* 1835mm. *Overall height:* 1315mm. *Weight:* 1450kg; 928 S: 1500kg.

ACKNOWLEDGMENTS

The publishers would like to thank the Porsche Archives for supplying most of the photographs used in this book, and also the following for photographs on the pages listed:
Neill Bruce: pp 28–29, 38–39, 44–45, 55, 56–57, 60, 61, 68–69, 90–91, 102–3, 104–5, 106–7, 114–115, 117, 118, 119 top, 120–121, 124–125, 138–139, 146–147, 148–149, 152–153, 156–157, 186–187, 194–195, 196–197, 200–201.
Chris Harvey: pp 67 inset, 78–79, 94, 96, 97, 98–99, 116 bottom, 122 center, 134–135, 155, 164 center, 173 bottom, 182–183.
SAM/Autopresse: pp 35 top right, both, 36–37, 48 top, 50–51, 51 center, 64 top, 66–67 main, 70–71, 74–75, 80 top and bottom, 83, 84, 86–87, 88 left, 100, 101 top, 122 top and bottom, 123, 126–127, 128–129, 130–131, 133, 140–141, 142–143, 144, 190–191, 192–193, 198, 204–205.
SAM: pp 108–109, 110 bottom, 111, 160–161, 164 bottom, 165, 168–169, 173 top, 174, 175, 178–179, 180–181.

INDEX

CARS

FERDINAND PORSCHE